Coaching
VOLLEYBALL
Technical and
Tactical Skills

Cecile Reynaud

In cooperation with

American Sport Education Program

HUMAN KINETICS

Library of Congress Cataloging-in-Publication Data

Coaching volleyball technical and tactical skills / American Sport
Education Program with Cecile Reynaud.
    p. cm.
  Includes index.
  ISBN-13: 978-0-7360-5384-6 (soft cover)
  ISBN-10: 0-7360-5384-0 (soft cover)
  1. Volleyball--Coaching. I. Reynaud, Cecile, 1953- II. American Sport
Education Program.
  GV1015.5.C63C616 2011
  796.325--dc22
                    2010049782

ISBN-10: 0-7360-5384-0 (print)
ISBN-13: 978-0-7360-5384-6 (print)

The Web addresses cited in this text were current as of February 2011, unless otherwise noted.

Acquisitions Editor: Annie Parrett; **Developmental Editor:** Laura Floch; **Assistant Editor:** Elizabeth Evans; **Copyeditor:** Patricia L. MacDonald; **Indexers:** Robert and Cynthia Swanson; **Permission Manager:** Martha Gullo; **Graphic Designer:** Nancy Rasmus; **Graphic Artist:** Julie L. Denzer; **Cover Designer:** Keith Blomberg; **Photographer (cover):** © Human Kinetics; **Photographer (interior):** Neil Bernstein; **Photo Asset Manager:** Laura Fitch; **Visual Production Assistant:** Joyce Brumfield; **Photo Production Manager:** Jason Allen; **Art Manager:** Kelly Hendren; **Associate Art Manager:** Alan L. Wilborn; **Illustrations:** © Human Kinetics; **Printer:** Premier Print Group

We thank The Bobby E. Leach Center at Florida State University in Tallahassee, FL, for assistance in providing the location for the photo shoot for this book.

Copies of this book are available at special discounts for bulk purchase for sales promotions, premiums, fund-raising, or educational use. Special editions or book excerpts can also be created to specifications. For details, contact the Special Sales Manager at Human Kinetics.

Printed in the United States of America   10 9 8 7 6 5 4 3 2 1

Human Kinetics
Web site: www.HumanKinetics.com

United States: Human Kinetics
P.O. Box 5076
Champaign, IL 61825-5076
800-747-4457
e-mail: humank@hkusa.com

Canada: Human Kinetics
475 Devonshire Road Unit 100
Windsor, ON N8Y 2L5
800-465-7301 (in Canada only)
e-mail: info@hkcanada.com

Europe: Human Kinetics
107 Bradford Road
Stanningley
Leeds LS28 6AT, United Kingdom
+44 (0) 113 255 5665
e-mail: hk@hkeurope.com

Australia: Human Kinetics
57A Price Avenue
Lower Mitcham, South Australia 5062
08 8372 0999
e-mail: info@hkaustralia.com

New Zealand: Human Kinetics
P.O. Box 80
Torrens Park, South Australia 5062
0800 222 062
e-mail: info@hknewzealand.com

E4975

contents

preface

If you are a seasoned volleyball coach, surely you have experienced the frustration of watching your players perform well in practice, only to find them underperforming in matches. In your own playing days, you likely saw the same events unfold. In practice, your teammates, or perhaps even you, could pass the serve and hit the ball around the block and into the court just fine. You could perform these skills properly, but you could not transfer that kind of performance to the match. Although this book will not provide you with a magical quick fix to your players' problems, it will help you prepare your players for match day. Whether you are a veteran coach or are new to coaching, *Coaching Volleyball Technical and Tactical Skills* will help you take your players' games to the next level by providing you with the tools you need in order to teach them the sport of volleyball.

Every volleyball coach knows the importance of technical skills. The ability to serve and pass a variety of serves accurately; hit different types of sets to various areas of the court; and dig the ball up, keeping the opponents frustrated by never allowing the ball to hit the floor, can significantly affect the outcome of a match. This book discusses the basic and intermediate technical skills necessary for your players' success, including offensive and defensive skills. You will learn how to detect and correct errors in your players' performances of those skills and then help them transfer the knowledge and ability they gain in practice to matches.

Besides covering technical skills, this book also focuses on tactical skills, including offensive skills such as hitting the ball with different speeds, as well as setting the ball at different areas along the net. Your players will learn to identify which shots work best for them and in what situations based on the opposing team's defense. The book discusses the tactical triangle, an approach that teaches players to read a situation, acquire the knowledge they need to make a tactical decision, and apply decision-making skills to the problem. To advance this method, the book covers important cues that help athletes respond appropriately when they see a play developing, including important rules, match strategies, and the strengths and weaknesses of opponents.

In addition to presenting rigorous technical and tactical training to prepare your athletes for match situations, this book also provides guidance in how to improve your players' match performance by incorporating gamelike situations into daily training. We describe many traditional drills that can be effective as well as show you how to shape, focus, and enhance drills and minigames to help players transfer their technical skills to tactical situations that occur during matches. For example, you can change a tedious serving and passing drill into an exciting, competitive contest by keeping score of the number of perfect passes and how many times the team can attack a quick set out of the middle of the court.

Coaching Volleyball Technical and Tactical Skills also covers planning at several levels—the season plan, practice plans, and game plans. We offer a set of eight-session practice plans based on the games approach that covers the length of the practice session, the objective of the practice, the equipment needed, the warm-up, practice of previously taught skills, teaching and practicing new skills, the cool-down, and evaluation.

Of course, playing in matches is what your practices eventually lead to. This book shows you how to prepare long before the first match by establishing practice and match routines and addressing such issues as communicating with players and parents, scouting your opponents, and motivating your players.

PART I

Teaching and Evaluating

Being a good coach requires more than simply knowing the sport of volleyball. You have to go beyond the sport and find a way to teach your athletes how to be better players. To improve your players' performance, you must know how to teach and evaluate them.

In chapter 1 we go over the fundamentals of teaching sport skills. We first provide a general overview of volleyball and talk about the importance of being an effective teacher. Next, we define some important skills, helping you gain a better understanding of technical and tactical skills before discussing the traditional and games approaches to coaching.

We build on the knowledge of how to teach sports skills by addressing the evaluation of technical and tactical skills in chapter 2. We discuss the importance of evaluating athletes and review the core skills you should assess and how you can best do so. This chapter stresses the importance of preseason, in-season, and postseason evaluations and provides you with tools you can use to evaluate your players.

By learning how to teach and evaluate your players, you will be better prepared to help them improve their performance.

chapter 1

Teaching Sport Skills

The sport of volleyball is a game most people have played at some time in their lives, whether in the backyard, on the beach, at picnics with family and friends, or competitively with an organized team. The objective of the game is fairly simple—keep the ball off the ground on your side of the court, and use up to three contacts to hit it back over the net into the opposing team's court. The team that does this successfully will score a point. The team with the most points at the end of the game, or set, wins that particular game, and the team that wins the most sets wins the match. This sport, originally called *mintonette*, was invented in 1895 in Massachusetts by William G. Morgan for businessmen at the YMCA who wanted a less strenuous sport than basketball.

Volleyball has developed into a high-powered sport and is one of the most popular team sports. It is played at all levels by millions of people all over the world. Having six players on one side of the net moving in a small court only 900 square feet (81 square meters) in size while trying to stop the opponents from hitting the ball into their court requires good physical and mental skills. Volleyball is the ultimate team sport—the players must coordinate their movements by reading, reacting, and moving as quickly as possible while the volleyball is in play. To make the sport even more complex, the ball is always in the air when it is contacted by a player, beginning with the serve. Several skills are performed while the players are not even on the floor when they contact the ball, as in attacking or blocking. This makes this sport very unique in that there is virtually no time to stop and think before contacting the ball, nor can a player hold onto the ball or move while in possession of the ball.

Offensively, the players receive a serve from the opposing team and pass the volleyball to their setter. That player will then set the ball to one of their attackers, who will jump in the air to hit the ball over the net back into the opposing team's court. Defensively, the players must position themselves in such a way that the ball will deflect off their hands when blocking at the net back into the opposing team's court, and off their arms or hands up into their own court when they are in the backcourt digging. Making sure the players have the proper techniques for each skill will improve their ability to be successful. As the players gain experience in the sport, they usually start to specialize in certain positions on the court, such as setters, liberos, right-side (or opposite) hitters, middle hitters, and left-side (or outside) hitters. Tactically, the game can be compared to football, with the net serving as the line of scrimmage. The three front-row players are trying to hit the ball around or off the three defensive players at the net, known as blockers, and the strategies used to do this efficiently are what makes the game exciting to watch and play.

Effective Teaching

Whether you have played the game of volleyball or not, effective coaching requires you to learn the sport in a different way. Great volleyball players do not necessarily make good coaches, and great coaches may not have been fantastic players. Although it may be helpful to have played the game at a high level and to have experience using complicated tactics and strategies, the ability to teach and train a team of athletes will be an entirely different challenge. You must master the transition from playing the game to teaching the game, a more difficult step than most people realize. An athlete gradually gains a sense of how each skill feels—how she has to move and think to perform successfully. As a teacher, you have to search for ways to help athletes gain that sense, or feeling, of how to perform skills, and you must understand that different athletes often perceive and learn the same skill in different ways.

Additionally, you cannot be an effective teacher until you can accept responsibility for the performance of your athletes and team yet not take a poor performance personally nor make it all about you. If you hide behind the excuse that your athletes just can't play, you will never be motivated to find the teaching strategy that will produce improvement. But if you adopt the following credo—"The team will reflect everything the coach has taught the players, or everything the coach has allowed them to do"—you will understand that every player can improve. Even if an athlete's skill level is average, you can

- motivate her to hustle and give great effort on every contact,
- set up training opportunities for the athlete until she is able to perform the skills consistently, and
- inspire the athlete to help the whole be greater than the sum of the individual parts.

And if you continually search for new ways to teach the same skill, you will eventually find a meaningful phrase, drill, or concept that triggers an athlete's reactions in such a way that she finally starts showing improvement in areas where she previously struggled. As a coach you have the responsibility to find a way to teach, motivate, and inspire each athlete to improve her skills. This concept alone—your acceptance of responsibility for each athlete's performance—will produce creative, exciting, and extremely effective teaching, the kind of teaching that in turn results in improved skills and better performance by both the individual and, ultimately, the team.

Technical and Tactical Skills

A coach has the responsibility of patiently and systematically explaining and drilling the athletes on the basic skills that make up the game. These skills, called technical skills, are the fundamentals that provide each player with the tools to execute the physical requirements of the game. Each day at practice, you must also create situations on the court in which players need to use their technical skills in a gamelike situation, forcing them to make decisions that simulate the applications of the skills and the choices they will have to make in a game. These skills, called tactical skills, are the bridge between practice performance and game performance. Although the proper execution of technical skills is necessary for success, the ability of athletes to make appropriate decisions, known as tactical skills, is the key to having everything come together when it counts—in the actual game.

Obviously, other types of skills, such as pure physical capacity, mental skills, communication ability, and character traits, all contribute to athletic performance (Rainer Martens, *Successful Coaching, Third Edition*, Champaign, IL: Human Kinetics, 2004, p. 186-188). Although all these skills are important, effective teaching of the technical and tactical skills of the game still provides the foundation for successful volleyball coaching.

This book focuses on the essential basic to intermediate technical and tactical skills in volleyball. The goal is to provide a resource that will help you improve your understanding and instructional methods as you strive to teach your players this exciting sport.

Technical Skills

Technical skills are defined as "the specific procedures to move one's body to perform the task that needs to be accomplished" (Martens, *Successful Coaching*, p. 169). The proper execution of the technical skills in volleyball is, obviously, crucial to successful performance. Most coaches, even those with little experience, know what the basic technical skills of volleyball are: serving, passing, setting, attacking, blocking, and digging. But the ability to teach athletes how to perform those skills usually develops only over a long period, as a coach gains knowledge and experience.

The goal of this book is to speed up the timetable of teaching skills, improving your ability to

- o clearly communicate the basic elements of each skill to the athletes,
- o construct drills and teaching situations to rehearse those skills in practice,
- o detect and correct errors in the athletes' performance of skills, and
- o help athletes transfer knowledge and ability from practice into games.

Effective coaches have the capacity to transfer their knowledge and understanding of skills into improved performance of those skills by their athletes. This book outlines a plan that will help you do just that by teaching you how to become a master of the basic to intermediate technical skills of volleyball and assisting you in providing your athletes with the resources necessary for success.

Tactical Skills

Mastery of the technical skills of volleyball is important, but athletes must also learn the tactics of the game. Tactical skills are defined as "the decisions and actions of players in the contest to gain an advantage over the opposing team or players" (Martens, *Successful Coaching*, p. 170). Basic volleyball resources might focus on the technical skills of the game and may overlook the tactical aspects. Coaches even omit tactical considerations from practice because they focus so intently on teaching technical skills. For volleyball players to develop better as overall players, they need to learn techniques and tactics together. One way you can approach tactical skills is by focusing on three critical aspects, "the tactical triangle":*

- Reading the play or situation
- Acquiring the knowledge needed to make an appropriate tactical decision
- Applying correct decision-making skills to the problems at the correct time

This book as a whole provides you with the knowledge you need in order to teach players how to use the tactical triangle. Part III covers important cues that help athletes respond appropriately when they see a play developing, including important rules, game strategies, and opponents' strengths and weaknesses that affect game situations, as well as ways to teach athletes how to acquire and use this knowledge. Part III will also help you teach athletes how to make appropriate choices in a given situation and show you how to empower players to recognize emerging situations on their own and make sound judgments.

Perhaps the greatest frustration for a coach is to witness athletes making errors in games on skills they have repeatedly done well in practice. For example, an attacker can successfully hit the ball hard and down into the opposing team's court in practice, but in a game situation when a ball is set to her in a less than perfect manner or she is in front of two strong blockers, she is not able to hit the ball past the blockers. The transfer of skills from practice to the game can be difficult, but you can reduce errors by placing the athletes in gamelike situations in practice to work on tactical skill decisions. Only after rehearsing the tactical decision repeatedly in practice will the athletes be prepared to execute those decisions (while maintaining their execution of the related technical skills) in the game.

Traditional Versus Games Approach to Coaching

As mentioned previously, transferring skills from practices to games can be difficult. A sound background of technical and tactical training prepares athletes for game situations. But you can surpass this level by incorporating gamelike situations into daily training, further enhancing the likelihood that players will transfer skills from practices to games. To understand how to accomplish this, you must be aware of two approaches to coaching—the traditional approach and the games approach.

---

*Adapted, by permission, from R. Martens, 2004, *Successful coaching*, 3rd ed. (Champaign, IL: Human Kinetics), 215.

Part IV of this book provides examples of both the traditional approach and the games approach to coaching. Although each style has its particular advantages, the concept favored in this book is the games approach. The games approach provides athletes with a competitive situation governed by clear objectives and focused on specific individuals and concepts. The games approach creates a productive and meaningful learning environment in which athletes are motivated by both the structure of the drills and the improvements they make. Finally, the games approach prepares athletes for competition because they will have already experienced settings that closely resemble the tactical situations they will see in the game.

Traditional Approach

Although the games approach to coaching has much merit, the traditional approach to coaching also has value. The traditional approach often begins with a warm-up period, followed by individual drills, group drills, and then a substantial team period (or scrimmage) at the end of the practice. The traditional approach can be helpful in teaching the technical skills of volleyball. But unless you shape, focus, and enhance the team training with gamelike situational drills and games, the athletes may be unable to transfer the skills they learn in the drills into the scrimmage situation in practice or, worse, into effective performance, especially of tactical skills, in games.

Games Approach

The games approach emphasizes the use of games and minigames to help coaches provide their athletes with situations that are as close as possible to how a real game is played (Alan G. Launder, *Play Practice*, Champaign, IL: Human Kinetics, 2001). But this method requires more than just putting the players on the court, throwing out a ball, and letting them play. You should incorporate the following three components any time you use the games approach:

1. Shaping
2. Focusing
3. Enhancing

Shaping play allows you to modify the game in a way that is conducive to learning the skills for that particular concept. You can shape play by modifying the rules, the environment (playing area), the objectives of the game, and the number of players (Launder, p. 56). In scrimmage situations the stronger players often dominate, and the weaker players merely get through the scrimmage without playing a strong, active role. The goal is to increase each player's opportunities to respond, so if you shape play by reducing the playing area or number of players, every athlete will have the opportunity to gain more contacts as well as to learn and practice the skills for her specific position on the court.

You also need to *focus* the athletes on the specific objectives of the game. Players are more apt to learn, or at least be open to learning, if they know why they are playing the game and how the tactics they are rehearsing fit into the bigger picture. Provide the athletes with clear objectives of the skill, drill, or game and a straightforward explanation of how those objectives will help them become better volleyball players not just in practice but also in competition.

Finally, you must play an active role throughout practices, *enhancing* play either by stopping the game for the whole team at a teachable moment or by taking individual players aside and instructing them about how they could improve their decision making or technical skills in that situation.

An example of a games approach to teaching tactical skills in volleyball is a game called narrow-court triples. To set up the court, place an extra antenna in the middle of the net and a line on the floor down the middle of the court (lengthwise on both sides of the net). One side of the court will have three players on it, with two back deep to receive a serve and the third player at the net ready to set the pass. Three other players are on the other side of the net, with one of them serving the ball from behind the end line. Since the court has been made smaller, the server will need to be more accurate. The opposing team receives the serve and will pass it to the setter near the net. The setter will set the ball to one of the two hitters on her side of the net, or she can dump the ball over the net to try to score. The receiving team has a small area to cover and pass the ball, so they should experience more success.

The defensive team has only half the court to block and dig, so they can narrow their focus on the setter and two attackers. They will learn to read the hitter's movements and position themselves around the blocker so they will be able to dig up the volleyball. They must control the ball in a smaller court, so they will need to become more accurate with their dig up to their setter. This small court with fewer players teaches the athletes to be more accurate with their serving and attacking and narrows their focus on defense to cover a smaller area. A smaller court and fewer players also means more contacts per player in the same amount of time. Once the athletes go back to a regulation-size court, they will see the difference in how much they have learned.

Coaching volleyball is a challenging yet rewarding job. Volleyball coaches are responsible not only for the development of good players but also for the development of young men and women on and off the court. The emphasis of this book is on the concepts and strategies of teaching the essential basic to intermediate technical and tactical skills of volleyball, using both the traditional and games approaches. The foundation of effective teaching this book provides will help you master the art of helping your athletes refine and improve the array of skills and techniques, and their varied applications, that make up the fast-paced, complex, exciting game of volleyball.

chapter 2

Evaluating Technical and Tactical Skills

Volleyball is the ultimate team sport. Players need to master many technical skills and know how to apply those skills in tactical situations. Most of the focus in team practices and individual training sessions is on the development and improvement of volleyball skills. Coaches, however, must also be concerned about objectively analyzing and evaluating those individual skills and using that information to develop the team's season and game plans. For example, decisions about starting lineups, having players specialize in certain positions, and developing offensive and defensive tactics can be made only if coaches have the necessary information to make sound decisions.

In building a team, coaches should use specific and accurate evaluation tools to assess the development of the individual parts that make up the whole of the team. You must remember that basic physical skills contribute to the performance of the technical and tactical skills of volleyball. In addition, a vast array of non-physical skills, such as mental capacity, communication skills, and character training, overlay athletic performance and affect its development and should also be considered (Rainer Martens, *Successful Coaching, Third Edition*, Champaign, IL: Human Kinetics, 2004). But even though all these skills are important, the focus here is on evaluating the technical and tactical skills of volleyball. Please refer to *Successful Coaching, Third Edition*, to learn more about how to judge those other more intangible skills.

In this chapter we examine evaluation guidelines, exploring the specific skills that should be evaluated and the tools to accomplish that evaluation. Evaluations as described in this chapter will help you produce critiques of your volleyball players that are more objective, something you should continually strive for.

Guidelines for Evaluation

Regardless of the skill you are measuring and the evaluation tool you are using, you should observe the basic guidelines that govern the testing and evaluation process. These are as follows:

- Understanding the purpose of evaluation
- Motivating for improvement
- Providing objective measurement
- Effectively providing feedback
- Being credible

Understanding the Purpose of Evaluation

First, the athletes need to know and understand the purpose of the test and its relationship to the game of volleyball. If you are evaluating a technical skill, the correlation should be easy. But when you are evaluating physical skills or mental, communication, and character skills, you must explain the correlation between the skill and the aspect of the game that will benefit. Doing so speaks to the importance of giving players ownership over their development.

Motivating for Improvement

Coaches must motivate the athletes to improve. Understanding the correlation of the skill to volleyball will help, but sometimes the matches seem a long way away during practices and training. For physical skills, elevating the status of the testing process can help inspire the athletes. If you can create a gamelike atmosphere with many players watching as you conduct the testing, athletes will compete with more energy and enthusiasm than they would if you ran the tests in a more isolated fashion. Goal boards and record boards listing all-time-best performances can also motivate the athletes. The best of these boards have several categories, such as the top 5 or top 10 performances, to give more athletes a reasonable chance to compete for a spot on the board. Separating the team by positions is suggested.

The best motivation, though, is striving for a personal-best effort in physical skills testing or an improved score, compared with the last evaluation, on measurements of technical, tactical, communication, and mental skills. When an athlete compares herself today to herself yesterday, she can always succeed and make progress, regardless of the achievements of teammates. And when an athlete sees personal progress, she will be motivated to continue to practice and train. This concept, while focusing on the individual, does not conflict with the team concept. Rather, you can enhance team development by simply reminding the team that if every player gets better every day, the team will be getting better every day.

Providing Objective Measurement

All testing and evaluation must be unbiased, formal, and consistent. Athletes will easily recognize flaws in the testing process and subsequently lose confidence in the results. Coaches must be systematic and accurate, treating every athlete the same way, for the test to have integrity and meaningful results. No athlete should receive credit for a skill if she does not execute the test regimen perfectly.

You must mandate good form and attention to the details of the test. The same is true of evaluation tools that are not quantitatively measured. A volleyball coach who wants to evaluate technical skills must use the same tool for all athletes at their position and score them fairly and consistently for the players to trust the conclusions reached.

Effectively Providing Feedback

Coaches must convey feedback on testing and performance to the athletes professionally and, if possible, personally. No athlete wants to fail, and all are self-conscious to a certain extent when they don't perform to their expectations or the expectations of their coach. At the same time, each athlete has areas in which she needs to improve, and you must communicate those needs to the athlete, especially if she does not see or understand that she needs to make the improvement. Private regular meetings with athletes are crucial to the exchange of this information. Factual results, comparative charts ranking each athlete, historical records of previous test results, and even video analysis of the athlete's performances can discretely communicate both the positive areas of improvement and the areas where progress needs to be made. Discuss both results and goals for each athlete as well as a plan for how the athletes will reach their goals. If you have a large number of athletes, you can accomplish these individual meetings in occasional and subtle ways—by asking an athlete to stay for a few minutes after practice or a workout, by going out to practice early and creating an opportunity to talk to a player individually, or by calling a player into the office at regular times just to talk. These one-on-one meetings are by far the best method to communicate to athletes the areas in which they need to improve.

Being Credible

Finally, you must apply the principles you are asking of your players to the process of evaluating them. You must be an expert in terms of your knowledge of the technical and tactical skills of your sport so you can accurately and consistently analyze and evaluate the skills that you see your players perform. You must understand the value and importance of the physical skills to convey the importance of these skills to the game. You must exhibit outstanding communication skills to be effective in your teaching, and you must exhibit those same skills in your dealings with other staff members and coaching peers, especially when you are visible to the players, so that you can establish credibility with the players regarding communication.

Evaluating Skills

Clearly, players must know the technical skills demanded by their sport, and they must know how to apply those skills in tactical situations when they compete. You must remember, however, that basic physical skills contribute to the performance of the technical and tactical skills, and so they must be consciously incorporated into an athlete's training plan. In addition, an array of nonphysical skills such as mental capacity, communication skills, and character training also overlay all athletic performance and affect its development.

As you evaluate your athletes, one concept is crucial: Each athlete should focus on improving her own previous performance as opposed to comparing her performance to that of teammates. Certainly, comparative data help an athlete see where she ranks on the team and among other players in the same position or role, and this data may motivate or help the athlete set goals. However, all rankings will place some athletes on the team below others, and the danger of focusing solely on this type of evaluation system is that athletes can easily become discouraged if they consistently rank in the bottom of the team or position. Conversely, if the focus of the evaluation is for every player to improve, compared with personal scores at the last testing, then every player on the team has the opportunity to be successful. Whether you are looking at physical skills or nonphysical skills, encourage your athletes to achieve their own personal bests every time they are tested or evaluated.

Evaluating Physical Skills

The essential physical skills for volleyball are strength, core strength, speed, agility, power, and flexibility. The training and evaluation of those six physical skills are especially important in the off-season and preseason periods, when athletes are concentrating on overall improvement. In-season evaluation, however, is also important to ensure that any off-season gains, especially in strength, do not deteriorate because the players and coaches are devoting much of their time and attention to specific game plan preparation and practice.

Testing should occur at least three times a year—once immediately before the volleyball season begins to gauge the athletes' readiness for the season and provide an initial or baseline score; once at the end of the season to measure the retention of physical skills during competition; and once in the off-season to evaluate the athletes' progress and development in the off-season program. You will be constantly evaluating your athletes throughout the season to make slight adjustments as needed.

Of course, training programs can positively affect several skills. For example, improvements in leg strength and flexibility will almost certainly improve speed. Furthermore, no specific workout program will ensure gains for every athlete in each of the six skill areas. Consequently, measurement of gains in these areas is critical for showing you and the individual athletes where they are making gains and where to place the emphasis of subsequent training programs.

Strength

Strength testing can be done safely and efficiently using various methods. The risk of injury for the athlete is minimal because she is not in the weight room lifting a maximal load. After a proper warm-up, the athlete performs a three-in-a-row standing broad jump test to assess lower-body strength. The athlete stands at a line with a tape measure stretched out in front and does three rapid consecutive broad jumps off of and landing on both feet. Record the total distance jumped, and repeat the test again. A third trial may be included if you are averaging the result for a score, or the best of the trials may be used as the score.

To test upper-body strength, the athlete can perform a two-hand basketball chest throw. The athlete stands at a line and chest-passes the basketball as far as possible along a tape measure stretched out in front on the floor. Make sure someone is standing alongside the tape measure to see or mark where the ball lands so an accurate measurement can be taken. The athlete should repeat this for a total of three throws. Again, you may average the result for a score, or the best of the trials may be used. Athletes can also do a one-minute push-up test (complete full-body push-ups). Each athlete performs as many complete (in good form) push-ups as possible in one minute. A second and perhaps third trial may be done as well, with a rest period between. The same scoring options apply.

Athletes will begin to appreciate the need for good overall strength as they get stronger and discover they have more control over what their bodies are doing. They will be able to move quicker, jump higher, and have more control over their skills as they play this fast-paced sport. They will be able to maintain their focus and control when matches last several hours.

Core Strength

Like the proverbial chain that is only as strong as its weakest link, the core of the body ultimately determines whether an athlete can put it all together and translate her strength, speed, and agility into a successful performance on the volleyball court. The core refers to the midsection of the body—the abdominal muscles, the lower-back muscles, and the muscles of the hip girdle—that connect lower-body strength and functions with upper-body strength and functions. Core strength is essential for volleyball, particularly since several of the skills are done while the athlete is in midair, but it is extremely difficult to isolate and test. The test for core strength is to have the athlete perform bent-knee sit-ups for one minute. Make sure the arms are folded across the chest to limit unnecessary pulling on the back of the neck. Again one to three trials may be used, with rest periods in between, either averaging the result for a score or using the best of the trials as the score.

The core must also be strong for volleyball athletes to play with great explosiveness—combining strength, power, and speed into serving, attacking, and blocking. Every physical training program for volleyball, therefore, must include exercises that strengthen and develop the core. This training program must go beyond sit-ups and crunches, which are important but not comprehensive enough to develop true core strength. Volleyball athletes must incorporate active exercises such as lunges, step-ups, and jump squats to focus on development of the core. Implements such as weighted medicine balls, stability balls, and resistance bands may be incorporated into the training program as well.

Speed

Speed testing for volleyball can focus on running a sprint shuttle the width of the court (30 feet, or 9 m) three times, with the time recorded. The size of the court is used as the measurement in order to relate the test as closely as possible to the game situation. Have the athlete start in a ready position on the sideline. Start the stopwatch when the athlete begins sprinting to the opposite sideline. The athlete will reach down and touch that sideline with one hand, turn and run back to the starting sideline, touch that sideline, and then sprint back to the other sideline, running through it to stop the clock. This shuttle consists of three trips across the court. The athlete will complete two or three trials and use the best time for the score.

Even though the volleyball court is a small area relative to some other sports courts, it is critical that athletes achieve maximum speed in their movement on the court. Players may have to run down an errant pass, move quickly to pass a hard serve, or use quick footwork to move to block or hit a slide. Players can spend a lot of time training in other areas, but they need to know that their overall success as volleyball players will depend on how fast they can move their bodies from point A to point B.

Agility

Agility is important in most sports. It is thought of as a rapid body movement with a change of direction, usually based on a response to some type of cue. Volleyball requires that athletes change direction quickly in short spaces and use quality footwork to get into proper position to receive a serve, set an out-of-system pass, attack a set, cover a hitter, move to block the opposing team's attacker, or dig up an opponent's spike. Agility and footwork are physical skills that must be trained and measured. A simple agility test for volleyball is the T-test. Set three cones 15 feet (4.6 m) apart on a straight line. Place a fourth cone 10 feet (3 m) back from the middle cone so that the cones form a T. For volleyball athletes, this basically means one cone on each sideline, one in the middle of those two, and one at the end line. The athlete starts behind the cone at the base of the T, or at the end line. The coach gives the signal to go and starts the stopwatch. The athlete runs forward to the middle cone, touches the cone, side-slides to the left cone (always facing the net), touches that cone with the left hand, side-slides to the far cone on the right, and touches that one with the right hand. The athlete then side-slides back to the middle cone, touches that one, runs backward to the base of the T, and touches the cone there, stopping the watch. This test measures the athlete's ability to plant, change directions quickly, and keep the core low in the athletic body position frequently mentioned throughout the skills in this book.

In many situations in the sport of volleyball, players must maintain a balanced body position but still be able to quickly change direction on the court. A player in the back row playing defense will need to be ready to chase a deflected ball hit off a blocker's hands as well as move to a ball that hits the net, which changes the anticipated flight of the ball.

Power

Power is another primary physical skill required for volleyball. The emphasis here is on the lower-body explosiveness that helps athletes jump high when attacking and blocking, chase down a bad pass to set, or quickly get to a ball dug off the court. The two simplest and best tests for power are the standing long jump and the vertical jump. Administer both tests with the athlete in a stationary position so that the test measures pure explosiveness on one maximum effort unassisted by a running start. Allow the athlete to take several trials, using the best effort as the recorded score.

For the vertical jump, place a tape measure up the wall vertically. The athlete stands with her side to the wall, both feet flat on the ground, and reaches up with the hand closest to the wall. The point of the fingertips is marked or recorded. This is called standing reach height. The athlete then stands slightly away from the wall and jumps vertically as high as possible from a standing start, using both the arms and legs to assist in projecting the body upward. The athlete attempts to touch the wall at the highest point of the jump and reach. The difference in distance between the standing reach height and the jump height is the score for the vertical jump. The best of three attempts is recorded. A Vertec is a good piece of freestanding equipment to measure the vertical jump with the most accuracy.

Since the sport of volleyball is played over a net set at a certain height, it is essential that athletes use the power in their legs to elevate their bodies off the floor so they can attack the volleyball at a higher contact point, therefore increasing their success rate of hitting the ball down into the opposing team's court. Being able to jump high to get their hands across the net to block balls hit by the opponent is also a highly desired skill.

Flexibility

Flexibility is the most neglected physical skill but one of the most important. Increases in flexibility will help an athlete improve performance in just about every other physical skill. Flexibility is difficult to measure, but the classic sit-and-reach test provides a reasonable indication of an athlete's range and gives her a standard to improve on. This test involves sitting on the floor with legs stretched out straight ahead. The heels of the feet are placed on each side of a line, with a tape measure stretched out in front and the heels placed at the 12-inch (30 cm) mark. Both knees should be kept flat on the floor (the tester may assist by holding them down). With the palms facing downward and the hands on top of each other or side by side, the player reaches forward over the legs and feet and along the tape measure as far as possible. Ensure that the hands remain at the same level, not one reaching farther forward than the other. After some practice reaches, the subject reaches out and holds that position for one or two seconds while the distance is recorded. Make sure there is no bouncing movement—the stretch must be slow, steady, and held. The measurement can be either a plus or a minus from the 12-inch mark. If the athlete reaches past her toes, the measurement is plus X inches; if she can't reach her toes, the measurement is minus X inches.

Although volleyball players are mostly on their feet, they often need to extend their bodies to dig a ball or play a deflected ball. Good flexibility will help keep an athlete from sustaining injuries such as a strained groin or hamstring muscle and hopefully protect the joints from more serious injuries.

Evaluating Nonphysical Skills

Athletic performance is not purely physical; a number of other factors influence it. You must recognize and emphasize mental skills, communication skills, and character skills to enable your athletes to reach peak athletic performance.

Despite the importance of the physical, mental, communication, and character skills, however, the emphasis in this book is on the coaching of essential technical and tactical skills. For an in-depth discussion of teaching and developing both physical and nonphysical skills, refer to chapters 9 through 12 in Rainer Martens' *Successful Coaching, Third Edition*.

Mental Skills

Volleyball is a quick-moving game that requires players to play hard but smart; maintain focus on their technique while implementing a game plan according to their opponents' strengths and weaknesses; stay positive with their teammates when opponents have the momentum; and stay focused on the next play instead of thinking about what just happened.

Most important to volleyball players' success, however, is the mental ability to understand the game and read cues that allow them to execute the proper skill at the right time. They must work hard on every point and continually monitor what is successful and not successful. Players must be ready to adapt to what their opponents are doing offensively and defensively. A consistent performance of technical skills requires knowledge of the game, discipline, and focus on the right cues while maintaining composure as a team. The term *mental toughness* might be the best and simplest way to describe the concentration and determination required to effectively execute the technical skills and appropriate tactical skills in the course of a long volleyball match.

Communication Skills

Volleyball also requires communication skills at several levels—among the players on the court and between the coaches and the players during practices and matches. As a coach, you must convey adjustments to the match plan and strategy during time-outs and in between sets. Because communication skills are essential in volleyball, you should spend considerable time coordinating your system of communication as it pertains to offensive and defensive systems on the court and out-of-system problem solving.

Character Skills

Finally, character skills help shape the performance of the team. Volleyball is a game that requires (and reveals) character as officials make calls, the score changes back and forth, and players are substituted in and out during a match. Good character is critical for teammates to play hard for one another.

Evaluation Tools

Volleyball coaches should video record practices and matches to analyze and evaluate athletes' performance of basic technical and tactical skills. Video is useful because the action is so quick it is difficult, if not impossible, to watch each of the players on every rally. Video allows you to repeatedly review players in practice or in a match, enabling you to evaluate each player on each play. The video also becomes an excellent teaching tool in individual or team meetings because the players can see themselves perform and listen to your comments evaluating that performance. In addition, live delayed video feeds (such as a TiVo) during practices can help athletes evaluate and correct their own performances.

You can use many different systems to evaluate what you see on video. The most common system isn't really a system at all—it is the subjective impression you get when you watch the video, without taking notes or systematically evaluating every player on every play. Because of limitations of time and staff, many coaches use video in this manner, previewing the video, gathering impressions, and then sharing those impressions with the player or players as they watch the video together immediately at courtside or at a later time.

Many coaches, depending on the level of play, have video and computer software that systematically breaks down the video by skills, players, certain rotations, plays, and any number of criteria a coach is interested in. The focus can be on specific techniques and tactical decisions by the players. The grading process can be simple; for example, you can simply give the athlete a plus or a minus on each play and score the total number of plusses versus the total number of minuses for the game. Alternatively, you can score the athlete on each aspect of the play, giving her a grade for technique and a grade for her tactical decision making. More elaborate grading systems keep track of position-specific statistics. Regardless of the level of sophistication or detail of the grading instrument, most coaches use a statistical system of some kind for evaluating player and team performance. Most grading systems are based on a play-by-play (or rep-by-rep in practices) analysis of performance, possibly coupled with an analysis of actual practice or match productivity totals such as the ones listed previously. Here are some basic statistics you may want to keep on your players, either individually or as a team:

- *Points scored per game (set)*: total aces plus total blocks plus total kills divided by total games (sets)
- *Hitting efficiency*: kills minus attack errors divided by total attack attempts
- *Kill percentage*: total number of kills divided by total attack attempts
- *Ace-to-error ratio (A-E ratio)*: total number of aces divided by total number of errors
- *Passing efficiency*: total number of points (based on a three-point system) divided by total number of passes attempted. The three-point system is as follows: three points for a perfect pass to the target area; two points if a pass is close to the target area, but far enough away that setter cannot set the middle attacker; one point if another player (other than the setter) has to step in and set the ball; and zero points if the serve results in an ace.
- *Perfect pass percentage*: total number of perfect passes (a three using the three-point system) divided by total number of passes
- *Points per rotation*: the difference between the number of points your team scored in each rotation and the number of points the opponents scored in each rotation; the results for each rotation will be a plus or minus

ATHLETE EVALUATIONS

Coaches on USA Volleyball High Performance teams evaluate their players in specific areas, such as physical skills, passing, setting, attacking, defending, and blocking. They also evaluate the players' understanding of the sport of volleyball along with their ability to process information while the ball is in play. Following is a comprehensive list of different types of evaluations coaches may want to use with their teams.

- *Physical skills*: approach-jump height, block-jump height, shuttle run, upper-body strength, and lower-body strength
- *Passing skills*: footwork, platform, overhead passing, accuracy, and communication
- *Setting skills*: footwork, hand and arm technique, accuracy, movement, isolation of hitters, out-of-system effectiveness, and communication
- *Attacking skills*: footwork, arm-swing technique, timing, shot selection, out-of-system effectiveness, transition effectiveness, and communication
- *Defending skills*: anticipation, reading the setter and hitter, footwork, court and body positioning, ball control, covering, floor skills technique, and communication
- *Blocking skills*: footwork, hand penetration, anticipation and reading of situation and hitter, and communication
- *Cognitive skills*: preparation, coachability, self-motivation, understands directions, attempts to execute, competitiveness, accepts role, assertiveness, team player, leadership, and conduct
- *Knowledge of the game*: team offense, team defense, and game and court sense

Figure 2.1, a and b, shows examples of an evaluation tool that allows you to isolate technical and tactical skills. The tool breaks down the whole skill into its component parts, enabling a more objective assessment of an athlete's performance than can be produced by statistics. By using these figures and the technical and

Figure 2.1a   Technical Skill Evaluation: Spiking (right-handed)

| | SKILL RATING | | | | | |
| | Weak | | | Strong | | |
Key focal points	1	2	3	4	5	Notes
Approach						
Accelerates, slow to fast	1	2	3	4	5	
Right, left, right, left	1	2	3	4	5	
Left foot forward on takeoff	1	2	3	4	5	
Ball in front of hitting shoulder	1	2	3	4	5	
Lands balanced on both feet	1	2	3	4	5	
Arm swing						
Both arms full swing, back and up	1	2	3	4	5	
Reaches high	1	2	3	4	5	
Arm-swing speed	1	2	3	4	5	
Contact with the ball	1	2	3	4	5	
Snaps wrist	1	2	3	4	5	
Follows through	1	2	3	4	5	

Figure 2.1b   Tactical Skill Evaluation: Selecting the Best Hitter Option by the Setter

| | SKILL RATING | | | | | |
| | Weak | | | Strong | | |
Key focal points	1	2	3	4	5	Notes
Reads the situation	1	2	3	4	5	
Avoids distractions as discussed in "Watch Out!"	1	2	3	4	5	
Uses the appropriate knowledge about the team strategy and game plan	1	2	3	4	5	
Uses the appropriate knowledge about the rules	1	2	3	4	5	
Uses the appropriate knowledge about physical playing conditions	1	2	3	4	5	
Uses the appropriate knowledge about opponents' strengths and weaknesses	1	2	3	4	5	
Uses the appropriate knowledge about self and team	1	2	3	4	5	

tactical skills in parts II and III as a guide, you can create an evaluation tool for each of the technical and tactical skills you want to evaluate during your season. In figure 2.1a, using the technical skill of spiking as an example, we have broken down the skill by pulling out each of its key points.

As you may already know, evaluating tactical skills is more difficult because there are many outside influences that factor into how and when the skill comes into play. However, as a coach, you can use a similar format to evaluate your players' execution of tactical skills. You will need to do the legwork in breaking down the skill into targeted areas; in figure 2.1b, we have used a generic format to show you how you can break tactical skills down for the setter using the skills found in chapters 5 and 6 as a guideline.

The sample evaluation tool shown in figure 2.1, a and b, constitutes a simple way to use the details of each technical and tactical skill, providing an outline for both the player and coach to review and a mechanism for understanding the areas in which improvement is needed. The tool can also be used as a summary exercise. After a match, after a week of practice, or after a preseason or spring practice session, an athlete can score herself on all her essential technical and tactical skills, including all the cues and focal points, and on as many of the corollary skills as desired. You can also score the athlete and then compare the two scoresheets. The ensuing discussion will provide both the player and you with a direction for future practices and drills and will help you decide where the immediate focus of attention needs to be for the athlete to improve her performance. You can repeat this process later so that the athlete can look for improvement in the areas where she has been concentrating her workouts. As the process unfolds, a better consensus between the athlete's scoresheet and your scoresheet should occur.

You must evaluate athletes in many areas and in many ways. This process of teaching, analyzing, evaluating, and motivating an athlete to improve her performance defines the job of the coach: taking the athlete somewhere she could not get to by herself. Without you, the athlete would not have a clear direction of the steps that need to be taken or how to proceed to become a better player. The coach provides the expertise, guidance, and incentive for the athlete to make progress. The evaluation of the athlete's technique might be substantially critical. You need to be careful how criticism is presented, however, and avoid purely negative comments. Try to catch your athletes doing the skills correctly as much as possible and give feedback on that basis.

One final rule, however, caps the discussion of evaluating athletes. Athletes in every sport and every age group want to know how much you care before they care how much you know. You need to keep in mind that at times you must suspend the process of teaching and evaluating to deal with an athlete as a person. You must spend time with your athletes discussing topics other than their sport and their performance. You must show each athlete that you have an interest and a concern for her as a person, that you are willing to listen to each athlete's issues, and that you are willing to assist if doing so is legal and the athlete wishes to be helped. Events in an athlete's personal life can overshadow her athletic quests, and you must be sensitive to that reality. You need to make time to get to know your players as people first and athletes second. Athletes will play their best and their hardest for a coach who cares. Their skills will improve, and their performance will improve, because they want to reward the coach's caring attitude for them with inspired performance. They will finish their athletic careers for that coach having learned a lifelong lesson that care and concern are as important as any skill in the game of volleyball.

PART II

Teaching Technical Skills

Now that you know how to teach and evaluate sport skills, you are ready to dive into the specific skills necessary for success in volleyball. This part focuses on the basic and intermediate skills necessary for your players' success, including offensive technical skills related to serving, passing, setting, and hitting and defensive technical skills related to blocking and digging.

Chapters 3 and 4 present the material in a way that is clear and easy to understand. More important, you can immediately incorporate the information into your practices. Whether you are a seasoned veteran or a new coach, you will find the presentation of skills in this part helpful as you work with your athletes.

For each skill we first present a list of what we call the key points, which are the most important aspects of the skill. This list is a road map to the proper execution of the skill. We give a detailed explanation of these key points, including instructional photos and diagrams to guide you along the way.

At the end of each skill description is a table of common errors that includes instructions for how to correct those errors in your athletes. We also include a useful "At a Glance" section to guide you to other tools in the book that will help you teach your athletes this particular skill—whether it is another technical skill they must be able to perform to be successful or a tactical skill that uses this technical skill.

Offensive Technical Skills

This chapter covers the offensive technical skills players must know to be successful. In this chapter, you will find the following skills:

Serving

Serving is the only skill in volleyball where the individual player is in complete control of the ball. Although there are many different types of serves, common guiding principles should be applied to every serve. The objective of the serve is, minimally, to put the ball in play and, maximally, to score a point. The easiest way to score a point is to make the serve difficult to pass. Being able to serve different types of serves will keep the opposing team off balance with their passing. Any type of serve with good speed will give the opponents less time to react to the ball coming over the net. This, in turn, gives them less time to get in a good position to pass the ball properly or communicate with a teammate if the ball is served to a seam between two players. An aggressive serve is a way of keeping the opponents "out of their offensive system" and out of rhythm. Other variables to consider in serving include the velocity of the serve, where the server is located along the end line as well as the distance behind the end line, and the target or zone where the ball is served into the opposing team's court. Obviously players will miss serves periodically. Remember, it is better to miss the serve long or wide than to serve it into the net and not give the opponents an opportunity to decide whether or not to play the ball.

There are several guiding principles that you and your players must be aware of when serving:

○ There is a point scored on every serve.
○ The serve is the only skill in volleyball where the player has control over all factors, such as location, velocity, and trajectory.
○ If there is a serving error, the other team scores.
○ An aggressive serve has a better chance of taking the opponents out of their offensive system or rhythm.
○ There should be more aces than errors.
○ Players should use the same routine each serve, which includes taking a deep breath, selecting a target, and serving.
○ Simple, efficient mechanics lead to repeatability and more success.
○ Always practice serves in gamelike situations.

Underhand Serve

An underhand serve is a method of putting the ball in play over the net by holding the ball below the waist, tossing it slightly out of the hand, and hitting underneath it with the other hand to send it over the net. The underhand serve is the easiest type of volleyball serve and is usually taught to young, beginning players who may not be physically strong enough to serve the ball over the net using an overhand motion.

KEY POINTS

Following are the most important components of an underhand serve:

- Position square to the target
- Short toss
- Contact with the ball
- Follow-through to target

POSITION SQUARE TO THE TARGET

Figure 3.1 **Player positioned square to the target for the underhand serve.**

The player should take a position somewhere along the end line where she is comfortable serving from and where she will move into the court to play defense. She should be facing the serving target on the other side of the net, with her front foot (foot opposite her serving hand) pointing toward the target and her body square to the target (see figure 3.1). The player should be stable, with her knees slightly bent in a balanced athletic stance. The upper body should be leaned forward slightly, with the weight on the back leg.

SHORT TOSS

The ball is held in the palm of the nonserving, or nonhitting, hand. The player extends the tossing hand out in front of her serving shoulder and holds the ball at about hip height. The toss is very short out of the hand, just above hip height (see figure 3.2). The toss is easier to control than in the overhead serve, which helps young players.

Figure 3.2 **Player making a short toss for the underhand serve.**

(continued)

CONTACT WITH THE BALL

The ball must be contacted in the air when tossed out of the hand, and it is important that the server look at the ball as the serving hand makes contact to ensure a solid serve. The hand position used to contact the ball needs to provide a firm, flat surface. The server can use a fully closed fist, a half-open fist, or even a stiff open hand (see figure 3.3). Ball contact should be just below the middle of the back of the ball, allowing it to travel forward, up, and over the net. The serve can include a step that transfers the player's weight from the rear to the front foot (see figure 3.4), or the player can shift the body weight forward without taking a step. Both options provide additional power in getting the ball over the net.

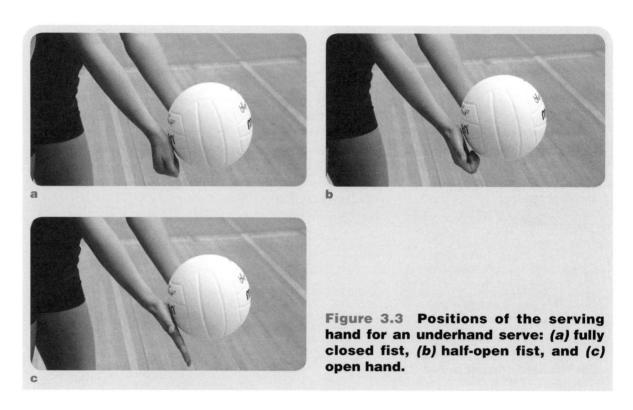

Figure 3.3 Positions of the serving hand for an underhand serve: *(a)* fully closed fist, *(b)* half-open fist, and *(c)* open hand.

Figure 3.4 **Player position prior to contacting the ball for an underhand serve with a step to shift body weight.**

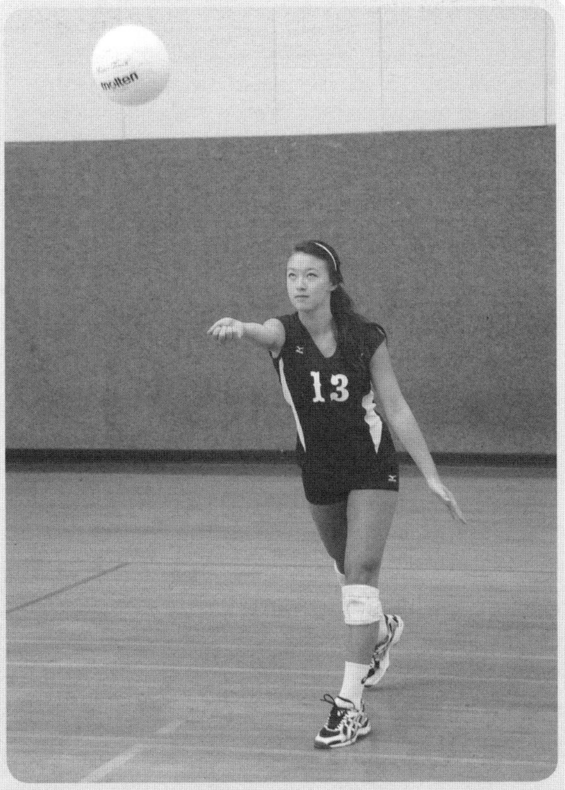

FOLLOW-THROUGH TO TARGET

The follow-through of the serving hand (the hand that makes contact with the ball) should be shoulder high and toward the court as if reaching over the net (see figure 3.5). This is similar to a release and follow-through in bowling. The server should maintain this position momentarily before entering the court to play defense.

Figure 3.5 **Player following through toward the intended target.**

(continued)

Common Errors

Following are several common errors you may run into when teaching your athletes the underhand serve.

Error	Error correction
Server is not facing the intended target.	Make sure the server concentrates on getting the feet, hips, and shoulders square to the target before the serve.
Server has the wrong foot forward.	To maintain balance and have more power, the foot opposite the serving hand should be forward so body weight can be transferred by shifting the weight forward or taking one small step.
Toss is inaccurate.	The ball should be tossed just slightly out of the hand and in line with the hitting shoulder before contact.
Serve lacks power.	The ball should be tossed slightly in front of the hitting hand toward the net so that shifting the body weight can help provide more power. Tell the player to speed up the arm swinging through to contact the ball.
Server's elbow is bent on contact.	Make sure the server concentrates on keeping the arm straight when swinging it back and then forward, making the longer lever more accurate.
Server's wrist or hand is loose.	It is important to have a strong, solid hand and wrist for better accuracy. Have the player practice serving straight ahead at a wall to make sure there is control.

The sidearm serve is another method of introducing the ball into play by hitting it over the net to the opponents from a sideways position with a short toss. The sidearm serve can also be used with young players. Players not yet strong enough to get the ball over the net using an overhand motion may be taught this technique in which the body rotates, or torques, providing even more power than the previous underhand serve.

PERPENDICULAR POSITION TO THE NET

The player should take a position somewhere along the end line where she is comfortable serving from and where she will move into the court to play defense after the serve. The player should position her feet approximately shoulder-width apart, with her nonhitting arm side to the net (see figure 3.6). She should be stable, with her knees slightly bent in a balanced athletic stance. The player's upper body should lean forward slightly, with her weight on her back leg (the one that is farthest from the net).

KEY POINTS

Following are the most important components of a sidearm serve:

- Perpendicular position to the net
- Short toss and body rotation
- Contact with the ball
- Follow-through to target

Figure 3.6 **Player's body positioned perpendicular to the net for the sidearm serve.**

(continued)

SHORT TOSS AND BODY ROTATION

The player holds the ball waist high in the palm of the nonhitting hand, away from the body, in line with the nonhitting shoulder and slightly toward the net. The toss is very short out of the hand, with contact quickly following.

As the toss is released, the hips and then the shoulders rotate toward the target, providing torque into the contact and giving the serve more power (see figure 3.7). This puts the weight on the front foot (see next section on weight transfer), with the upper body facing the net during and after contact, allowing the athlete to run into the court to a defensive position.

a   b

Figure 3.7   **Player making *(a)* a short toss and *(b)* rotating the body for the sidearm serve.**

CONTACT WITH THE BALL

The server should look at the ball as it is contacted. The hitting arm is held out to the side of the body away from the net and will swing through the ball toward the net (like slamming a door). The contact hand position can be anything from a fully closed fist, to a half-open fist, to an open hand as long as the contact surface is firm and flat (see figure 3.8). The contact point on the hand should be facing toward the target area.

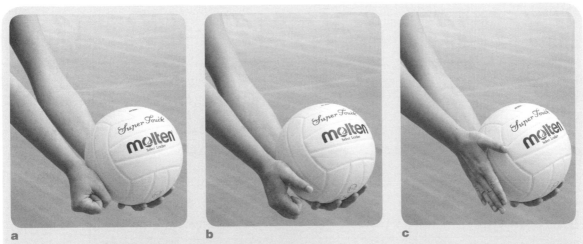

a　　　　　　　　　b　　　　　　　　　c

Figure 3.8 **Positions of the serving hand for a sidearm serve:** *(a)* **fully closed fist,** *(b)* **half-open fist, and** *(c)* **open hand.**

Figure 3.9 Player contacting the ball for the sidearm serve with a step to shift body weight.

The player shifts her weight during the toss and contact. This can be done with a slight step onto the front foot toward the net (see figure 3.9) or simply a weight transfer from the back foot to the front foot nearest the net. The knees should be bent, with shoulders slightly forward.

(continued)

FOLLOW-THROUGH TO TARGET

The follow-through of the serving hand (the one that makes contact with the ball) should be shoulder high and over the net and into the court (see figure 3.10). The server should maintain this position momentarily before entering the court to play defense.

At a Glance

The following parts of the text offer additional information on the sidearm serve:

Underhand serve	25
Standing floater serve	34
Jump floater serve	39
Topspin serve	43
Roundhouse serve	46
Jump spin serve	50
Forearm pass	55
Overhead pass	59
Aggressive serving	142
Team serve reception	146

Figure 3.10 **Player following through toward the intended target for the sidearm serve.**

Common Errors

Following are several common errors you may run into when teaching your athletes the sidearm serve.

Error	Error correction
Server loses balance.	The player must use a balanced athletic stance, with the knees bent and feet shoulder-width apart.
Server makes poor contact with the ball.	The toss must be accurate and in line with the hitting hand as the body rotates. Tell the server to look at the ball to make sure the contact is solid.
Serve lacks power (ball does not go over the net).	Have the player swing the arm faster to give the serve more speed. Also work on core exercises to increase the strength of the trunk of the body.
Serve lacks power (ball does not go over the net).	Follow-through needs to be complete, with the body rotated and the hand toward the net facing the target over the net.

KEY POINTS

Following are the most important components of a standing floater serve:

- o Position square to the target
- o Toss, arm swing, and body rotation
- o Contact with the ball
- o Follow-through to target

This serve is the basic overhand serve technique used by most players, from beginners to international athletes. If a player is strong enough to throw the ball over the net from the end line with an overhand motion, she can learn how to execute this type of serve. It is such an effective serve because when done correctly, the ball floats (without spinning) and has an unpredictable path that makes it very difficult to pass accurately.

POSITION SQUARE TO THE TARGET

The player should take a position somewhere along the end line, from which she will move into the court to play defense. The player should begin with the foot on the nonhitting side forward and her weight on the back foot (see figure 3.11). The front foot, hips, and shoulders should face the target where she wants to serve the ball. The knees should be bent slightly, with the body in a balanced athletic stance. The ball should be held in the pads of the fingers of the nonhitting hand, about shoulder high and in line with and slightly in front of the serving shoulder.

Figure 3.11 **Player positioned square to the target for the standing floater serve.**

TOSS, ARM SWING, AND BODY ROTATION

As she tosses the ball, the server should take a slight step forward with the front foot (see figure 3.12) or simply begin to transfer her weight from the back to the front foot. The ball for a floater serve is tossed, or more accurately, lifted, only as high as the server can reach with the serving hand when extended. The ball should be in the air only briefly, with lift–hit timing (see the next section for information on contacting the ball). As the ball is lifted for the toss, the hitting-hand elbow is drawn back high (at or above the shoulder), which rotates the hitting shoulder away from the ball. At the height of the toss, the hips and then shoulders begin rotating toward the net, followed by the elbow and then the hand reaching to the point of contact.

a   b

Figure 3.12 **Player (a) tossing the ball for a standing floater serve and (b) taking a step to shift her weight.**

(continued)

CONTACT WITH THE BALL

The eyes should focus on the ball, and the server should see the ball as it is contacted. The player contacts the ball with a flat palm on the back of the ball, slightly below center, and the palm faces the target upon contact. The player should keep the fingers away from the ball and hit straight through. As we learned in the previous section, just before contact, the weight is shifted forward, then the elbow and then the forearm are brought forward, with the wrist extended and the hand rigid upon contact (see figure 3.13). The ball should be in front of and in line with the hitting shoulder.

Figure 3.13 Player contacting the ball for the standing floater serve.

FOLLOW-THROUGH TO TARGET

The follow-through of the hitting hand (palm is the contact area) should be high, with the palm to the target (see figure 3.14). The server should hold this position momentarily before entering the court to play defense.

Figure 3.14 Player following through to the target for the standing floater serve.

(continued)

Common Errors

Following are several common errors you may run into when teaching your athletes the standing floater serve.

Error	Error correction
Server contacts the ball with uneven surface, using the knuckles or fingers.	Contact surface is the flat, rigid surface of the palm of the hand, which keeps the ball from spinning and makes it float.
Server's wrist is loose.	Tell the player to keep the wrist and forearm rigid on contact.
Toss has spin.	Have the server hold the ball with the inside pads of the fingers and lift the ball up without any spin.
Toss is too low or too high.	Tell the server to see how high the serving hand will be on full reach and toss to that height.
Server steps forward with the same foot as the hitting arm.	Make sure the player starts with the feet in a staggered stance. Shifting the weight forward or stepping forward onto the front foot will provide power for the serve.
Slow swing causes loss of power.	The player needs to swing the serving hand through faster to increase the speed of the serve and make solid contact with the flat palm of the hand.
Server lacks control.	Remind the server to watch the ball as it is contacted to make sure there is solid contact. The palm should be facing toward the target upon contact.
Toss is inconsistent.	The server needs to get the feet in a good stance to transfer the body weight, with the front foot at the end line, but lift and serve the ball without taking a step. This will force the server to make a good toss. The server could also start with the hitting hand and elbow already rotated back so there is one fewer motion and one fewer variable. The toss must be in line with the hitting shoulder. Have the server let the lifted ball drop several times to ensure it is consistently tossed to the correct spot.

Jump Floater Serve

The jump floater serve is the same as the standing floater serve except there is an approach and jump to make contact with the ball. This type of serve allows the server to contact the ball at a higher point, making the trajectory of the serve flatter over the net and keeping the ball in the air for a shorter period, giving the passer less time to react and adjust to the serve. If a player is strong enough to throw the ball over the net overhand from the end line, then she can learn how to execute this type of serve. It is such an effective serve because when done correctly, the ball floats (without spinning) and has an unpredictable path, which makes it very difficult to pass accurately.

POSITION SEVERAL STEPS BEHIND THE END LINE

The player should take a position somewhere along the end line, from which she will move into the court to play defense. The player must be far enough behind the end line that she can make her approach and jump without going over the end line and committing a foot fault. The player should begin with the foot on the nonhitting side forward and the weight on the back foot. The ball should be held in both hands, about waist high and in line with and slightly in front of the serving shoulder (see figure 3.15).

KEY POINTS

Following are the most important components of a jump floater serve:

- Position several steps behind the end line
- Approach for the serve
- Toss slightly toward the net
- Jump and swing
- Contact with the ball
- Follow-through to target, landing on both feet

Figure 3.15 **Player positioned several steps behind the end line in preparation for the jump floater serve.**

(continued)

APPROACH FOR THE SERVE

For a full three-step approach, the player steps forward with the foot on the nonhitting side (see figure 3.16a), followed by a step onto the hitting-side foot (see figure 3.16b), and then plants the nonhitting-side foot (slightly in front, closer to the net) and jumps up off both feet (see figure 3.16c). This is the same basic footwork and approach used in attacking the ball at the net, which we cover on page 88. An alternative is a two-step approach. From the same starting position, the first step is taken with the hitting-side foot, and then the nonhitting-side foot is planted so the player can jump off both feet.

a b c

Figure 3.16 **Player taking a full three-step approach for the jump floater serve.**

TOSS SLIGHTLY TOWARD THE NET

The ball may be tossed either with both hands or with the nonhitting hand as you saw in figure 3.16, slightly out in front of the hitting shoulder as the server begins to take the second step of the three-step approach. For a two-step approach, the toss is on the first step. The toss should be 3 to 4 feet (.9 to 1.2 m) high and slightly toward the net so the server can jump up and reach high to hit it.

JUMP AND SWING

As the player lifts the ball for the toss, the hitting-hand elbow is drawn back high, which rotates the hitting shoulder away from the ball, as you saw in figure 3.16b. As the server jumps, and at the height of the toss, the hips and shoulders begin rotating around a central axis toward the net, followed by the elbow and the hand to the point of contact. The ball should be in front of and in line with the hitting shoulder.

CONTACT WITH THE BALL

Throughout the entire motion, the server should focus on the ball and should see the ball being contacted. The contact point is on the back of the ball, slightly below center, with the palm of the hand. The wrist should be rigid and cocked back slightly to keep the fingers away from the ball. The server should hit straight through the ball, with the palm to the target throughout (see figure 3.17).

At a Glance

The following parts of the text offer additional information on the jump floater serve:

Underhand serve	25
Sidearm serve	29
Standing floater serve	34
Topspin serve	43
Roundhouse serve	46
Jump spin serve	50
Forearm pass	55
Overhead pass	59
Aggressive serving	142
Team serve reception	146

Figure 3.17 Player contacting the ball for the jump floater serve.

(continued)

FOLLOW-THROUGH TO TARGET, LANDING ON BOTH FEET

The follow-through of the hitting hand should be high and into the court, with the palm to the target, while the player lands balanced on both feet (see figure 3.18). The server's forward momentum should cause her to land inside the end line after contact with the ball. She will then continue to move into her defensive position on the court.

Figure 3.18 **Player following through the ball and landing in a balanced position on both feet after hitting the jump floater serve.**

Common Errors

Following are several common errors you may run into when teaching your athletes the jump floater serve.

Error	Error correction
Toss is inconsistent.	Practice this serve by tossing and jumping to serve without the approach. Make sure the toss is in line with the hitting shoulder.
Toss is too far in front or behind.	Practice this serve by tossing and jumping to serve without the approach. Remind the server to carry the ball forward and lift toward the net.
Server gets the footwork confused.	Use a spike approach. Start with the more controllable two-step-approach footwork.

The topspin serve is an overhand serve technique that can be hit with tremendous power and is used by intermediate to advanced players. This serve travels over the net with good speed and topspin, bringing it down into the court more quickly than a floater serve. Although the path of the ball is more predictable than for a floater serve, the ball will drop faster and land in front of many passers who are used to having the ball come right to them. It may also appear to be traveling past the end line, but the spin of the ball may bring it down into the court, keeping it from going out of bounds.

KEY POINTS

Following are the most important components of a topspin serve:

- Position square to the target
- Toss and body rotation
- Contact with the ball
- Follow-through to target

POSITION SQUARE TO THE TARGET

The player should take a position somewhere along the end line, from which she will move into the court to play defense. The player should begin facing the net, with the foot opposite the serving arm forward and the weight on the back foot. The ball should be held in the nonhitting hand at about shoulder height and in front of the hitting shoulder, between the body and the net (see figure 3.19).

Figure 3.19 **Player positioned square to the target for the topspin serve.**

(continued)

TOSS AND BODY ROTATION

The toss for a topspin serve is 2 to 3 feet (.6 to .9 m) directly over and in line with the hitting shoulder. The ball is held in the palm of the nonserving hand and tossed upward, spinning forward toward the net with topspin. As the server tosses the ball, the hitting-hand elbow is raised high and back, rotating the shoulder and hips away from the ball (see figure 3.20). As the ball drops into the contact zone, the hips and shoulder rotate forward toward the net, followed by the elbow and then the hand to the point of contact.

Figure 3.20 Player tossing the ball overhead with topspin.

CONTACT WITH THE BALL

The player must watch the ball to make good contact. Contact is made with the heel of the hand first and the fingers spread to allow a large area for contact with the ball. The contact point is on the back of the ball, slightly farther below center than for a floater serve. At the top of the arm swing, the wrist and fingers snap over the top of the ball toward the target on the other side of the net. This serve can be hit with a simple weight shift from the rear foot onto the front foot (see figure 3.21) or with a short step with the front foot to provide power. The back will be arched just before contact.

Figure 3.21 Player contacting the ball for the topspin serve using a weight shift from the back to front foot.

FOLLOW-THROUGH TO THE TARGET

The abdominal muscles will contract and the body will bend forward at the waist, providing more power to this serve. The follow-through of the hitting hand should be high and into the court, with the wrist snapped toward the target and then continuing down to the hitting side of the body. The server should hold this position momentarily before moving into the court to play defense.

Common Errors

Following are several common errors you may run into when teaching your athletes the topspin serve.

Error	Error correction
Ball goes into the net.	The toss is too far in front. The ball should be tossed closer to the body and up over the hitting shoulder.
Ball floats with no spin over the net.	The ball needs to be tossed high overhead with topspin and contacted with a wrist snap.
Server has no wrist snap.	Have the player hit the ball down to the floor, bouncing it up to the wall with spin to practice the correct wrist snap to produce topspin.
Ball goes deep out of bounds.	Remind the server to snap the wrist more and contact higher on the ball instead of underneath.

KEY POINTS

Following are the most important components of a roundhouse serve:

- Perpendicular position to the net
- Toss slightly in front
- Arm swing and body rotation
- Contact with the ball
- Follow-through to target

The roundhouse serve falls somewhere between the sidearm serve and the overhand serve and can be used by all levels of players. Players who may not yet be strong enough to serve the ball over the net using a regular overhand motion may use this serve. It uses more body torque (rotation), which provides more power than an underhand or sidearm serve. The roundhouse serve may also be used by players experiencing shoulder problems.

PERPENDICULAR POSITION TO THE NET

The player should take a position somewhere along the end line facing the sideline, from which she will move into the court to play defense. The player stands with her nonhitting side toward the net and with the feet, hips, and shoulders perpendicular to the net, meaning parallel to the sideline (see figure 3.22). Knees should be slightly bent throughout the serve.

Figure 3.22 Player positioned perpendicular to the net for the roundhouse serve.

TOSS SLIGHTLY IN FRONT

The server holds the ball out away from the body in the nonhitting hand at waist height and slightly forward of the body toward the net. The hitting hand and arm are held back near the rear hip. The ball is lifted as in the floater serve to just as high as the server can reach, in front of the body, toward the net, and in line with the hitting shoulder (see figure 3.23). The ball is contacted with the palm of the hand as the serving arm swings up and around to hit it.

ARM SWING AND BODY ROTATION

The player pulls back the hitting arm near the hip and keeps the upper body counterrotated to provide extra power (see figure 3.24). As the weight is shifted to the front foot and the hips and then shoulders begin to rotate toward the net, the extended hitting arm rotates from the hip up to shoulder height to contact the ball above the head in line with the hitting shoulder.

Figure 3.23 Player tossing the ball slightly in front of the hitting shoulder.

Figure 3.24 Player's arm swing and body rotation for the roundhouse serve.

(continued)

CONTACT WITH THE BALL

The hand position when contacting the ball can be a fully closed fist to a half-open fist or an open hand as long as the contact surface is firm and flat. The eyes should focus on the ball during contact. At contact, the nonhitting arm is dropped, the weight is forward, and the hitting hand should be high and should move forward into the court (see figure 3.25). This serve can be hit with a short step onto the front foot or simply a weight transfer from the back foot to the front foot. The feet, hips, and shoulders rotate toward the court as contact is made, which provides power for this serve.

Figure 3.25 **Player contacting the ball for the roundhouse serve using a weight transfer.**

At a Glance

The following parts of the text offer additional information on the roundhouse serve:

Underhand serve	25
Sidearm serve	29
Standing floater serve	34
Jump floater serve	39
Topspin serve	43
Jump spin serve	50
Forearm pass	55
Overhead pass	59
Aggressive serving	142
Team serve reception	146

FOLLOW-THROUGH TO TARGET

The hitting arm follows through high and into the court, with the palm toward the target, and is held there momentarily (see figure 3.26). The server's feet, hips, shoulders, and body should face the target before she moves into the court to a defensive position.

Figure 3.26 **Player following through toward the target for the roundhouse serve.**

Common Errors

Following are several common errors you may run into when teaching your athletes the roundhouse serve.

Error	Error correction
Toss is inconsistent.	Make sure the toss is in front of the body, between the body and the net and in line with the hitting shoulder.
Ball goes into the net.	The contact point on the ball should be a little below center to make sure it goes up and over the net.
Serve is misdirected.	At the time of contact, the hitting surface should be rigid and facing the target area.
Serve lacks power.	Have the player swing faster and rotate the body with more and faster torque to add power.

KEY POINTS

Following are the most important components of a jump spin serve:

o Position facing the net
o Toss with the serving hand
o Approach and arm swing
o Contact with the ball
o Landing and follow-through

The jump spin serve is a great serve, and when hit with enough control and speed, it can be difficult to receive. It can be used by any player with enough strength and ability to control the ball. The player makes a full spike approach behind the end line, hitting the ball with topspin down into the opposing team's court. Although the ball can be served hard, the trajectory is predictable, with the topspin bringing it down into the court quickly. Many times the ball will drop in front of the player trying to pass it. It is also a crowd pleaser when executed well.

POSITION FACING THE NET

The player should take a position somewhere along the end line, from which she will move into the court to play defense. The player starts facing the net and deep enough behind the end line to make a full attack approach (see figure 3.27).

Figure 3.27 Player positioned facing the net for the jump spin serve.

TOSS WITH THE SERVING HAND

The player holds the ball in the palm of the serving hand, low and in line with the hitting shoulder to begin the serve, with the body weight balanced. The server tosses the ball with topspin, using the shoulder as a fulcrum, out in front of the body, high and toward the net, slightly inside the court end line. The toss can be as high as she can control it and keep it in line with the hitting shoulder (see figure 3.28).

Figure 3.28 The toss for the jump spin serve is as high as the player can control and is in line with her hitting shoulder.

APPROACH AND ARM SWING

The approach for the jump spin serve is used to transfer the horizontal movement into an increased vertical jump. The player begins the approach as soon as she tosses the ball by taking four steps (a three-step approach may also be used, but four steps allow more momentum to be built before the jump). The server starts with the hitting-side foot on the first step as the tossing arm drops back and then steps with the nonhitting-side foot as the tossing arm swings forward and the ball is released. The third step is taken, followed closely by the fourth step (both feet land almost at the same time) to plant for the broad jump up to the ball as it reaches the peak of the toss. In the plant position the knees are bent, preparing to jump, and both arms are extended high and back; on takeoff, both arms swing quickly and aggressively forward and up to the ball, as shown in figure 3.29.

Figure 3.29 Player jumping up to the ball for a jump spin serve.

(continued)

CONTACT WITH THE BALL

At the top of the jump, the serving shoulder should be rotated back away from the ball. The nonhitting arm is used as a guide and is extended up and toward the tossed ball. The serving-arm elbow should be high, with the palm of the hand open and facing away from the body, and the wrist should be loose (see figure 3.30a). The server's body will float forward from the takeoff point.

The contact point on the ball is on the back, slightly below center, and the ball is contacted with an open hand, fingers spread (see figure 3.30b). The wrist snaps quickly up and over the ball toward the target to create topspin, and the body pikes in the air on contact, providing additional power. Contact should be high and in front of the head but in line with the hitting shoulder. The guide-arm elbow will pull down toward the body, which will start the hip and right shoulder torque, or rotation. The hitting shoulder is now directly beneath the ball, with the serving-arm elbow preparing to extend and swing through to throw the serving hand at the ball for contact. The rotation of the body is complete, and the hitting arm is fully extended.

a   b

Figure 3.30 **Player contacting the ball for the jump spin serve.**

LANDING AND FOLLOW-THROUGH

The player lands balanced on both feet well inside the end line of the court (see figure 3.31). As long as the ball is contacted behind the end line or the player jumps from behind the end line to contact the ball in the air, it is perfectly legal to land inside the court. The wrist and hand follow through toward the ground. The player will then run to her defensive position on the court.

Figure 3.31 **Player landing and following through for the jump spin serve.**

Common Errors

Following are several common errors you may run into when teaching your athletes the jump spin serve.

Error	Error correction
Serve is inconsistent.	Teach this serve by starting at the attack line. Have the player toss the ball up near the net, make an approach, and hit it over. Continue to move back from the net until the player is jump serving from behind the end line.
Toss is too far in front, and the ball hits the net.	Server must chase the ball with an aggressive approach so the shoulder is under the ball at contact. To practice this serve, first have the player try tossing the ball up with topspin and hitting the serve without using an approach. You can also try using a line on the court or a floorboard to help align the ball toss from outside the hip up in front of the hitting shoulder.
Toss is too far behind, and the ball goes out of bounds.	Have the player toss the ball up with topspin toward the net. Server must chase the ball with an aggressive approach.
Toss is inconsistent.	Start teaching this serve by adding 1 step to the approach at a time (start with no steps, then 1 step, then 2 steps until the full approach is taken). Also place the server on a line perpendicular to the net to ensure the ball toss is out in front of the approach; tell the server to keep the shoulder on that line during the approach.

Passing

Passing is used in its many variations to receive serves, free balls, down balls, or even tips or attacks. The forearm pass is the most common form and is usually used for any ball coming over the net that is too low to play using an overhead pass. Passing is one of the most important skills in volleyball and is a key to whether a team is successful. Being able to receive a serve and accurately pass it to the setter, whether using a forearm or an overhead pass, will determine the offense the team will be able to use. Poor passing will limit the team's options in setting the attackers. Successful passers have good vision, movement, and eye–hand coordination. They are confident and communicate quickly and effectively with teammates before and during the play. Two techniques for passing are discussed here, with forearm passing being the most popular and overhead passing being for more advanced players.

There are several guiding principles that you and your players must be aware of when passing:

- Angle of arms at contact is the key—the ball knows angles.
- Keep the head in front of the feet.
- Arms and body act independently.
- Arms move faster than the body to pass from outside the midline.
- One motion to the ball.
- Less movement means more repeatability.
- Passing needs to be consistent under pressure.

Forearm Pass

A forearm pass is used in volleyball to receive a ball coming over the net from a serve or a free ball. The hands and arms are held together to make a flat, solid platform to contact and direct the ball to the setter or target area on the court near the net. This skill is critical to master to be successful in the sport of volleyball.

READY POSITION

The feet should be in a slightly staggered stance and shoulder-width apart, with the right foot slightly forward and the knees bent (see figure 3.32). The body should be in a medium-high body position, enabling the player to move quickly. The upper body is bent forward, with the head in front of the feet. The hands should be hanging down in front of the knees, with the shoulders loose, the elbows locked, and the hands open and palms to the net. This position will look much like a shortstop in baseball waiting for the batter to hit the ball. The hips and feet should be facing the direction the ball is coming from (i.e., the server). When assuming this ready position, the player should quickly assess where she is in the court in relation to teammates and the sideline and end line of the court so she can make a good decision on whether to play a ball, let a teammate play it, or let it go out of bounds.

READING THE SERVER

When preparing to receive a serve and the official gets ready to blow the whistle, the player should be in the ready position and focusing on the server. The player should watch where the server is looking and determine where the server is intending to serve the ball by watching the toss height, direction, and contact on the ball. Attention to these details will help determine what type of serve to expect and where the ball may end up. The player should continue focusing on the ball from when it leaves the server's hand until it is passed. The receiver should observe the ball direction, trajectory, speed, and spin and communicate with teammates what she sees.

LEVEL MOVEMENT TO THE BALL

As soon as the direction of the ball is judged, the player shuffles quickly toward the ball, keeping the feet apart, with the right foot forward and the body balanced, in an effort to beat the ball to the spot where it will land. The player should strive to get the feet to the ball and keep the body behind the ball as much as possible—in other words,

KEY POINTS

Following are the most important components of a forearm pass:

- Ready position
- Reading the server
- Level movement to the ball
- Ball contact with the platform
- Platform held toward target

Figure 3.32 **Player in the ready position for a forearm pass.**

(continued)

block the ball with the midline of the body. The body movement to the ball should be level to keep the head and eyes from moving up and down. This is important to see the ball clearly, and the player doesn't waste time rising up and getting back down.

BALL CONTACT WITH THE PLATFORM

The surface of the forearms that the player uses to contact the ball is called the platform. The player should keep the ball, platform, and target in view and be stopped and balanced on contact whenever possible. The intended target for a serve reception (or free ball) is just to the right side of the middle of the court (see figure 3.33), so the player should angle the platform in that direction and transfer the weight to the right foot in the direction of this target area as contact is made. Remember that the platform with the arms is made just before contact with the ball. If the arms are put together too early, it inhibits the player's ability to get to the ball quickly and efficiently.

The ball should be contacted using the fleshy part of inner arms for good rebound surface between the wrists and elbows. The base of the thumbs should be together, with the wrists extended downward. The elbows should be straight and the arms flat. The platform should be out away from the body and under the volleyball, with the shoulders shrugged. The player should angle the arms and shoulders to the target area by dropping the inside shoulder (nearest the target). Ideally, contact should be made when the ball is between waist and knee height (see figure 3.34). This will allow the passer more time to prepare for the contact and will also give a floater serve time to stop moving or floating and drop in a more predictable path. If the ball is too high as it approaches, the passer should move back quickly by stepping back and turning the body away from the target while keeping the platform solid and facing the target. The eyes should continue focusing on the ball as it nears the platform to ensure good solid contact, then the focus shifts to the target.

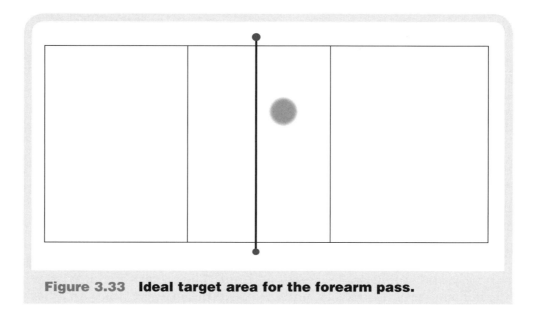

Figure 3.33   Ideal target area for the forearm pass.

Figure 3.34 **Contacting the ball for a forearm pass.**

Figure 3.35 **Player holding the platform toward the target after contacting the ball for a forearm pass.**

PLATFORM HELD TOWARD TARGET

When the ball has been contacted, the player continues to hold the platform toward the target momentarily while maintaining a balanced position (see figure 3.35) and then moves forward to attack the ball or cover a teammate attacking the ball. If a player cannot hold this position, it means she was not balanced when she made the pass. If this happens, the player and coach should take time to observe the path of the passed ball and make an adjustment for the next pass if needed.

(continued)

Common Errors

Following are several common errors you may run into when teaching your athletes the forearm pass.

Error	Error correction
Player bends her elbows.	Remind the player to keep the passing skill simple—there is no need to have the elbows bent. Keeping the arms straight will make the pass more accurate. It also takes more time to unbend the elbows to pass, therefore losing valuable time.
Player "shanks" a pass, or the ball flies off her arms outside the court.	The player must get her body behind the ball to keep this from happening. Have the player chase down the shanked ball a few times, and she will be more likely to keep the ball between her body and the net when making contact.
Player puts her hands together too soon.	This limits the player's ability to move quickly to the ball. Remind the player to run to the ball first and then put the hands together as the ball arrives, just before contact.
Player passes the ball just over the net, and the opponents attack it.	The player needs to adjust the level of the arms to the correct angle depending on the distance from the net and the speed of the ball. This will become easier with more experience.
Player passes the ball straight up instead of forward toward the net.	The player needs to let the ball come down below the waist instead of trying to pass it while it is at shoulder height. She may need to take a step or two back to keep the ball low and in front of her to push it forward toward the target.

Overhead Pass

The overhead (overhand) pass can be used by any player to receive a ball coming over the net. Volleyball rules at most levels have changed, allowing more leniency on receiving a serve or spike with an overhead pass. This first contact does not necessarily need to be a clean contact. The ball travels faster on the volleyball serve, so only players who have strong hands should attempt this. Players must understand that they need to keep their fingers protected and away from the oncoming ball.

The overhead pass is also used to pass a free ball to a setter. However, using the overhead pass to receive serves differs slightly from the setting skill. It can be less restrictive than the regular second-contact set since double contact is allowed only on the first contact of the ball coming over the net.

Following are situations in which a player would use the overhead pass for serve reception.

- Short serves, since the ball is not traveling at a high speed and the trajectory of the serve is usually higher, slower, softer, and therefore more forgiving.
- When the ball is above the player's waist or shoulders and is not traveling too fast. Players may begin in a starting position closer to the net so they can transition to hit faster.
- Any time the passer can get directly under the ball. It is hard to execute an overhead pass unless the ball is directly above the forehead.
- Any time the offense needs to be sped up to beat the blockers. Since the ball is contacted at a higher point, this will get the ball from the passer to the setter more quickly.

READY POSITION

The player should get in a ready position before the serve in the middle of the court (halfway between the center line and the end line) so the serve can be received overhead without going out of bounds (see figure 3.36).

MOVEMENT TO THE BALL

As the ball is served, the player should move to where the ball will descend and get into position so she can make contact with it in front of her forehead.

Figure 3.36 Ready position for an overhead pass.

(continued)

CONTACT WITH THE BALL

The player should put her hands up in front of her forehead just before contact to ensure that she can move to the ball quickly without the arms inhibiting her ability to move fast; however, the ball will most likely be traveling very fast, so the player must get her hands up quickly. The hands are positioned slightly closer together than when setting and with the fingers spread (see figure 3.37a). The wrists should be stiff and fingers spread wide to make a large surface for the ball to contact (see figure 3.37b). Once the ball is contacted, the hands and arms move upward to direct the ball to the setter or target area near the middle right side of the court and several feet off the net (see figure 3.37c). The ball should be passed approximately antenna height, or 10 feet (.3 m) off the ground on the way to the target area or setter.

a   b   c

Figure 3.37 **Player contacting the ball for an overhead pass.**

FOLLOW-THROUGH TOWARD CEILING

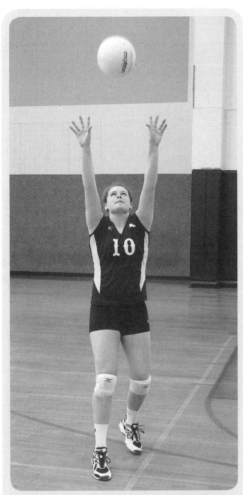

Figure 3.38 Player holding the follow-through toward the ceiling on the overhead pass.

After contact with the ball, the player follows through by keeping the hands up in the air. The hands and fingers should follow through in the direction of the target (see figure 3.38).

At a Glance

The following parts of the text offer additional information on the overhead pass:

Forearm pass	55
Front set	63
Back set	68
Lateral set	72
Jump set	76
One-hand set	80
Forearm set	84
Aggressive serving	142
Team serve reception	146
Setting a quick set	155
Attacking or dumping the second ball	158
Receiving a free ball	177
Using a libero	180

(continued)

Common Errors

Following are several common errors you may run into when teaching your athletes the overhead pass.

Error	Error correction
Ball goes through the player's hands.	The hands must be strong enough to prevent this. Have the player receive balls thrown at her forehead using this technique, with thumbs and forefingers in a triangle formation. Be careful not to throw too hard until the player understands how close together her hands need to be.
Ball goes straight ahead instead of up in the air to the target.	The follow-through with the hands and fingers needs to be up toward the ceiling. If the ball is coming right at the face, the passer must bend the knees deeply to drop the head and hands under the ball to direct it upward.
Player's hands are not strong enough to set the ball.	Have the player attempt fingertip push-ups to build strength in the hands.

The front set, which is essentially an overhead pass, is a specific application of the overhead pass skill and is used by a setter as a method of delivering a hittable ball to an attacker. The front set is used to get the ball to the attacker so she can get a good hard swing at the ball without getting into the net or going over the center line. The front set is the most accurate method of getting a hittable ball to the attacker since the passer is using two hands rather than the forearms. Since the forearms can sometimes have different angles depending on the way the arms are put together to form a platform, the overhead set is usually more accurate.

KEY POINTS

Following are the most important components of a front set:

- o Ready position
- o Position at the net
- o Hand position above the forehead
- o Contact with the ball
- o Follow-through toward ceiling

READY POSITION

The setter will need to move quickly into position from where she is located on the court to the target position near the net in order to set the ball to an attacker. The setter's upper body should lean forward, and her feet should be in a staggered stance, typically with the right foot slightly forward, ready to move when it is appropriate, such as when the ball is contacted on the serve or dug up by a teammate. The weight is on the balls of the feet and distributed evenly. The setter must be able to read the situation and the moving ball so she can move quickly to the correct position at the net. She must also be aware of her teammates on the court so they do not overlap on serve reception.

POSITION AT THE NET

If the setter is not already in position before the serve or dig, she should move quickly and efficiently toward her target zone at the net and be stopped and balanced, with the body in a medium-high ready position and the feet and forehead behind and under the ball, so she is prepared to contact the ball when it arrives (see figure 3.39). The setter's shoulders and hips should be facing the left side (zone 4; see figure 3.40 for an example of the court zones) of the court, where she will set the majority of the balls. Her feet should be shoulder-width apart, with the right foot slightly forward and the knees bent to help prevent her from setting the ball accidentally over the net. With the foot closest to the net forward, the shoulders are more likely to be facing the appropriate position, keeping the ball from drifting over the net to the opposing blocker.

Figure 3.39 Setter positioned at the net for a front set.

(continued)

5	4	2	1
6	3	3	6
1	2	4	5

Figure 3.40 Court zones.

It is important that the setter contact the ball in a neutral, balanced body position every time so she can set a variety of sets without "showing" it, in an effort to deceive the opponents as to where she plans to set the ball. This position should also allow the setter to see the opposing blockers' movement as well as her own passers and their platforms as they get ready to pass or dig the ball to the target area. As the setter arrives at the position to set the ball, she should make a quick eye check (just moving the eyes) out to the left antenna to know exactly where she is on the court.

HAND POSITION ABOVE THE FOREHEAD

Once at the proper location and just before contact, the setter should put her hands up. She should open the hands wide, with the fingers spread and relaxed, forming a triangle with the thumbs and index fingers above and in front of the forehead in a ball-shaped position (see figure 3.41). The elbows should be bent at about 90 degrees in a comfortable position angled out to the sides. The setter should look up through the triangle to see the ball coming into the hands. The hands should be up above the forehead early—well before the ball arrives.

Figure 3.41 Setter's hand position for a front set.

CONTACT WITH THE BALL

All the pads of the fingers should make contact with the ball, with the primary contact being with the index and middle fingers and thumbs on the lower back portion of the ball (see figure 3.42a). The ball does not touch the palms of the hand, nor should it come to rest in the hands. The ring and little fingers help the thumbs control the direction of the set. The weight and impact of the ball will move the wrists back toward the forehead slightly, and then the setter extends both wrists and elbows in a forward and upward direction immediately upon contact with the ball (see figure 3.42b). A soft touch can be created with the wrists by absorbing and releasing the ball quickly. The setter should also simultaneously push and extend the legs and arms forward and upward. The acceleration into the ball controls the distance and height of the set. The farther the distance from the target, the more acceleration and use of the legs are needed.

a   b

Figure 3.42 **Setter contacting the ball using a front set.**

(continued)

FOLLOW-THROUGH TOWARD CEILING

The setter transfers her weight into the ball and onto the front foot (right foot when along the net). Note that the setter will always be facing the left front of the court so she can disguise her sets and to make it easier for right-handed hitters to spike the ball. For a high set to the antenna, the entire body extends up toward the ceiling (see figure 3.43). The ball is directed to land in a spot about 2 to 3 feet (.6 to .9 m) off the net, and the fingers and hands follow through after the ball. For a set of a shorter distance, the fingers and wrists flick the ball, and the elbows extend a shorter distance up toward the ceiling, while the legs may not extend much at all. The setter should hold the follow-through momentarily to assure an accurate set and then move quickly to cover the hitter. If the setter cannot hold the position, she may not have been in the proper and balanced position to make the set to begin with.

Figure 3.43   Setter following through toward the ceiling after the front set.

Common Errors

Following are several common errors you may run into when teaching your athletes the front set.

Error	Error correction
Setter makes inaccurate sets.	The setter needs to be stopped and in a balanced position, ready to set the ball, with the hands up in a triangle formation before the ball arrives.
Setter is not in the correct position to set the ball.	Have the setter focus on specific sprint workouts to improve her foot speed so she can beat the ball to the target area near the net.
Ball falls through the setter's hands.	Have the setter practice holding the hands up in the triangle formation above the forehead. Then have the setter stand 1 foot (.3 m) away from a wall and set the ball against the wall 50 times. The repetitions will help the setter create muscle memory of the correct hand position.
Setter sets the ball over the net.	The setter's right foot (foot closest to the net) must be forward when making contact, with the setter aiming for the ball to land in a spot 2 to 3 feet (.6 to .9 m) off the net and inside the sideline.
Ball drops short of making it to the hitter.	The setter can develop arm strength by doing push-ups and upper-body weightlifting. The setter can also practice power by setting a weighted ball to herself or off a wall.
Setter makes an illegal hit.	The setter must contact the ball evenly on both hands to make a legal set on the second contact. Make sure both hands and arms have equal strength and are level in the triangle (ready to set) position.

KEY POINTS

Following are the most important components of a back set:

○ Ready position
○ Position at the net
○ Hand position above the forehead
○ Weight transfer
○ Contact with the ball
○ Follow-through back and toward ceiling

Because most hitters are right-handed, the setter usually faces the hitter on the left side of the court when setting the ball. It is easier for a right-handed hitter to hit the ball when it just needs to fall in front of her hitting shoulder instead of going across her body. There are going to be instances, however, when the hitter is behind the setter, so the setter must be able to back-set to the hitter as they spread out the offense. The back set needs to be disguised as long as possible in order to hold the middle blocker in her position and not release to the hitter early, since the goal of the setter is to get the hitter up against only one blocker. The back set is similar to the front set except for the follow-through.

READY POSITION

The setter will need to move quickly into position from where she is located on the court to the target position near the net in order to set the ball to an attacker. The setter's upper body should lean forward, and her feet should be in a staggered stance, typically with the right foot slightly forward, ready to move when it is appropriate, such as when the ball is served or dug. The weight is on the balls of the feet and distributed evenly. The setter must be able to read the situation and the moving ball so she can move quickly to the correct position at the net. She must also be aware of her teammates on the court so they do not overlap on serve reception.

POSITION AT THE NET

The setter should move quickly and efficiently from where she is located on the court to the target position near the net to set the ball to an attacker. Just as for a front set, the setter must be stopped and balanced, with the body leaning forward in a medium-high ready position, with the feet and forehead behind and under the ball so she is ready to contact it when it arrives (see figure 3.44). Weight is on the balls of the feet, distributed evenly, and the feet are staggered at about shoulder-width apart, with the foot closest to the net (right) forward and knees bent to help prevent setting the ball over the net accidentally. Having the right foot forward keeps the shoulders facing the same side of the court instead of open to the net. The setter's shoulders and hips face the left side (zone 4; refer back to figure 3.40 on page 64 for an example of the court zones) of the court, where she will set the majority of the balls.

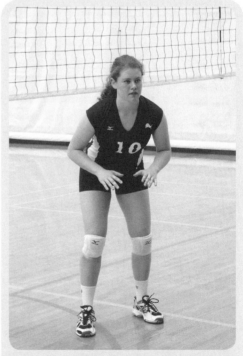

Figure 3.44 Setter positioned at the net for a back set.

It is important that the setter contact the ball in a neutral, balanced body position every time so she can set a variety of sets without showing it, in an effort to deceive the opponents as to where she plans to set the ball. This position should also allow the setter to see the opposing blockers' movement as well as her own passers and their platforms as they get ready to pass or dig the ball to the target area. The setter should make a quick eye check (just moving the eyes) out to the left antenna as she arrives at the ball to know exactly where she is on the court.

HAND POSITION ABOVE THE FOREHEAD

Once at the proper location and just before contact, the setter opens the hands wide, with the fingers spread and relaxed, forming a triangle with the thumbs and index fingers above and in front of the forehead in a ball-shaped position (see figure 3.45). The elbows should be bent at about 90 degrees in a comfortable position angled out to the sides. The setter should look up through the triangle to see the ball coming into the hands and look under the triangle to spot her hitter and teammates. The hands should be up above the forehead early—well before the ball arrives.

WEIGHT TRANSFER

At contact, the setter moves the hips forward and underneath the ball, arches the back, and transfers the weight to the front foot (foot closest to the net). This slight movement forward assists in changing the direction of the ball.

Figure 3.45 Setter's hand position for a back set.

(continued)

CONTACT WITH THE BALL

All the pads of the fingers should make contact with the ball, with the primary contact being with the index and middle fingers and thumbs on the lower back portion of the ball (see figure 3.46a). The ball does not touch the palms of the hand, nor should it come to rest in the hands. The ring and little fingers help the thumbs control the direction of the set. The weight and impact of the ball will move the wrists back toward the head slightly, and then the setter extends both legs and her wrists and elbows in a backward and upward direction toward the ceiling, squeezing the elbows behind the ears, to cause the ball to be directed behind the setter's body (see figure 3.46b). The acceleration into the ball controls the distance behind the setter and the height of the set. The farther the distance from the target, the more acceleration and use of the legs are needed.

At a Glance

The following parts of the text offer additional information on the back set:

a   b

Figure 3.46 **Setter contacting the ball using a back set.**

FOLLOW-THROUGH BACK AND TOWARD CEILING

The setter follows through with the arms, hands, and fingers in the direction of the set—back behind the head and toward the ceiling (see figure 3.47). The setter's hips and shoulders should stay square to the left-front target position throughout the follow-through. The setter watches the path of the ball with her head tilted back and holds the follow-through momentarily. The setter will then need to quickly turn toward the net to cover the hitter.

Figure 3.47 Setter following through back and toward the ceiling for the back set.

Common Errors

Following are several common errors you may run into when teaching your athletes the back set.

Error	Error correction
Setter leans back early to set the ball.	The setter's body must stay in a neutral position until contact is made. To help the setter practice this, stand on the other side of the net and say either "front set" or "back set" at the last second so she cannot lean in one direction.
Ball is set straight up.	Have the setter work on flexibility and moving the hands and arms up and behind the head toward the ceiling on extension.
Setter makes inconsistent sets.	Help the setter by giving her specific feedback on where the ball lands or, even better, where it needs to land (e.g., "Two feet farther out toward the sideline" or "One foot closer to the net").

KEY POINTS

Following are the most important components of a lateral set:

- Ready position
- Position at the net
- Hand position above the forehead
- Shoulder drop
- Contact with the ball
- Follow-through laterally toward ceiling

A lateral set can be used if the ball is passed or dug tight to the net. For the lateral set, the setter either faces the net or has her back to the net. The ball is contacted above the setter's forehead as in other sets, but the follow-through is lateral, or off to the side. An important aspect of the lateral set is that the setter must be careful to make sure the ball is contacted evenly and released from both hands at the same time to avoid a double contact violation. The follow-through, although off to the side, is the same as for a front or back set, with the hands ending high and toward the target.

READY POSITION

The setter will need to move quickly into position from where she is located on the court to the target position near the net in order to set the ball to an attacker. The setter's upper body should lean forward, and her feet should be in a staggered stance, typically with the right foot slightly forward, ready to move when it is appropriate, such as when the ball is served or dug (see figure 3.36 on page 59). The weight is on the balls of the feet and distributed evenly. The setter must be able to read the situation and the moving ball so she can move quickly to the correct position at the net. She must also be aware of her teammates on the court so they do not overlap on serve reception before the ball is contacted on the serve.

POSITION AT THE NET

Once the setter has sprinted to the net, she will need to get herself in the best position to make a set to one of her hitters. She can rotate her body so that her shoulders and hips face the net, or she can keep her back to the net so that her shoulders and hips face away from the net. The setter must be stopped and balanced, with the body leaning forward in a medium-high ready position, with the feet and forehead behind and under the ball so she is ready to contact it when it arrives. Weight is on the balls of feet, distributed evenly, and the feet are staggered at about shoulder-width apart with the knees bent.

It is important that the setter contact the ball in a neutral, balanced body position every time so she can set a variety of sets without showing it, in an effort to deceive the opponents as to where she plans to set the ball.

HAND POSITION ABOVE THE FOREHEAD

Once at the proper location and just before contact, the setter opens the hands wide, with the fingers spread and rigid, forming a triangle with the thumbs and index fingers above and in front of the forehead in a ball-shaped position. The elbows should be bent at about 90 degrees in a comfortable position angled out to the sides, without making contact with the net if the setter is facing it. The setter should look up through the triangle to see the ball coming into the hands. The hands should be up above the forehead early—well before the ball arrives.

SHOULDER DROP

When contacting the ball, the setter drops the shoulder closest to the target and slightly bends laterally at the waist in the direction she is setting the ball. This should allow the ball to contact both hands evenly to prevent an illegal double contact.

CONTACT WITH THE BALL

All the pads of the fingers should make contact with the ball, with the primary contact being with the index and middle fingers and thumbs on the bottom of the ball (see figure 3.48a for this position when facing the net and figure 3.48b for this position when the setter's back is to the net). The ball does not touch the palms of the hand, nor does it come to rest. The ring and little fingers help the thumbs control the direction of the set as the arms extend upward.

It is critical for both hands to have even contact with the ball for this to be a legal set. An illegal contact will be called if one hand spends more time on the ball than the other hand. Both hands and arms must extend at the same time to a spot on the ceiling 2 to 3 feet (.6 to .9 m) off the net toward the intended attacker's position.

Figure 3.48 **Setter contacting the ball for a lateral set (a) when facing the net and (b) when the back is to the net.**

(continued)

FOLLOW-THROUGH LATERALLY TOWARD CEILING

The setter follows through, with the upper body bending laterally and hands and fingers toward the ceiling in the direction of the set (see figure 3.49a for this position when facing the net and figure 3.49b for this position when the setter's back is to the net). The setter continues to watch the path of the ball and holds the follow-through momentarily before moving quickly to cover the hitter.

At a Glance

The following parts of the text offer additional information on the lateral set:

Overhead pass	59
Front set	63
Back set	68
Jump set	76
Front-row attack	88
Back-row attack	93
Quick attack	97
Slide	102
Covering the hitter	121
Aggressive serving	142
Defending against the slide	168
Defending against the back-row attack	174

a   b

Figure 3.49 **Setter following through laterally and toward the ceiling for the lateral set (a) when facing the net and (b) when the back is to the net.**

Common Errors

Following are several common errors you may run into when teaching your athletes the lateral set.

Error	Error correction
Setter makes net fouls.	The setter needs to learn to move carefully around the net. She may need to work next to a wall to learn if her arms and elbows are sticking out too much.
Setter makes an illegal hit (double hit).	It is important that both hands stay on the ball the same amount of time, so the body needs to bend at the waist in the direction of the set to allow that to happen.
Setter is not able to consistently control the location of the set for the attacker to hit.	The setter needs to practice numerous repetitions, with a coach or teammate giving feedback on the location of the set. She should be able to self-correct if she knows where the ball is landing.

In a jump set, the setter jumps off the ground and then sets the ball. This is an advanced move that increases the tactical advantage if the setter is accurate with the location of the set. One reason for using this skill is that the ball is in the air a shorter amount of time, giving the attacker a better opportunity to hit around the blocker. The jump set can be used to speed up the offense because the ball is delivered more quickly out of the setter's hands since she is setting the ball in the air instead of waiting for it to come down to her standing on the floor. It may also be used if the setter is positioned in the front row and is considered a threat to attack the ball on the second hit. This puts more pressure on the blockers to determine whether the setter will hit the ball over or set to another attacker. If the setter is left-handed, this is even more effective since the setter can decide to swing at the ball as an attacker or dump the ball over instead of setting it. The blockers and defensive players need to pay closer attention to the setter when she jump-sets. The jump set may also be used for a ball passed or dug tight to the top of the net or to prevent a pass from going over the net.

When using the jump set, it is important that the setter be able to make an accurate set. Although it can be a spectacular tactical move, it will work only if the setter can still make a great set while jumping. If she is inexperienced or not skilled enough, she may be called for an illegal hit or just make a poor set. The setter must have good upper-body strength and good body control for this skill to be done correctly since she is not using her legs to push off the floor while setting, and she needs to be in control to stay out of the net and make an accurate set.

READY POSITION

The setter will need to move quickly into position from where she is located on the court to the target position near the net in order to set the ball to an attacker. The setter's upper body should lean forward, and her feet should be in a staggered stance, typically with the right foot slightly forward, ready to move when it is appropriate. The weight is on the balls of the feet and distributed evenly. The setter must be able to read the situation and the moving ball so she can move quickly to the correct position at the net. She must also be aware of her teammates on the court so they do not overlap on serve reception.

POSITION AT THE NET

The setter should move quickly and efficiently from where she is located on the court to the target position near the net to set the ball to an attacker. Just as for a front set, the setter must be stopped and balanced, with the body leaning forward in a medium-high ready position, with the feet and forehead behind and under the ball so she is ready to jump and contact the ball when it arrives (see figure 3.50). Weight is on the balls of feet, distributed evenly, and the feet are staggered at about shoulder-width apart, with the foot closest to the net (right) forward and knees bent to help prevent setting the ball accidentally over the net. Keeping the right foot forward and facing the left front of the court will keep the shoulders square to the sideline, and the ball is less likely to drift over the net accidently into the blocker's hands. The setter's shoulders and hips face the left side (zone 4; refer to figure 3.40 on page 64 for an example of the court zones) of the court, where she will set the majority of the balls.

Figure 3.50 **Setter positioned at the net for a jump set.**

It is important that the setter contact the ball in a neutral, balanced body position every time so she can set a variety of sets without showing it, in an effort to deceive the opponents as to where she plans to set the ball. This position should also allow the setter to see the opposing blockers' movement as well as her own passers and their platforms as they get ready to pass or dig the ball to the target area. Once the setter is in proper position, she can quickly take her eyes off the approaching ball to check her position on the court and her distance from the sideline she is facing. She just glances at the net antenna in front of her to gain this valuable information.

JUMP AND HAND POSITION

The setter's knees will be slightly bent, and she will use her arms to help her jump straight up toward the ball. The timing of this jump will depend on the setter's jumping ability, specifically how high she can jump and how long she can hang in the air. After jumping and reaching the peak of the jump, she will open the hands wide, with the fingers spread and relaxed to form a triangle, with thumbs and index fingers above and in front of the forehead in a ball-shaped position. The elbows should be bent at about 90 degrees, but the elbow next to the net will remain at her side so it doesn't touch the net if she is close to it. The setter looks up through the triangle to see the ball coming into the hands. It is important that the setter jump straight up so as to not interfere with the approach of a quick hitter coming toward the net to hit the ball.

(continued)

CONTACT WITH THE BALL

All the pads of the fingers should make contact with the ball, with the primary contact being with the index and middle fingers and thumbs on the bottom of the ball (see figure 3.51a). The ball does not touch the palms of the hand, nor should it come to rest. The ring and little fingers help the thumbs control the direction of the set. While the setter is in the air, the weight and impact of the ball will move her wrists back toward the forehead slightly. The setter extends her wrists and elbows in a forward and upward direction immediately on impact with the ball and before returning to the floor while simultaneously pushing and extending the arms forward and upward (see figure 3.51b). The acceleration of the elbow and wrist extension into the ball controls the distance and height of the set.

a   b

Figure 3.51   Setter contacting the ball for a jump set.

FOLLOW-THROUGH AND LANDING

After contact, the player should land from the jump, balanced on both feet, and move quickly to cover the hitter. Landing balanced on both feet shows that she was in the proper balanced position in the air to make a legal and accurate set to her hitter.

Common Errors

Following are several common errors you may run into when teaching your athletes the lateral set.

Error	Error correction
Setter makes net fouls.	Have the setter practice jump setting next to a wall, keeping the elbow closest to the net parallel to her body at her side and then extending both arms at the same time.
Setter makes inaccurate sets.	The first priority is an accurate set. It may look impressive, but if jump setting is not accurate, have the player stay on the ground to set the ball.
Setter jumps forward while setting.	Have the player practice jump back sets to make sure her body position is neutral in the air and she is not floating after jumping. Also, have a person standing on the floor in front of the setter while she practices jump setting to keep her from drifting forward.
Setter lands on one foot.	Identify the setter's range and when she should use a jump set. If she cannot get into the correct position to jump straight up and land balanced on both feet, she should not be using the jump set in that situation.

A one-hand set is used only when the ball is passed tight to the net or is going over the net, and the setter cannot set the ball with both hands. In this situation, the setter is just trying to keep the ball from going over the net until the hitter can get up in the air to hit it. The setter and hitter will be in the air at the same time, with the setter using the pads of the fingers and thumb of the right hand (similar to a tipping hand position on page 151) to keep the ball in play. The setter must be ready for the blocker to try to attack the ball at the same time she is jumping up to keep it on her side for the hitter. This can be dangerous for the setter in terms of keeping her fingers from being hit. She will have to decide whether or not to put her unprotected hand up or to possibly close the hand into a half fist or a fist just to play the ball up in the air.

KEY POINTS

Following are the most important components of a one-hand set:

o Ready position
o Position at the net
o Jump and hand position
o Contact with the ball
o Follow-through and landing

READY POSITION

The setter will need to move quickly into position from where she is located on the court to the target position near the net in order to set the ball to an attacker. The setter's upper body should lean forward, and her feet should be in a staggered stance, typically with the right foot slightly forward, ready to move when it is appropriate. The weight is on the balls of the feet and distributed evenly. The setter must be able to read the situation and the moving ball so she can move quickly to the correct position at the net. She must also be aware of her teammates on the court so they do not overlap on serve reception.

POSITION AT THE NET

The setter should move quickly and efficiently from where she is located on the court to the target position near the net to set the ball to an attacker. Just as for a front set, the setter must be stopped and balanced, with the body leaning forward in a medium-high ready position, with the feet and forehead behind and under the ball so she is ready to jump and contact the ball when it arrives. Weight is on the balls of feet, distributed evenly, and the feet are staggered at about shoulder-width apart, with the foot closest to the net (right) forward and knees bent to help prevent setting the ball accidentally over the net. The body position should be facing the left side (zone 4; refer to figure 3.40 on page 64 for an example of the court zones) of the court, where she will set the majority of the balls. This position should also allow views of the opposing blockers' movement as well as her own passers and their platforms as they get ready to pass or dig the ball to the target area. Having her body in a neutral position will also keep opponents from determining which direction she intends to set the ball.

Once the setter is in proper position, she can quickly take her eyes off the approaching ball to check her position on the court and her distance from the sideline she is facing. She just quickly glances at the net antenna in front of her to gain this valuable information.

JUMP AND HAND POSITION

Once the player is in the correct position under the ball, she will swing her arms and use her legs to get her body up in the air. The timing of the jump will depend on how quick the setter is, how high she can jump, and how long she can stay up in the air. It is important that the player jumps straight up so she does not interfere with a quick hitter's approach as she moves toward the net to hit the ball. Since this is an attempt to save a bad pass, the hand position doesn't have to be perfect. Essentially, the setter just needs to jump in the air, and the hand closest to the net opens in a ball-shaped position (similar to a tipping, or dinking, hand position) facing the ball coming toward it (see figure 3.52).

At times it may be more effective to close or half-close the hand. Essentially, the setter's main goal is to ensure she makes legal contact, which means the ball cannot come to rest in her hand. So, in some situations, making contact with the open heel of the hand may provide a flat surface to get the ball up to the hitter legally.

Figure 3.52 **Setter jumping up to the ball for the one-hand set.**

(continued)

CONTACT WITH THE BALL

All the pads of the fingers should make contact with the ball. For the one-hand set, the setter is essentially trying to save a poor pass, so she can just tap the ball up for the hitter to make contact. The ball cannot come to rest on the pads of the fingers, so a quick tap will get the ball back in the air quickly for a quick hitter (see figure 3.53). She may also push the ball up to the outside hitter to keep the ball off the net, but setting the ball outside requires a very strong hand position.

FOLLOW-THROUGH AND LANDING

After contact, the arm, hand, and fingers briefly follow through toward the ceiling. The setter should attempt to land balanced on both feet and then quickly move to cover the hitter.

Figure 3.53 Setter contacting the ball for a one-hand set.

Common Errors

Following are several common errors you may run into when teaching your athletes the one-hand set.

Error	Error correction
Setter makes an illegal set.	Have the setter work on hand strength to make sure she can keep her hand and wrist rigid enough to make the set.
Setter makes net fouls.	Have the setter practice setting with one hand next to a wall to make sure she learns to control her elbow, keeping it parallel to the net.
Setter is called for a back-row attack.	The setter may be called for a back-row attack if she contacts the ball while it is on top of the net. The setter must intercept the ball before it gets in that position.

The setter may need to use her forearms to set the ball to the hitter instead of her hands if the ball is passed too low or too fast to the net. This is an emergency skill and should be used only when the player cannot receive the ball above the forehead. Essentially, the setter just passes the ball off her forearms to get it to land in a target area about 5 feet (1.5 m) off the net and 5 feet inside the sideline so the attacker can hit it.

READY POSITION

The setter will need to move quickly into position from where she is located on the court to the target position near the net in order to set the ball to an attacker. The setter's upper body should lean forward, and her feet should be in a staggered stance, typically with the right foot slightly forward, ready to move when it is appropriate. The weight is on the balls of the feet and distributed evenly. The setter must be able to read the situation and the moving ball so she can move quickly to the correct position at the net. She must also be aware of her teammates on the court so they do not overlap on serve reception.

POSITION AT THE NET

The setter should move quickly and efficiently toward the passed or dug ball and be stopped, balanced, and in a medium-high ready position to contact the ball when it arrives. The foot closest to the net (right) should be forward to help prevent passing the ball accidentally over the net, and the weight should be on the balls of the feet. The setter's body should face the left side (zone 4; refer to figure 3.40 on page 64 for an example of the court zones) of the court, where the majority of balls will be set. This position also allows the setter to see the opposing blockers' movement as well as her own passers and their platforms as they get ready to pass or dig the ball to the target area. The setter should make a quick eye check (just moving the eyes) out to the left antenna to determine exactly where she is on the court after getting into position to play the ball. This set does not need to be disguised since it is an emergency set; the opponents know the ball will probably be directed to the outside hitter or a back-row attacker.

ARM POSITION

The setter should place the forearms together and under the ball to create a platform just as the ball is coming down near her (see figure 3.54). This platform will be exactly the same as for the forearm pass introduced earlier in this chapter on page 55. The setter will need to be in a low enough position that she can make a good play on the ball to pass it up for an attacker to hit.

Figure 3.54 **Setter's arm position for a forearm set.**

CONTACT WITH THE BALL

The setter lifts the platform up under the ball and toward the intended target (5 feet off the net and 5 feet inside the court) (see figure 3.55). Setting the ball in this way is not quite as accurate as when using the hands, so the target area is off the net to make sure the ball does not get so close to the net that the attacker makes a net foul or the ball accidentally goes over the net.

The setter should contact the ball using the fleshy part of the inner arms for good rebound surface, between the wrists and elbows. The base of the thumbs should be together, with the wrists extended downward. The elbows should be straight and the arms flat and out away from the body and under the volleyball, with the shoulders shrugged. Dropping the inside shoulder (nearest the target) will angle the arms and shoulders to the target area. Ideally, contact should be made when the ball is between waist and knee height.

Figure 3.55 **Setter contacting the ball for a forearm set.**

(continued)

FOLLOW-THROUGH WITH ARMS

The setter lets the arms follow through up near the shoulders, with the hands still together, while extending the legs to help get the ball up in the air so the attacker can take a good swing at it (see figure 3.56). The setter then moves toward the attacker to help cover her if she is blocked.

Figure 3.56 Setter following through with the arms on the forearm set.

At a Glance

The following parts of the text offer additional information on the forearm set:

Forearm pass	55
Front set	63
Front-row attack	88
Back-row attack	93
Covering the hitter	121
Aggressive serving	142
Reading the attacker	165
Defending against the back-row attack	174
Using a libero	180

Common Errors

Following are several common errors you may run into when teaching your athletes the forearm set.

Error	Error correction
Setter sets the ball over the net.	Make sure the setter keeps the foot closest to the net forward to keep the shoulders square to the outside hitter.
Ball travels too far outside the court.	The setter's platform with the forearms needs to face the target on contact. In addition, the angle of the platform may need to be elevated.
Ball is not set high enough.	Have the setter extend the length of the follow-through, providing more power and lift to the ball.

Attacking

The attack, also called a spike or a hit, is the most popular and exciting skill in the sport of volleyball. Most players want to work on the technique for their attack as much as possible. It is a very difficult skill in which the player jumps in the air to hit a moving ball over the net while avoiding the opposing blockers. The attacker's goal is to direct the ball around, over, or off the blockers' hands or to hit the ball down into the opposing team's court away from the defenders.

The attacker can hit sets from her on-hand or off-hand side. *On-hand* refers to a ball that comes from the right side of the court to a right-handed hitter. This is the easiest ball to hit since an attacker can contact it before it travels across her body. *Off-hand* refers to a ball that comes from the left side of a right-handed hitter. These balls are more difficult to hit because they must travel across the attacker's body and drop in front of her right shoulder before she can hit it. For a player to hit any ball she is set, she must have her body in the correct position every time. She can do this using efficient footwork and by getting the hitting arm fully extended, with the ball slightly in front of her hitting shoulder.

There are several guiding principles you and your players must be aware of when attacking:

- Attackers should be able to put the ball away.
- Attackers should be able to keep the ball in play.
- Attackers should make as few unforced errors as possible.

KEY POINTS

Following are the most important components of a front-row attack:

o Ready position
o Approach to the ball
o Contact with the ball
o Follow-through and landing

An attack from the front row is a skill that involves a player jumping up to hit the ball over the net. The attacker moves to a ball that is set to her and then jumps up to contact the ball above the net, sending it down into the opposing team's court. This skill requires a good sense of timing and coordination to jump up and hit the ball with an open hand around or through opposing players who are trying to stop the attack from coming over the net (block).

READY POSITION

Getting in a ready position to attack requires the player to move from one area on the court to another to get into a position to make an approach to the ball (the approach is discussed in more detail in the next section). The attacker may be transitioning off the net from a blocking position, from a serve reception pass or formation, or from a defensive position. The attacker should watch the ball going to the setter while getting her body into a medium-high body position and moving to a place on the court to begin the approach. The shoulders should be forward of the feet, the arms hanging loose and relaxed beside the body. The attacker should be ready to move quickly, with the feet in a staggered stance and weight on the nonhitting-side foot for a four-step approach, as shown in figure 3.57, or with the weight on the hitting-side foot for a three-step approach. This is a good time for the attacker to quickly glance across the net to observe the court positions of the defensive players so she has more information on where to successfully hit the ball into their court to score a point.

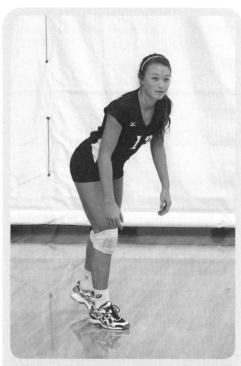

Figure 3.57 **Attacker in a ready position for a front-row attack.**

APPROACH TO THE BALL

The attacker should study the ball as it comes from the setter or another player, determine where the ball is going, and then make a decision on when to start her approach. The goal is to approach the ball so she can contact it in the same place relative to her body every time. Ideally, this is when the ball is slightly out front of her hitting-arm shoulder. In general, most attackers will start the approach roughly when the ball is at its peak after being set. Adjustments can be made earlier or later from that point depending on the hitter's quickness and the type of set delivered.

Most attackers find that using a four-step approach to attack the ball allows them to adjust to the ball and attack from just about anywhere on the court if the ball is not exactly where it is supposed to be set. The four steps also increase the speed of the approach and allow for a higher jump. However, some players prefer a quicker three-step approach or in some cases need to utilize a quicker two-step approach, such as a middle blocker in a fast transition off and back to the net for a quick set.

First Two Steps

For the four-step approach, the first step is slow and in the direction the ball is falling; the second step is faster and moves the attacker into the foot plant, which is explained next, with the ball coming down slightly in front of and over the hitting shoulder. The arms are relaxed, hanging down during the first step and swinging back on the second step.

Foot Plant

In figure 3.58, the attacker is moving forward into the foot plant where eventually, in the final foot plant position, the feet and hips should be at a 45-degree angle to the net, with the nonhitting-side foot slightly ahead of the hitting-side foot. The knees are bent, and the body is slightly bent forward at the waist. The attacker's eyes should still be focused on the ball. Both arms are straight and drawn high and back.

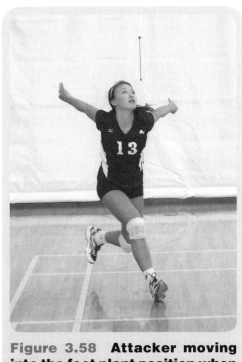

Figure 3.58 **Attacker moving into the foot plant position when approaching the ball using a four-step approach.**

(continued)

Takeoff

The takeoff should be balanced off both feet, which are planted at a 45-degree angle at the net as shown previously, with both arms swinging from behind the body to lift up in the air in front to assist in making the jump as high as possible (see figure 3.59). During the takeoff, the arms swing aggressively forward and upward; while in the air, the attacker should draw the hitting shoulder and arm back, with the elbow and hand in a high position. The nonhitting arm will pull down near the chest as the hitting hand (wide open) swings forward to make contact with the ball. The hitting-hand wrist should be loose and ready to snap over the top of the ball, giving it topspin and speed. Speed and power are produced by rotating the hips and shoulders around a vertical axis, providing speed to the arm when making contact with the ball.

Figure 3.59 Attacker's takeoff when approaching the ball using a four-step approach.

CONTACT WITH THE BALL

The attacker should contact the ball at the top of the jump in front of the hitting shoulder, with the arm fully extended (see figure 3.60). Contact is made with the full hand and fingers spread. The contact is quick, with the heel, palm, and fingers snapping quickly over the ball. This whiplike action will cause topspin on the ball, increasing speed and directing it down toward the floor more quickly. Since the ball is round, the contact area can vary based on the direction the attacker wants to hit the ball. If the attacker wants to hit the ball down the line, she contacts the back of the ball; if she wants to hit the ball at a sharp angle, she contacts the ball more on the side to direct it at a different angle. Make sure the hitter looks at the ball to contact it solidly.

Figure 3.60 Attacker contacting the ball for a front-row attack.

FOLLOW-THROUGH AND LANDING

Figure 3.61 **Attacker's follow-through and landing after attacking the ball in the front row.**

The hitting arm and hand should follow through toward the intended target for the attack. If the ball is set in the proper position off the net (2 to 3 feet, or .6 to .9 m), the attacker does not have to worry about her hand hitting the net on the follow-through. Sets that are too close to the net do not allow the hitter to take a full swing at the ball because they cause the hitting arm and hand to contact the net.

After contact, the attacker should land in a balanced position on both feet (see figure 3.61). This shows that the attacker approached the ball correctly and was able to use her full power in hitting. It is also important for the health of the player's knees. After landing safely, the hitter will need to be ready to block, attack, or play defense again based on the outcome of the hit.

At a Glance

The following parts of the text offer additional information on a front-row attack:

(continued)

Common Errors

Following are several common errors you may run into when teaching your athletes how to use a front-row attack.

Error	Error correction
Attacker makes net fouls.	The ball is set too close to the net for a full swing, or the attacker is broad-jumping forward into the net. Help ensure the setter keeps the ball away from the net by placing tape on the floor during practice to give the setter an area off the net where the ball should be set.
Attacker is called for a center-line violation.	The ball is set too close to the net, or the hitter is broad-jumping too far forward toward the net. Make sure the setter keeps the ball far enough away from the net so the attacker can hit the ball and land safely without going over the center line.
Attacker hits the ball out-of-bounds outside the opponent's court.	The attacker needs to work on reaching high to contact the top portion of the ball as well as on improving the wrist snap to give the ball more topspin and a downward trajectory, bringing it down into the opponent's court.
Attacker hits the ball into the net.	Contact is made too high on the top of the ball, or the ball has dropped too low before the attacker swings the arm for contact. The attacker needs to swing earlier (or faster), and contact needs to be at a spot on the ball that will get it over the net. Also, the ball may be set too close to the net for the attacker to hit it over the net, or the attacker is late starting the approach. There is a better chance for success for a small (short) attacker to hit it over the net if the ball is set farther off the net and the approach is begun at the correct time. The attacker may be approaching too slow, allowing the ball to drop too low. Have the attacker speed up the approach so she can contact the ball while it is above the net.
Attacker lands on one foot.	The attacker must approach the set with the ball landing in front of the hitting shoulder. Landing on one foot means the approach was not accurate and limits the ability to hit the ball to various areas of the court.
Attacker's approach is too far under the ball.	The ball is set too far off the net, or the attacker needs to start the approach a little later, once she identifies where the ball will be dropping.
Attacker's hit lacks power.	Have the attacker speed up the arm swing, or check to make sure the feet are at a 45-degree angle on takeoff for more body torque and power. Also make sure that the opposite foot is forward from the hitting arm during the takeoff. This will allow the body and shoulders to rotate, providing more power for the attacker.

Back-Row Attack

The back-row attack is made by a player in the back-row. The player must take off from behind the attack line (10 feet, or 3 m, away from the center line). This type of attack can be very effective when the opponents are strong blockers and can block the front-row hitters. It also adds a fourth or fifth attacker and helps balance the attack. The back-row attack is essentially the same as a front-row attack, except the approach starts deeper off the net and a little sooner. Also, the set should be antenna height, or 3 to 4 feet (.9 to 1.2 m) above the top of the net, to make sure the attacker can hit against fewer blockers. Setting the ball higher will allow more time for a block to form in front of the hitter, taking away the benefit of attacking from the back row.

KEY POINTS

Following are the most important components of a back-row attack:

- Ready position
- Approach to the ball
- Contact with the ball
- Follow-through and landing

READY POSITION

Getting in a ready position to attack requires the player to move from one area on the court to another to get into a position to make an approach to the ball (the approach is discussed in more detail in the next section). The back-row attacker will be transitioning from serve reception or a defensive position. The attacker should watch the ball going to the setter while moving into a medium-high body position. The shoulders should be forward of the feet, the arms hanging loose and relaxed beside the body. The attacker should be ready to move quickly, with the feet in a staggered stance and weight on the nonhitting-side foot for a four-step approach (or with weight on the hitting-side foot for a three-step approach).

APPROACH TO THE BALL

The attacker should study the ball as it comes from the setter or other player, determine where the ball is going, and then make a decision on when to start her approach. A ball being set to a back-row attacker should land on or slightly in front of the attack line. The goal is to approach the ball so she can contact it in the same place relative to her body every time, which, ideally, is slightly out of front of her hitting arm and shoulder. In general, most back-row attackers will start the approach just before the ball is set. Adjustments can be made earlier or later from that point depending on the hitter's quickness and the type of set delivered.

First Two Steps

The back-row attacker's approach begins sooner than it would for a front-row attack. The first two steps are taken before the setter releases the ball because the set is much lower and the attacker has less time for the approach. For higher back-row attacks, hitters will start the approach roughly when the ball is at its peak after being set. Adjustments can be made earlier or later from that point depending on the hitter's quickness and the height of the set delivered.

(continued)

Foot Plant

In figure 3.62, the attacker is moving forward into the foot plant where eventually, in the final foot plan position, the feet should be at a 45-degree angle to the net and behind the 10-foot (3 m) attack line, with the nonhitting-side foot slightly ahead of the hitting-side foot. The hips and hitting shoulder are rotated back away from the net. The knees should be bent and the body slightly bent forward at the waist. Both arms are straight and drawn high and back.

Figure 3.62 Back-row attacker moving into the foot plant position when approaching the ball using a four-step approach.

Takeoff

The takeoff should be balanced off both feet, with both arms swinging from behind the body to lift up in the air in front to assist in making the jump as high as possible (see figure 3.63). During the takeoff, the arms swing aggressively forward and upward; while in the air, the attacker should draw the hitting shoulder and arm back, with the elbow and hand in a high position. This rotation should be around a central axis. The nonhitting arm will pull down near the chest as the hitting hand (wide open) swings forward to make contact with the ball. The hitting-hand wrist should be loose and ready to snap over the top of the ball, giving it topspin and speed. Speed and power are produced by rotating the hips, shoulders, and arm when making contact with the ball. Also note that on the takeoff for the back-row attack, there is some broad jump, allowing the attacker to travel forward, and the attacker may land well in front of the attack line.

Figure 3.63 Back-row attacker's takeoff when approaching the ball using a four-step approach.

CONTACT WITH THE BALL

Figure 3.64 **Back-row attacker contacting the ball.**

The attacker should contact the ball at the top of the jump in front of the hitting shoulder with the arm fully extended (see figure 3.64). Contact is made with the full hand and fingers spread. The contact is quick, with the heel, palm, and fingers snapping quickly over the ball. This whiplike action will cause topspin on the ball, increasing speed and directing it down toward the floor more quickly. Since the ball is round, the contact area can vary based on the direction the attacker wants to hit the ball. If she wants to hit the ball down the line, she contacts the back of the ball; if she wants to hit the ball crosscourt, she contacts the ball more on the side to direct it at a different angle. Make sure the attacker looks at the ball when contacting it.

FOLLOW-THROUGH AND LANDING

The hitting arm and hand should follow through toward the intended target for the attack. Make sure the ball is set to the proper height and position just inside the attack line so the hitter does not have to worry about stepping on the line and being called for a violation. If the sets are too high, the hitter loses the ability to hit quickly around the blocker.

After contact, the attacker should land in a balanced position on both feet. This shows that the attacker approached the ball correctly and was able to use her full power in hitting. It is also important for the health of the player's knees. After landing safely, the hitter will need to be ready to quickly move back to her defensive position or attack again based on the outcome of the hit.

At a Glance

The following parts of the text offer additional information on a back-row attack:

(continued)

Common Errors

Following are several common errors you may run into when teaching your athletes how to attack from the back row.

Error	Error correction
Attacker hits the ball into the net.	This means the attacker was not ready to attack the ball, the ball dropped too much, or the attacker started the approach too late or too slow. The attacker should contact the ball with a good wrist snap at the top of the jump, and the contact point should be below center. It could also mean the attacker started the approach too far back in the court. The attacker should start a few steps behind the attack line and land inside the attack area after hitting the ball.
Attacker hits the ball deep out of bounds.	The attacker contacted the back or bottom of the ball or hit it flat with no wrist snap. Instead, the attacker should contact the ball with a good wrist snap at the top of the jump and the contact point should be below center.
Attacker collides with a front-row attacker.	It is important that the setter set the ball to a back-row attacker only when there is not an attacker waiting to hit a high ball in the same area along the net. The attacker needs to set the ball in the same zone (middle back or right back) as for a quick attacker in the front row, so it will be a quick hitter jumping to be an optional hitter and then the back-row hitter jumping behind her as the second option.
Attacker is called for a line violation.	The attacker stepped on or over the attack line when taking off to hit the ball. The set needs to be deep enough off the net so the attacker can jump from behind the attack line and hit the ball without fouling. After hitting, she can land on the line or in front of it.
Attacker's hit lacks power.	The attacker needs to keep the ball out in front of her and not get under it. This error could also be caused by lack of shoulder torque or rotation.
Attacker is not ready for the set.	Back-row attackers need to get available to attack and communicate to the setter that they are ready to hit the ball by calling out the name of the back-row set.

Quick Attack

A quick attack is used when the opponent has strong blockers and there is a need to get the ball by them before they have a chance to set up a solid block. This set is most often hit by a middle attacker. This attack requires an accurate pass and an excellent setter because of the critical timing. In a true first-tempo quick attack, the hitter is up in the air before the set is actually released, and the setter must put the ball in her hand quickly and with great accuracy. Being able to use this type of attack will also open up the outside hitters by keeping the middle blocker more occupied with the threat of your middle attacker. However, remember that a team should only attempt tactically what it can do technically, and this is a perfect example of that principle.

KEY POINTS

Following are the most important components of a quick attack:

- Ready position
- Approach to the ball
- Contact with the ball
- Balanced landing

READY POSITION

Getting in a ready position to make a quick attack requires the player to move from one area on the court to another to get into a position to make an approach to the ball (the approach is discussed in more detail in the next section). The attacker who hits a quick attack will usually be transitioning from a blocking or serve-reception position. The player should quickly get into a position near the center of the court near the attack line in a medium-high body position. The shoulders should be forward of the feet, the arms hanging down beside the body, loose and relaxed. The feet should be in a balanced, staggered stance ready to move forward quickly, with the weight on the hitting-side foot when using a full three-step approach (or on the nonhitting-side foot when using a two-step approach).

APPROACH TO THE BALL

The middle hitter should be sure to turn her head to watch the ball as it travels to the setter from the passer or digger. As the ball goes toward the net and past the hitter, she should follow, or chase, the ball toward the setter. Although the hitter should primarily be watching the ball, she should begin the approach, keeping the setter in full view as well as being aware of the opposing blocker. The attacker should approach directly in front of the setter but without passing up the ball. For example, if the pass is 3 feet (.9 m) off the net, the attacker should approach 3 feet away from the setter to allow the hitting shoulder to stay open and to allow the setter to place the ball in front of the hitting shoulder. The attacker should give the setter a verbal cue by yelling "quick" or "one" on the way in to make sure the setter knows the middle attacker is available and the quick hit is an option.

In most cases, when hitting a quick set, attackers will use a three-step approach to attack the ball, which allows them to transition off the net quickly and get back toward the net and up in the air to hit the ball. However, there are some situations where a two-step step approach is used, such as after transitioning only a short distance off the net after attempting to block a ball coming over.

(continued)

First Step

During the first step in the three-step approach, both of the attacker's arms make a short backswing during the approach and into the foot plant. The first step is made toward the point the attacker will jump up to hit the ball.

Foot Plant

As the player gets to the area where she will jump up to hit the ball, her body will be leaning backward slightly to transfer the forward momentum to her vertical jump. Both feet contact the floor at the same time, known as the foot plant, and should be at approximately a 45-degree angle to the net (see figure 3.65). The foot plant is important to keep the body from continuing to drift forward into the net. Both arms are drawn back and then up as the attacker plants and begin her jump up to hit the ball.

Figure 3.65 **Attacker's foot plant when approaching the ball using a three-step approach for the quick attack.**

Takeoff

The takeoff should be behind the ball and far enough away from the net that the attacker can hit the ball around the blocker. The arms swing forward and upward quickly. The left foot should be slightly forward, with the feet at about a 45-degree angle to the setter, which will open up the hitter's shoulder to the setter (see figure 3.66). The attacker should jump quickly, getting the hitting hand high in the air as the ball is arriving in the setter's hands. This will give the setter a target (the hitter's open hand) to set the ball to.

Figure 3.66 **Attacker's takeoff when approaching the ball using a three-step approach for the quick attack.**

(continued)

CONTACT WITH THE BALL

Contact is made with the full open hand and only a quick forearm rotation, keeping the elbow high (see figure 3.67). This quick snap does not need a full follow-through, which keeps the hand out of the net. The setter should place the ball in front of the attacker's hitting shoulder (to allow the attacker to hit to the opposing team's left back) or in front of the left shoulder (to allow the attacker to hit to the right back, also called a cut shot or a cut back). This will allow the attacker to hit around the blocker. If the ball is set to the middle of the attacker's body, she cannot direct the ball very well in either direction and is likely to get blocked.

BALANCED LANDING

At a Glance

The following parts of the text offer additional information on a quick attack:

Front set	63
Back set	68
Lateral set	72
Jump set	76
One-hand set	80
Front-row attack	88
Team serve reception	146
Setting a quick set	155
Attacking or dumping the second ball	158
Reading the attacker	165
Defending against a quick attack	183
Defending against the setter's dump or attack	190

The attacker lands in a balanced position on both feet (see figure 3.68). This shows that the attacker approached the ball correctly and was able to use her full power in hitting. It is also important for the health of the player's knees. After landing safely, she will need to be ready to move quickly to block or attack again based on the outcome of the hit.

Figure 3.67 Attacker contacting the ball for a quick attack.

Figure 3.68 Attacker's landing after contacting the ball on a quick attack.

Common Errors

Following are several common errors you may run into when teaching your athletes how to use a quick attack.

Error	Error correction
Attacker missed timing with the setter.	This could be caused by poor passing, which increases the distance between the setter and hitter. Make sure the team is passing well enough to implement this type of attack by including a setter and middle attacker when practicing passing.
Attacker makes net fouls.	The middle attacker needs to keep herself far enough away from the net when approaching and jumping so she doesn't hit the net when she swings at the ball. Also, make sure the setter keeps the ball off the net at least 1 foot (.3 m).
Attacker is called for a center-line violation.	The middle attacker needs to keep away from the center line, approaching and jumping far enough away from the net that she won't go over the center line when she lands. Also make sure the setter keeps the ball off the net at least 1 foot (.3 m).
Attacker hits the ball into the net.	Have the setter watch the attacker's approach and arm extension to make sure she is setting the ball high enough. The target is the hitter's extended hand, so the height of the quick set will vary with each middle hitter.
Attacker hits the ball out of bounds.	Make sure the attacker does not jump too early or too late, but just when the ball gets into the setter's hands.
Attacker is late to the setter.	The attacker should not start the approach from any farther away from the net than the attack line. Work on having the attacker start at the net and then transition off to the attack line and then follow the ball coming in from a pass or a dig to jump and hit.
Attacker is blocked.	The setter needs to set the ball in front of the shoulder and far enough off the net so the attacker can hit around the block.

Slide

KEY POINTS

Following are the most important components of a slide:

- Ready position
- Approach to the ball
- Contact with the ball
- Balanced landing

The slide, in which the attack is made behind the setter, is successful if the attacker is technically able to hit quick sets in front of the setter. The set for this attack has the ball traveling at a lower trajectory, and the attacker is approaching and traveling in the same direction as the set, so the attacker has a longer window of opportunity to hit the ball. The advantage of this attack is that the attacker can hit the ball at various heights, speeds, and distances from the setter along the net. It is difficult for the blockers to know exactly where to set the block since the ball is moving parallel to the net and not dropping straight down to a predictable contact point for the hitter.

READY POSITION

Getting in a ready position to attack requires the player to move from one area on the court to another to get into a position to make an approach to the ball (the approach is discussed in more detail in the next section). The player who hits a slide will usually be transitioning from blocking or serve reception. The player should quickly get into a position near the center of the court near the attack line in a medium-high body position. The shoulders should be forward of the feet, the arms hanging down beside the body, loose and relaxed. The feet should be in a staggered, balanced stance ready to move forward quickly, with the weight on the hitting-side foot when making an approach to hit a slide. The number of steps will vary depending on where the ball is set and how far the hitter has to go to contact it along the net.

APPROACH TO THE BALL

The attacker should be sure to turn her head to watch the ball from the passer or digger to the setter. As the ball goes toward the net and passes the hitter's shoulder, she should follow, or chase, the ball toward the setter. Although she should primarily be watching the ball, the attacker should begin the approach, keeping the setter in full view as well as being aware of the opposing blockers.

In most cases, attackers use a variety of steps in their approach to attack the ball depending on where the ball is set along the net. The varied steps in the approach allow attackers to transition off the net and quickly approach, follow the ball, and jump in the air to hit it.

First Three Steps

The attacker should look as if she is approaching the setter directly in front of her to hit the ball to get the middle blocker's attention, but at the last second, the attacker plants her left foot (if a right-handed hitter) and turns to the right to complete the final two or more steps of the approach, running past the setter to follow the ball as she sets it behind her along the net. The approach should be almost parallel to the net, keeping the ball out in front and between the net and the hitter's body. When using the four-step approach, the first step is on the nonhitting foot, in front of and toward the setter. Then, the attacker quickly changes direction to take the second and third steps past the setter, parallel to the net toward the net standard. The arms will move as if the player is running, and the hitting arm will swing up and draw back as she takes off from the floor on her last step.

Takeoff

After the attacker takes her two steps past the setter, she takes off on her nonhitting-side foot (the one closest to the net) behind the ball, keeping the ball in front of the hitting shoulder between the hitter and the net. The foot should be planted at a 45-degree angle facing the net standard. The hitting-arm elbow should draw back into a high position, ready to reach as high as possible, with the hand open and ready to contact the ball as soon as the attacker jumps.

The takeoff should be far enough away from the net so the attacker can hit the ball (without hitting the net) off the outside blocker's hand or down the line or rotate more to hit the ball crosscourt and inside the blockers' hands. The hitter can take off whenever she thinks she can jump up and hit the ball drifting through the air. The attacker's momentum may cause her to land outside of the sideline. This footwork is similar to a layup in basketball and comes very naturally to many players.

CONTACT WITH THE BALL

While elevating the hitting-side knee and leg (away from the net) during the jump, the attacker draws her hitting arm and hand up and back, with the elbow higher than the hand, to contact the ball at the top of the jump. Contact with the ball is made with a fully open hand and a quick forearm rotation, keeping the elbow high (see figure 3.69a). The wrist should snap over the ball, giving it topspin. This quick snap does not need much follow-through, which keeps the hand out of the net.

The setter should set the ball along the net, and it is up to the attacker to get it in the proper position to hit it effectively. This will allow the attacker to hit around the blocker. Beginners should aim to rotate the shoulders slightly to face the ball and hit it down the line to make sure the ball stays in front of the hitting shoulder. (See figure 3.69b.) The slide attacker may rotate the hips and shoulders even more after the jump to hit the ball back crosscourt and inside the blockers' hands.

a   b

Figure 3.69 **Attacker contacting the ball on a slide.**

(continued)

BALANCED LANDING

The attacker lands in a balanced position on both feet even though the jump was off of one foot (see figure 3.70). This shows that the attacker approached the ball correctly and was able to use her full power in hitting. It is also important for the health of the player's knees. After landing safely, she will need to be ready to move quickly back into the court to block or attack again based on the outcome of the hit.

Figure 3.70 **Attacker's landing after contacting the ball on a slide.**

Common Errors

Following are several common errors you may run into when teaching your athletes how to use a slide.

Error	Error correction
Attacker gets blocked.	The attacker may have run past the ball so it is in front of the nonhitting shoulder instead of the hitting shoulder. A smart blocker knows the only shot the hitter then has available is to hit it back crosscourt.
Attacker passes the ball.	The player needs to use the proper approach timing to chase the ball, keeping it between her and the net and in front of her right shoulder.
Attacker has poor timing on the approach.	The ball should be passed to the setter at antenna height, allowing the attacker to establish timing.
Attacker lacks vertical jump.	The attacker should feel comfortable jumping off of one foot.

chapter 4

Defensive Technical Skills

This chapter covers the defensive technical skills players must know to be successful. In this chapter, you will find the following skills:

KEY POINTS

Following are the most important components of a block:

- Ready position
- Reading the situation
- Moving parallel to the net
- Jumping straight up
- Reaching over the net
- Balanced landing position

Blocking—the first line of defense in volleyball—is the act of jumping up and placing the hands above and over the net to keep the ball on the opposing team's side of the court. This can be done by positioning your blockers so they essentially eliminate a part of the court from the opponent, forcing the attacker to hit the ball into the block or to hit the ball in a different direction toward the back-row defenders or with different speed than she wanted to. Blockers may deflect the attack attempt back into the opposing team's court or back and up into their own court for a teammate to play the ball or may force the attacker to tip or hit the ball off-speed. A well-positioned block may never touch the ball, but it can channel the spike toward the defenders placed in the court around the blockers. The best blockers are players who understand the game and have good timing on their jump to get their hands across the net at the correct time. Good core strength will help blockers stabilize their bodies in the air while keeping their shoulders, arms, and hands in place when an attacker hits the ball into them.

READY POSITION

The blocker stands in a neutral, balanced athletic position about a forearm's length away from the net, with her feet shoulder-width apart and the knees slightly bent so she is ready to move or jump. The elbows should be shoulder high, with the forearms held up at a 45-degree angle to the net (see figure 4.1). The hands should be up just outside the shoulders, with the fingers spread wide and out in front, high enough so the blocker can see the back of her own hands without blocking her vision. Weight is slightly forward, and the heels should be slightly off the ground. For middle blockers anticipating blocking the quick attack, the closer the ball is passed to the net, the higher their hands should be held so they can get them across the net more quickly.

Figure 4.1 **Blocker in a ready position.**

READING THE SITUATION

Blockers need to watch the play develop, read and anticipate the attack possibilities, and use good timing and judgment to position themselves correctly. A blocker's eyes should be open wide, and she should concentrate on first seeing the big picture of what's happening on the opposing team's court. She should see the entire court, all the opposing players, and the movement of the ball. The blocker must watch the ball as it moves to the opposing passer or digger first and then the direction of her opponent's platform in order to judge the rebound angle of the ball. This is important because the opponent may make a bad pass, sending the ball directly back over the net, so the blocker must be ready to attack the ball in this situation.

After judging the quality of the pass, the blocker then looks at the setter to see if the direction of the set can be determined. (For clues, watch the setters closely during the warm-up to look for any preferences when setting a ball, and share this information with your players). After the ball is set, the blocker looks briefly to see the flight and trajectory of the ball to determine where it will come down and to which attacker so that the blocker can be in the right place at the right time.

MOVING PARALLEL TO THE NET

Once the blocker determines who the attacker is and the direction and trajectory of the ball, she should step parallel to the net with the foot nearest the location of the set, with her body and hands maintaining their positions, so the hands stay in full view of the blocker and are positioned above the bottom of the net. Blockers can use a two-, three-, or five-step footwork pattern based on the distance they need to move along the net to be in a position to front the hitter's shoulder at the point the ball will cross the net. For example, if the blocker needs to move to the right side of the court and needs only three steps to reach the attacker, she takes a step out with her right foot, then her left foot, then lands on both feet, toes perpendicular to the net with knees still bent, and is then ready to jump straight up (see figure 4.2). At this time, the blocker should also focus on the hitter's approach to the ball so she can get in the best position in front of the attacker's hitting shoulder to block the ball. If the ball is set toward the outside of the court, the outside blocker will "set the block" or determine where the blockers will jump in relation to the attacker and the middle blocker will join them, forming a double block.

Figure 4.2 **Blocker moving parallel to the net in order to front the attacker's hitting arm.**

(continued)

JUMPING STRAIGHT UP

The blocker should jump before the hitter swings to make sure her hands are over the net when the attacker contacts the ball. The farther the ball is set off the net, the later the blocker should jump. It is important to jump straight up, extending the ankles and knees, so the defensive players behind the blocker can position themselves around the block. It is also important to keep multiple blockers close enough together in the air so there is no seam, or hole, between their arms and hands for the attacker to hit through.

After jumping and right before the attacker makes contact, the blocker should pay attention to which way the attacker's head is facing and where she is looking. This is usually an indicator of the direction she intends to hit the ball. A single blocker should position her inside foot and hand in line with the ball across the net to block a ball being hit down the line and should position her outside foot and hand in line with the ball across the net to block a ball being hit crosscourt. The same is true for a double block—the outside blocker positions herself as just described for a single blocker and the middle blocker moves close to the outside blocker's inside foot, hip, and shoulder before jumping.

REACHING OVER THE NET

The blocker reaches her hands over the net low and tight to penetrate the plane of the net and to "seal" it by leading with the hands, closing up the area between her forearms (or hands if the blocker does not jump that high) and the top of the net so no balls can pass between. This will keep the ball from coming over the top of the net between the blocker's hands and arms and the net. The ultimate goal for a block is to stop the ball on the opposing team's side of the net whenever possible.

To block the ball, the body is in a slightly piked position, with the abdominal and core muscles tight. The arms should be extended and locked straight, with the shoulders shrugged, giving the blocker a strong position (see figure 4.3). This helps the blocker keep the shoulders and arms stable and in position over the net as the hard-hit ball contacts the hands. The hands act as paddles and are positioned usually less than a ball-width apart, with the fingers and wrists rigid, moving independently of one another. For an outside blocker, the outside hand is angled back into the court, while the inside hand faces the middle of the court. For a middle blocker, the inside

Figure 4.3 Blocker reaching over the net to block the attack.

hand, or hand nearest the middle of the court, will be angled back toward the hitter, cutting off the crosscourt hit. Thus, the palms will face the direction toward which the blocker wants the ball deflected back into the opposing team's court.

BALANCED LANDING POSITION

The blocker holds her hands high as she descends from her jump so that she is in front of the attacked ball as long as possible. She lands balanced on both feet with the knees bent so she can open up and move in whichever direction the ball was hit and be ready to transition off the net to become an available attacker (see figure 4.4).

Figure 4.4 **Blocker landing in a balanced position.**

At a Glance

The following parts of the text offer additional information on the block:

Front-row attack	88
Quick attack	97
Slide	102
Dig	114
Aggressive serving	142
Hitting off the block	152
Attacking or dumping the second ball	158
Positioning defensively as a team	162
Reading the attacker	165
Defending against the slide	168
Determining blocking strategies	171
Defending against the back-row attack	174
Receiving a free ball	177
Defending against a quick attack	183
Defending against the setter's dump or attack	190

(continued)

Common Errors

Following are several common errors you may run into when teaching your athletes how to block.

Error	Error correction
Blocker doesn't jump straight up or drifts past the attacker's shoulder.	The movement along the net requires that the blocker set the block by planting her outside foot. This acts like a brake on the lateral momentum and directs the jump straight up. Make sure the blocker focuses on the attacker so she can get into the correct position with the hands in front of the hitter's shoulder at the point the ball crosses the net. This will help the back-row defenders' read of the attack and where they need to position themselves.
Blocker jumps too early or too late.	The blocker should be in a "loaded" knees-bent, ready-to-jump position so she doesn't have to take more time to bend her knees before she jumps, which can make her late in getting her hands up and over the net. Pay close attention to the attackers when warming up to determine how fast their arm swings are. If the attackers have fast arm swings, the blockers may need to jump earlier than they normally would.
Blocker's hands do not penetrate the net.	Work on the blocker's jumping ability so she can get her hands over and across the top of the net. Use video from the side of the net to show the blocker where her hands are positioned. In practice, have the blocker wear brightly colored gloves so she will notice when her hands come off the net and out of her view.
Blocker doesn't watch the hitter closely enough to front the hitter's shoulder.	The blocker should pay attention to the attacker during her approach and know if she is hitting right- or left-handed. Then the blocker can make sure she is in front of the correct shoulder and in the angle where the ball will actually cross the net. In practice, have the blocker wear a baseball cap, forcing her to pay attention to the attacker instead of watching the ball up in the air. With head level, she can practice transferring focus away from the set ball and across to the anticipated hitter.

Error	Error correction
Blocker makes net fouls.	In practice, have the blocker practice moving along the net or along a wall without touching it. The hands and feet should stay in the same initial relationship to the net at all times. If the hands are pulled off the net, which may happen if the blocker's lead foot and shoulder come off the net as she takes her initial directional step, there is a better chance of the hands hitting the net when she moves back toward it.
Blocker swings at the ball.	The blocker's hands must stay in front of her body at all times, and she must focus on sealing and pressing the hands across the net to the ball. If the hands are not in front, the blocker will have to get them back to the net to block, which results in swinging the hands and arms forward into the net. Again, have the blocker wear brightly colored gloves in practice to make sure her hands stay in her line of vision and not behind her off the net.
Ball comes across the net near the inside hand.	The blocker may have positioned the block too far outside the attacker's shoulder and angle of attack. Have the blocker work on making sure her hand is over the net and angled slightly back toward the attacker so the ball will not glance off of the flat hand but will rebound into the opposing team's court.

KEY POINTS

Following are the most important components of a dig:

- Ready position
- Reading the situation
- Moving to where the ball will be hit
- Body position on the attacker's contact
- Hand and arm position
- Contact with the ball
- Follow-through to target

Figure 4.5 **Defensive player in a ready position.**

A dig is an individual defensive skill performed by a player to deflect the ball up off her forearms. The defensive player will read the play as it develops, position herself around the blockers, and prepare to keep a ball hit by an attacker off the floor. When the blockers and the back-row defenders work together to cover the court, it can make for very exciting action.

READY POSITION

Defensive players should face the attacker in a medium-low athletic ready position, with feet slightly wider than shoulder-width apart and arms and palms in front of the body (figure 4.5). They should be in a position on the court so they can read the situation and move to cover anywhere within their defensive area of responsibility in three steps. It is important for the defensive players to look around and be aware of where they are on the court in relation to the sideline nearest them and the end line. Knowing the location of these boundary lines allows them to decide whether the ball is going out of bounds and they don't need to play it.

READING THE SITUATION

Defensive players or diggers need to watch the play develop, read and anticipate the attack possibilities, and use good timing and judgment to position themselves correctly. A digger's eyes should be open wide, and she should concentrate on first seeing the big picture of what's happening on the opposing team's court. She should see the entire court, all the opposing players, and the movement of the ball. The digger must watch the ball as it moves and the direction of her opponent's platform in order to judge the rebound angle of the ball. This is important because the opponent may make a bad pass or dig, sending the ball directly back over the net, so the blocker must be ready to attack in this situation.

After judging the quality of the pass or dig, the digger then looks at the setter to see if the direction of the set can be determined. (For clues, watch the setters closely during the warm-up to look for any preferences when setting a ball, and share this information with your players.) After the ball is set, the digger should watch the attacker's approach angle, speed, and head position because an attacker will typically hit the ball in the direction of her approach or the way her head is facing. The digger should then communicate with her teammates of any specific things she notices so that all teammates are aware of where the ball is likely to be hit.

MOVING TO WHERE THE BALL WILL BE HIT

After reading and anticipating where the ball will be hit, the defensive player moves quickly to that area of the court while maintaining the same relatively low body position (see figure 4.6). The body should stay in the same level position so the head does not move up and down and interfere with her vision and her focus on the action. This will also increase movement speed since she won't have to rise to move and then return to a low position to play the ball. The movement should be either quick shuffle steps or a combination shuffle and crossover step to that position.

When moving to a ball, it is important that the digger maintain a position where she can see her teammates so she knows that when they go for a ball in the seam (between two players), they will not collide with each other. At no time should the defense back away from a ball hit into a seam so a teammate can take it. The defender closest to the attacker will go for the ball by crossing in front of the deeper defender. The defender who is farther away will cover the deep seam or move across the seam behind her teammate closer to the ball. This is covered in more detail in chapter 6 on defensive tactical skills.

Figure 4.6 **Defensive player moving to the area on the court where the ball will be hit.**

BODY POSITION ON THE ATTACKER'S CONTACT

At the time the attacker contacts the ball, the defensive player should be stopped, balanced with feet wider than shoulder width, and leaning forward so she is ready to move quickly for a ball hit in any direction (see figure 4.7). This is the same as the ready position previously shown in figure 4.5. Her head is in front of her feet, her hands are in front of her shoulders, her shoulders are in front of her knees, and her knees are in front of her toes. Her hands should be open, arms extended loosely in front of the knees, with palms facing the attacker.

As the ball is contacted, the rule of thumb is that the defensive player be in a low enough position to protect her shoes. This position will ensure that the player is low enough to get her arms under the ball. Diggers can raise up if they need to much faster than they can drop down to

Figure 4.7 **Defensive player's body position when the attacker contacts the ball.**

(continued)

dig a hard-driven ball. A digger's head should also be up so she can see the ball under the blocker's hands.

Also, when the defensive player is forced to extend her defensive position to get her arms under the ball, it is important that she stays on her feet until after she has touched the ball. This ensures that she doesn't make a commitment to the floor and then have to try to adjust her body to dig the ball. Generally, diggers should go to the floor only if they lose their balance and after the ball has been played. If the ball is touched by another teammate at the last second, the digger will need to still be on her feet to adjust to and pursue the deflected ball.

HAND AND ARM POSITION

As the ball comes toward the digger, she puts her hands together exactly where the ball is approaching and keeps her eyes on the fast-approaching ball as much as possible. Her arms are out in front of her body, with the base of the thumbs together and arms rotated out so the inside of the forearms provides a flat, solid area between the wrist and elbows for the ball to hit and deflect up to the target area.

If the ball is approaching a location outside the digger's body, she needs to move to the ball but not put her hands together yet. Diggers should be disciplined enough that they don't put their hands together too early because if they do, they will typically end up swinging the platform to the ball. Rather, they need to let the ball come to the platform. Also, putting the hands together too early will not allow diggers to move fast enough to the ball, and it will likely glance off the moving platform and rebound behind them.

Figure 4.8 **Defensive player contacting the ball for a dig.**

CONTACT WITH THE BALL

Upon contact with the ball, the digger should hold her arm and body position for a brief time, keeping the platform quiet (see figure 4.8). The target area for the dug ball is up and into the middle of the court at the attack line. The body must be low and the platform angled up (so the ball will go up and then land on this spot on the court) at contact for the ball to rebound correctly. The trajectory of the ball should be about 20 feet (6 m) high and hanging in the air, allowing time for the setter to transition from her defensive position, either as a blocker or a back-row defender, to set the ball. It will also allow time for the blockers to transition off the net and get in a ready position to become available attackers.

FOLLOW-THROUGH TO TARGET

Once the ball contacts the platform, the accuracy of the dig will be increased if the digger holds that position momentarily. This ensures a solid platform, angled to the target throughout the skill, and not just a rapid poke or swing at the ball.

Common Errors

Following are several common errors you may run into when teaching your athletes how to dig.

Error	Error correction
Defensive player digs the ball over the net.	The player needs to better understand the different rebound angles of the ball and the platform positions she needs to use to get under the ball and keep it on her side of the net. Generally, the closer the digger is to the net, the flatter (more parallel to the floor) the platform and the lower the hips must be. To practice this, have players dig live balls hit over the net, both short and deep, so they can get a feel for the positioning and the ball's response on each dig.
Defensive player goes to the floor before she plays the ball.	The player may not have enough leg strength to keep her knees bent and hold up her body weight. She may need to do some leg-strengthening work to increase her leg strength or lunges to work on quad strength and flexibility.
Ball glances off the defensive player's platform and rebounds off the court behind her.	The digger must contact the ball in front of her body. Work to make sure diggers understand they have to move to keep the ball in front of them, between the platform and the net.
Defensive player makes an inaccurate dig.	The player's hands and arms are most likely coming apart too soon. The player should hold her follow-through for 2 seconds (or until the ball reaches the setter) before releasing the hands and moving to cover the hitter.
Defensive player is moving as the attacker hits the ball.	Make sure the defensive players have the opportunity to "read" the attackers hitting over the net. The more they get to read and anticipate where the ball will be going, the more often they will be in the correct position when the ball is contacted, and the more accurate their digs will be. Experienced players seem to always be in the right place to dig the ball because they read the situation so well and are able to be stopped and balanced at contact, allowing a secondary move to pursue the ball if necessary after contact.

KEY POINTS

Following are the most important components of a run-through:

- o Ready position
- o Reading the situation
- o Moving to the ball
- o Contact with the ball
- o Continuing to move for a few steps

A run-through is used to pursue and play up a slower-moving ball when the attacker decides to tip the ball or the ball is deflected off the blocker or another digger. The defensive player must chase the ball down to get it back into the court. This is a very important skill to have because it is used many times in a match during broken plays. The player should stay low and run toward the ball, putting her arms together for the platform just before contact. The platform will need to be angled to the area the ball should be dug, or deflected.

READY POSITION

Defensive players should face the attacker in a medium-low athletic ready position in the back row, with feet slightly wider than shoulder-width apart and arms and palms in front of the body (see figure 4.9). They should be in a position on the court so they can read and move to cover anywhere within their defensive area of responsibility in three steps. It is important for the diggers to look around and be aware of where they are on the court in relation to the sideline nearest them and the end line. Teammates will have to react quickly to a ball that has been attacked, so they need to know whether a ball will land inside the court or outside the court and whether a teammate is closer to the ball and can play it instead of them.

Figure 4.9 Defensive player in a ready position for a run-through.

READING THE SITUATION

Defensive players need to watch the play develop, read and anticipate the attack possibilities, and use good timing and judgment to position themselves correctly. A digger's eyes should be open wide, and she should concentrate on first seeing the big picture of what's happening on the opposing team's court. She should see the entire court, all the opposing players, and the movement of the ball. The digger must watch the ball as it moves and the direction of her opponent's platform in order to judge the rebound angle of the ball. This is important because the opponent may make a bad pass or dig, sending the ball directly back over the net.

After judging the quality of the pass, the digger then looks at the setter to see if the direction of the set can be determined. (For clues, watch the setters closely during the warm-up to look for any preferences when setting a ball, and share this information with your players). After the ball is set, the digger should watch the attacker's approach angle, speed, and head position because an attacker will typically hit the ball in the direction of her approach or the way her head is facing. The diggers should then communicate with her teammates of any specific things she notices so that all teammates are aware of where the ball is likely to be hit.

MOVING TO THE BALL

After reading the situation and knowing where the ball will be hit by seeing it tipped by the attacker or going off a blocker's hands, the player moves quickly to that area of the court while maintaining the same relatively low body position, with the chest down toward the floor and her head in front of her feet. The body should stay in the same level position so the head does not move and interfere with her vision and her focus on the action. This will also increase movement speed since she won't have to raise up to move and then return to a low position to play the ball. There is no special footwork—the digger just runs with the shoulders down and arms ready to form a platform as she reaches the ball.

CONTACT WITH THE BALL

As the defensive player pursues the ball, she continues to run with her shoulders low. When she approaches the contact point, she reaches her arms out straight, most likely parallel to the floor, making sure the base of her thumbs are together (see figure 4.10). The ball should make contact on the forearms midway between the wrist and elbows. It is important that the shoulders and the platform be angled toward the target on contact. This does not mean the hands and wrists should swing toward the target, but just that the platform angle is facing the correct direction. The digger should keep the platform out for a few seconds before taking the hands apart.

Figure 4.10 **Defensive player contacting the ball for a run-though.**

(continued)

CONTINUING TO MOVE FOR A FEW STEPS

After contacting the ball, the defensive player should let her momentum continue in the same directional line (see figure 4.11). There is no need to stop or abruptly change directions. Once her momentum from the run has slowed down, the digger can turn to get ready to cover the hitter on her team.

Figure 4.11 **Defensive player continuing to move for a few steps after contacting the ball on a run-through.**

Common Errors

Following are several common errors you may run into when teaching your athletes how to run through a ball.

Error	Error correction
Defensive player stands up before she runs to the ball.	The player can practice this skill by running along the center line under the net while keeping her shoulders down. If she rises up to run she will make contact with the net. This is a good way to make sure she stays low.
Defensive player starts to run to where she thinks the ball will be hit.	Players can anticipate where they think the ball is going to go, but they must be disciplined enough to wait until they actually see it going there before moving. If the defender releases too early, the attacker may hit the ball back to where the defender came from (tipping deep instead of short, for example).
Defensive player swings her hands back to the target.	After ball contact, the platform and hands should stay in the direction the player is running. Have the player run down a line placed on the court. Toss a ball over the net on that line, and have the player drop the shoulder closest to the target to pass the ball back to the target at an angle while keeping the arms and hands on that line.

As the ball is set to an attacker, every other player on that team should move to an area of the court to dig up a spike coming back into the court off the opposing team's block. They should be in a ready position to dig the ball up on their own side of the court if it is blocked.

MOVING WHEN THE BALL IS SET

As soon as the ball is set to your team's attacker, each player has an assigned position on the court she must move to in order to cover that specific attacker. If everyone is in the correct position, the court should be balanced when the attacker hits the ball. This should give the hitter the confidence to swing at the ball knowing that if she gets blocked, her teammates will be there to cover her, get the rebound off the block, and give her (or another hitter) another swing at the ball.

BODY POSITION ON ATTACKER'S CONTACT

When the attacker makes contact with the ball, all the covering players should be stopped, balanced, and low (see figure 4.12). Defenders should stop even if they have not made it completely to their assigned positions. This will allow each to react to a deflected ball and immediately move in any direction she needs to in order to pursue the ball. When stopped, the player's feet are wide with the knees bent, shoulders forward, arms held out parallel to the floor, and head up. There is little time to react, so it is fine to have the hands and arms out and ready.

Figure 4.12 **Covering players' body position when the attacker contacts the ball.**

(continued)

TRANSITION BACK TO BASE POSITION

If the ball is not blocked, the covering players need to transition back to their defensive base-court positions, keeping their eyes on the ball on the other side of the net as they move. If the ball is blocked and one of the covering players digs it up, they need to then back away quickly and either make themselves available as a hitter or get ready to cover the next player the ball is set to. This is discussed in greater detail in chapter 6.

Players should focus on the opposing blockers arms and hands because if the attack is blocked by an opponent, this is the area the ball will come from, and it will do so quite fast. It is important for the player covering directly behind the hitter to communicate to the attacker what she sees. This may include telling the hitter how many blockers are up; if there is a hole, or seam, between two blockers; or whether she needs to hit the ball down the line or crosscourt. Typical calls include "Line!" "Angle!" "Seam!" "One up!" and "No block!" If the ball is blocked and comes back over the net, the target for the dig is back off the net to the middle of the court near the attack line. This is an area the setter can get to so she can set the ball to an attacker again.

Common Errors

Following are several common errors you may run into when teaching your athletes how to cover the hitter.

Error	Error correction
Player is out of position.	Walk through the correct attacking position that needs to be covered for each player on the court and make sure they all understand how to transition there from their offensive positions.
Player does not move to cover the attacker.	Attackers in the front row who do not get the set often take themselves out of the play by not moving to cover or by moving up to the net to get ready to block. Stop the play when this happens, and make sure they understand where they need to go. Continue stopping each play until all the players are moving into position. Have players yell, "Cover!" as the ball is set.
Player digs the ball over the net.	Players can get in position 3 feet (.9 m) from a wall, with their eyes focused on the wall at net height. Someone can stand behind them and toss a ball against the wall so it will fall down, and they have to dig it up away from the wall.

Dig Out of the Net

There are times when the ball may accidentally be passed or dug into the net, perhaps because of a poor serve reception or dig from a spiked ball. If the ball cannot be intercepted with control before it hits the net, the player can use the net as a rebound point. It is important to train players to see where the ball goes into the net so they know where to position themselves to make a good play when it comes out of the net.

SEEING THE BALL TRAVEL INTO THE NET

The defensive player should observe the ball trajectory as it moves toward the net. If the ball goes into the top half of the net, it will most likely come down near the net (see figure 4.13a). If the ball goes into the lower portion of the net, it is likely to rebound farther from the net (see figure 4.13b). Of course, the tightness of the net will have an impact on the distance the ball rebounds out of the net, so test this before play begins with a few tosses into the net. Also be aware that the player's hit into the net counts as the first contact for the team.

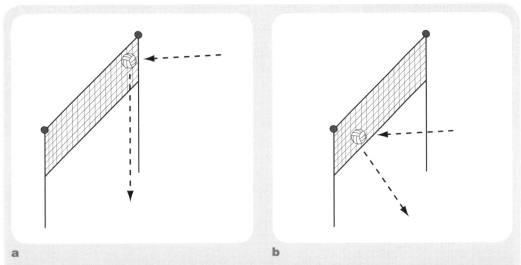

a   b

Figure 4.13 **Location of rebounds for a ball in the net: (a) the top half of the net and (b) the lower half of the net.**

(continued)

BODY POSITION AND CONTACT WITH THE BALL AT THE NET

When a ball goes into the net, the defensive player should move to a position facing the net and the court at a 45-degree angle so she can play the ball up and out of the net toward the target area in the middle of the court, at least 5 feet (1.5 m) off the net. The body should be in a low position with the feet wide, hips low, knees bent, and arms out with hands together ready to play the ball (see figure 4.14). The body should be low enough so the arms will be lower than the net. This gives the player more time to react to the ball. The player must be patient in letting the ball rebound out of the net since it will be dropping toward the floor. If necessary, she can drop her body even lower to play the ball up out of the net.

If the ball comes directly back toward the player, it may be necessary to bend the elbows to play the ball back away from the net, called a J stroke (see figure 4.15). This is the only time most players will bend the elbows in defense or passing a ball. Note that this hit counts as the second hit for the team, so the next contact will be the third and last and must put the ball over the net.

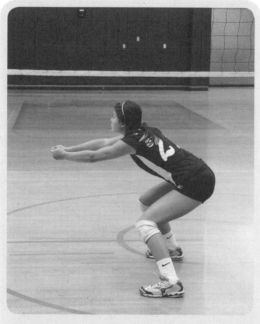

Figure 4.14 Defensive player's body position when preparing to dig a ball out of the net.

Figure 4.15 Defensive player using a J stroke.

TRANSITION TO NEXT POSITION

Once the ball has been hit out of the net and is traveling up toward the middle of the court, the next contact is the last contact your team can make, so a player must hit the ball over the net. The player who dug it out of the net is the only player who cannot participate in the next contact, so that player should be prepared to cover the teammate who hits the ball next.

At a Glance

The following parts of the text offer additional information on a dig out of the net:

Forearm pass	55
Overhead pass	59
Block	108
Dig	114
Using a libero	180
Chasing down a ball	187

Common Errors

Following are several common errors you may run into when teaching your athletes how to dig the ball out of the net.

Error	Error correction
Ball bounces out past the defensive player or drops in front of her.	The player needs to carefully watch the trajectory of the ball going into the net, which will dictate where it will come out of the net and the speed it will have. Practice by throwing balls into the net at various speeds and trajectories to teach players to anticipate how the ball will come out of the net each time.
Defensive player is called for an illegal contact or lift.	The player needs to be low enough that the ball will drop onto her arms and make a quick rebound movement. If the ball comes to rest on the arms, it is an illegal hit.
Defensive player digs the ball over the net or back into the net.	The player is most likely facing the net too squarely and should take a more angled position, with one shoulder, hip, and foot closer to the net than the other. This could also happen if the player's platform is too low and not parallel to the floor. You can practice the positioning for digs out of the net by having players positioned 3 feet (.9 m) from a wall, with their eyes focused on the wall at net height. Stand behind them and toss a ball against the wall so it will fall down, and they have to dig it up and away from the wall.

Overhead Dig

KEY POINTS

Following are the most important components of an overhead dig:

o Ready position

o Arm position and contact with the ball

o Follow-through held to target

To make a defensive play, players should position themselves on the court so they can keep the ball low and in front of their bodies, using the forearms as a platform to dig the ball up. There are some situations or team defenses, however, where players start closer inside the sideline or end line, or the attacker may have hit the ball with a higher, flatter trajectory, forcing the digger to dig the ball overhead. Although the hand positions may vary from open to clasped to interlocked, the outcome should be the same, with the ball traveling up to the middle of the court so the setter or another player can get the ball to an attacker for a good swing at the ball. The first contact on the ball in volleyball rules doesn't have to be a "clean hit," allowing a player just to get their hands up and make contact with the ball. The player will need to know the rules for their particular governing organization.

READY POSITION

Defensive players should face the attacker in a low defensive ready position, with feet slightly wider than shoulder-width apart. The shoulders should be low, with the chest toward the floor and the head in front of the feet (see figure 4.16). This is the best defensive position for reading and reacting to balls. The arms are out in front of the body, with the palms facing up.

Figure 4.16 Defensive player in a ready position for an overhead dig.

ARM POSITION AND CONTACT WITH THE BALL

From a low ready position on the court as the ball is coming toward the defender, there are two options for making contact with the ball. In the first, the digger gets both hands up, with the fingers spread and wrists and fingers stiff, similar to a blocking hand position (see figure 4.17a). Contact is made on the inside pads of the fingers (see figure 4.17b). This is a more advanced move, and much training should be done to make sure the player has strong enough hands and wrists to play this ball safely and accurately.

The second option is for the defensive player to put both hands together, which is sometimes referred to as a tomahawk. For this hand position, the player either cups the hands around one another (see figure 4.18a) or interlocks the fingers (see figure 4.18b) to keep the hands together during contact. The ball will make contact with the base of the hands or the forearms near the wrists. The forearm platform should be angled up toward the ceiling so the ball will rebound up.

a   b

Figure 4.17   **Defensive player contacting the ball with open hands.**

a   b

Figure 4.18   **Defensive player contacting the ball with the hands *(a)* cupped together or *(b)* interlocked for an overhead dig.**

(continued)

FOLLOW-THROUGH HELD TO TARGET

The player should maintain her arm position momentarily to make sure the ball goes in the intended direction, which is up in the air toward the target area, or middle of the court near the attack line (see figure 4.19). Bringing the hands down too quickly rushes the move and gives an unstable area for the ball to contact.

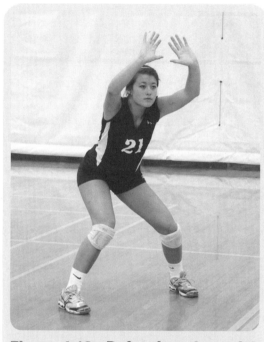

Figure 4.19 Defensive player following through to the target after hitting an overhead dig.

Common Errors

Following are several common errors you may run into when teaching your athletes how to do an overhead dig.

Error	Error correction
Ball goes through the defensive player's hands.	The player's wrists and hands may not be stiff enough or may be too far apart, resulting in the ball coming through her hands. Determine whether the players are strong enough to play the ball overhead with open hands or should use the tomahawk method.
Defensive player gets her hands up too late.	The digger's hands may be too low in the ready position. If the ball is being hit so fast or hard that the player cannot get her hands up fast enough, she should position herself deeper in the court on defense so she doesn't have to play many balls overhead.

Barrel Roll (Log Roll)

The barrel roll, or log roll, is used to make a defensive save in an emergency situation in order to play a ball up, recover, and quickly get back into a ready position. In the event that a player extends her body by taking a low lunge step to play a ball, she can cover a little extra distance and keep from stopping herself abruptly by rolling on the floor using this technique. This move is called a barrel roll or log roll because the body simulates a barrel or a log rolling. To use this technique, it is important that players feel comfortable with the floor; if they stay low enough during this move, they will develop more confidence in going to the floor after they have played the ball up.

KEY POINTS

Following are the most important components of a barrel roll (log roll):

- Ready position
- Moving to the ball
- Contact with the ball
- Sliding onto hip after contact
- Rolling through on back
- Getting on feet

READY POSITION

Defensive players should face the attacker in a low defensive ready position, with feet slightly wider than shoulder-width apart. The shoulders should be low, with the chest toward the floor and the head in front of the feet (see figure 4.20). This is the best defensive position for reading and reacting to balls. The arms and hands are out in front of the body, with the palms facing up. The defensive player should also be in a position on the court where she is able to move and cover her defensive area of responsibility in three steps.

MOVING TO THE BALL

After reading and anticipating where the ball will be hit, the defensive player moves quickly to that area of the court. The movement will be a quick step or two in the direction of the ball. Once the

Figure 4.20 **Defensive player in a ready position.**

player determines that the ball cannot be dug using normal digging technique, she will take one last step to get to the ball. This last step is a lunge where the player drops the hips low, extends the leg nearest the ball, and drives the body outside the foot base to reach the ball.

(continued)

CONTACT WITH THE BALL

The player should contact the ball with her platform using both arms when the ball is close enough, but she can also contact it with one arm in an effort to save the ball that may be just out of her lunge and reach. The platform should extend to the ball and should get under the ball before contact (see figure 4.21). The platform is held with the forearms together to give the ball a solid surface

Figure 4.21 **Defensive player contacting the ball for a barrel roll (log roll).**

to rebound off of. When possible, the player should try to have the platform (or single hand or forearm nearest the ball) facing up and toward the target area, which is the middle of the court near the attack line.

SLIDING ONTO HIP AFTER CONTACT

After contact, the player lets the outside hand slide along the floor to absorb the body's momentum instead of trying to stop the body abruptly, she rotates the outside knee toward the middle of the body so the hip and rear make contact with the floor as the hand slides (see figure 4.22). It is important to rotate the knee so it does not bang into the floor; in fact if this move is done correctly, the knee should not contact the floor at all.

Figure 4.22 **Defensive player sliding onto the hip after contacting the ball for a barrel roll (log roll).**

ROLLING THROUGH ON BACK

The player's momentum will keep the body moving while she rolls onto her back with one leg extended (see figure 4.23). The roll should be across the back so there is no chance of an injury to the neck or head. The player will then continue the roll onto her stomach.

Figure 4.23 **Defensive player rolling through on the back for a barrel roll (log roll).**

GETTING ONTO FEET

As the player completes the roll onto her stomach, she bends the leg coming across the body, puts the foot down, and pushes up with both hands (see figure 4.24). The player should be able to quickly get back to her feet and be ready for the next play, which is hopefully moving to cover a hitter.

Figure 4.24 **Defensive player getting onto the feet after a barrel roll (log roll).**

(continued)

Common Errors

Following are several common errors you may run into when teaching your athletes how to do a barrel roll (log roll).

Error	Error correction
Defensive player lands on her knee instead of taking a lunge step and rotating the knee in.	Try the skill in slow motion, making sure the player rotates the knee inward so it does not come in contact with the floor.
Defensive player doesn't extend far enough when taking a lunge step toward the ball.	Help the player learn the proper body position when extending to contact the ball by pulling her gently by the outside hand (direction she is extending) until the hips are no longer over the feet and she loses her balance.
Defensive player is afraid of the floor.	Work slowly on this skill without a ball from a very low position until she feels comfortable doing it. Make sure she has enough leg strength to hold her body off the floor until after the ball is contacted. Forward and lateral lunges are a good way to work on leg strength for this skill.

The collapse dig, or sprawl, is an emergency skill used to dig a hard-hit ball just before it hits the floor, typically when an attacker has hit the ball down toward the digger so it is going to land somewhere in front of her. There is no time to move the feet to the ball, only time enough to shoot the arms out along the floor to get them under the ball. The player's main priority in this situation is to get the arms to, under, and through the ball to play it up and keep it off the floor.

KEY POINTS

Following are the most important components of a collapse dig (sprawl):

o Ready position
o Moving to the ball
o Contact with the ball

READY POSITION

Defensive players should face the attacker in a low defensive ready position, with feet slightly wider than shoulder-width apart. The shoulders should be low, with the chest toward the floor and the head in front of the feet (see figure 4.25). This is the best defensive position for reading and reacting to balls. The arms and hands are out in front of the body, with the palms facing up. The defensive player should also be in a position on the court where she is able to move and cover her defensive area of responsibility in three steps.

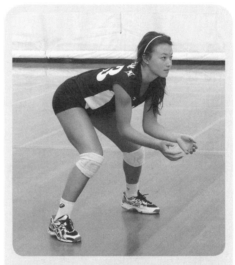

Figure 4.25 **Defensive player in a ready position.**

MOVING TO THE BALL

The digger's feet should already be wide, with the knees bent and the hips low to the ground, as she reads the situation and waits for the hitter to contact the ball. The digger should then take a low lunge step with the foot closest to where the ball is going to land so that the hips are lower than the knee (see figure 4.26). This is important for the player's safety so that her body collapses onto or slides along the floor from a lower position instead of landing on the floor from a higher point.

Figure 4.26 **Defensive player moving to the ball for a collapse dig (sprawl).**

(continued)

At a Glance

The following parts of the text offer additional information on a collapse dig (sprawl):

CONTACT WITH THE BALL

The player should put her hands together quickly as she lunges and just before she contacts the ball, as shown in figure 4.27a, with the base of the thumbs together and the forearms exposed to provide a solid platform. The platform will shoot or slide out along the floor under the ball. It is important that the platform get under and through the ball parallel to the floor so the ball will deflect up and not forward at a low trajectory. As the forearms contact the ball, the knee of the lunging leg rotates out so the body can collapse to the floor onto the stomach without hitting the knee or the hip bone on the floor, as shown in figure 4.27b. (This is opposite of what the knee does for the barrel roll.) The defensive player's arms will extend and slide out along the floor instead of trying to stop the body's momentum. This will prevent jamming the wrists and shoulders or stopping the move, which may affect the angle of the platform and the trajectory of the ball as it comes off the arms. Once the ball has been played up, the player simply pushes herself off the floor and resumes play.

a

b

Figure 4.27 **Defensive player contacting the ball on a collapse dig (sprawl).**

Common Errors

Following are several common errors you may run into when teaching your athletes how to do a collapse dig (sprawl).

Error	Error correction
Defensive player tries to stop herself from going to the floor completely.	Players must be comfortable going to the floor. If they start with their hips low enough, the body will be close to the floor. The move should be a quick collapse along the floor, shooting the arms out to play the ball. Trying to stop the move halfway is more dangerous to wrists and shoulders than going through with it.
Defensive player runs a few steps before executing this skill.	If a player has time to take steps to the ball, she should be using another digging skill. The collapse dig (sprawl) is designed for digging a ball that is coming within one step of the player but is moving so fast the player is unable to move her feet for a dig.

KEY POINTS

Following are the most important components of a pancake:

- o Ready position
- o Moving to the ball
- o Going to the floor on the stomach
- o Contact with the ball

The pancake is an emergency defensive move to get the hand flat and on the floor, like a pancake, with the palm down and under the ball just as it gets ready to hit the floor. The ball will hit the back of the hand and rebound up enough for a teammate to get to it to keep it in play. This is the last option to use when the player can't reach the ball any other way.

READY POSITION

Defensive players should face the attacker in a low defensive ready position, with feet slightly wider than shoulder-width apart. The shoulders should be low, with the chest toward the floor and the head in front of the feet (see figure 4.28). This is the best defensive position for reading and reacting to balls. The arms and hands should be out in front of the body, with the palms facing up. The defensive player should also be in a position on the court where she is able to move and cover her defensive area of responsibility in three steps.

Figure 4.28 **Defensive player in a ready position.**

MOVING TO THE BALL

The defensive player will see the ball coming over the net and attempt to get to the ball to make a play while staying on her feet. After a few steps, once it is determined the ball will drop to the floor outside the area she can reach, the player should go to the floor to save the ball. To get low, she moves her hips low to the ground and takes a long lunge step toward the ball, extending the leg and her body.

GOING TO THE FLOOR ON THE STOMACH

The player goes to the floor, facedown on the court on her stomach, and makes a final reach for the ball with her arm and hand. The hand is flat and placed with the palm down on the floor. The other hand is used to help lower the body to the floor and is on the ground in front of the shoulder, providing balance during the reach (see figure 4.29).

Figure 4.29 **Defensive player going to the floor to reach the ball for a pancake.**

CONTACT WITH THE BALL

The hand that reaches for the ball will be palm down on the floor, with the fingers spread to provide the most surface for the ball to contact (see figure 4.30). At this point in the skill, timing is critical. The player must time the move so her hand gets to the floor before the ball and the ball bounces straight up off the back of her hand. This move, if done correctly, allows the hand to just slide under the ball to keep it from hitting the floor. After contact, the player quickly gets back up on her feet, ready to continue her participation in the play.

Figure 4.30 **Defensive player making contact with the ball for a pancake.**

(continued)

Common Errors

Following are several common errors you may run into when teaching your athletes how to do a pancake.

Error	Error correction
Defensive player's hand gets to the floor too soon.	This is an extension move where the body is stretched to full extension to get the hand under the ball. If the body is not at full extension, the hand will get to the floor too soon.
Defensive player goes to the floor unnecessarily to use this skill.	The first priority defensively is for a player to stay on her feet to play the ball so she can continue in the play, covering a hitter. To do that, a player must move her feet quickly to get in the correct position to play a ball. If that is not possible and the player has gone as far as she can, then she can go to the floor and stretch out to make this move.
Both of the defensive player's hands go forward for the reach.	Make sure the player's opposite hand helps lower the body to the floor by catching the body weight near the shoulder.
Ball does not rebound up from the hand.	The hand and arm are most likely not in full contact with the floor, causing the ball to "die" upon contact or deflect in another direction and become unplayable.

PART III

Teaching Tactical Skills

Acquiring tactical skills may mean the difference between a beginning team and an experienced team. It is important to be comfortable in executing the technical skills with confidence while learning the tactics involved in volleyball. USA Volleyball urges coaches to "only attempt tactically what your team can do technically," a guiding principle for coaching this sport successfully. Coaches can empower their athletes by teaching them how to read situations. This is done best by training in gamelike situations as much as possible.

Part III focuses on tactical skills in volleyball such as those used in serving strategies (delivering different types of serves from and to varying parts of the court, at different trajectories and speeds) and individual attacking strategies (learning how to vary attack speeds and directions and to hit a variety of sets) as well as tactics used by players in various positions on the court. Like the technical skills chapters, these chapters have been designed so you can immediately incorporate the information into your teaching.

THINKING TACTICALLY

Throughout the presentation of tactical skills, you will see references to the need for athletes to know the game situation. As described in Rainer Martens' *Successful Coaching, Third Edition*, the game situation includes knowing if the opposing team's setter is in the front or back row, who and where the weakest passer and the strongest blocker is, and who and where your own strongest hitter is in a specific rotation. In other words, your team needs to know specific information when facing a specific situation. For example, when you need to set up the defense against a strong hitter, you may ask yourself, "How should we block this attacker? Do we need to block down the line or crosscourt? Will they tip or hit hard? Do we have the court balanced? Can we transition quickly out of these defensive positions?"

You and your team must know what key information you need in order to make the best decision. Following are a few questions to keep in mind when facing tactical situations during a game.

- What is your strategy?
- How does your game plan affect your strategy?
- How does the game situation (the score, the strengths and weaknesses of the individual players, the rotation the team is in, and so on) affect your game plan?
- How would I beat our defense if I were the hitter?

In the skills that follow, you will first be presented with an overview that paints a picture, or puts you and your athletes into a specific scenario in the game in which you would be likely to use that particular tactical skill. The "Reading the Situation" element offers important cues your athletes need to be able to read so they can make appropriate decisions for the situation. The "Watch Out!" element highlights the distractions that may affect your athletes' ability to make appropriate decisions and provides insight on what to look for. The section called "Acquiring the Appropriate Knowledge" provides the information your athletes need to understand in order to make the proper decision and successfully execute the skill, as presented in the overview. Finally, as in the technical skills chapters, the "At a Glance" section refers you to the other important tools in this book that will help you teach the skill.

chapter 5

Offensive Tactical Skills

This chapter covers the offensive tactical skills players must know to be successful. In this chapter, you will find the following skills:

Aggressive Serving

Aggressive serving wins volleyball matches! Although it is important to serve aggressively, players must also be smart when serving since a serving error will give a point to the other team. Understanding serving tactics will increase players' opportunities to score a point for their team. The serve is the only skill in volleyball where the player has control over every variable related to the execution of the skill, such as where she is serving from and to, the velocity and trajectory of the ball, and the specific type of serve executed. Your team will have a better chance at scoring from an aggressive serve, but players should be serving more aces than errors.

 ## WATCH OUT!

The following circumstances may distract your athletes:

- Serving immediately after a time-out is called by the opposing team
- Serving after the previous player missed a serve
- Serving at set or match point
- Spectators distracting them as they go back to the serving area
- Close score

READING THE SITUATION

How do you and your players gain the best advantage when serving? Teach your players to do the following:

- Identify the best areas to serve to and why.
- Use the same routine for serving each time.
- Be confident in their ability to make strong serves to different areas of the court.
- Aim to serve an ace every time.
- Serve to take away a strong offensive option or to completely take the opposing team out of their offensive system.
- Run into the court to play defense immediately after the serve.

ACQUIRING THE APPROPRIATE KNOWLEDGE

When serving, your athletes must understand the following:

Rules

You and your athletes need to know several main rules when serving:

- Rules about the time limit for a player to serve after the referee blows the whistle
- Rules about serving in the correct rotation
- Rules about overlapping
- Rules about the area that is available behind the end line to serve
- Rules about a foot fault
- Rules about catching a poor toss

REMINDER!

You and your players must understand the team strategy and game plan and assess serving based on those plans and the situation at hand. Make sure you and your players consider the questions on page 140.

Strengths and Weaknesses of Opponents

You and your players must account for the opposing team's strengths and weaknesses to know how to gain the best advantage when serving. Teach your players to consider the following about your opponents:

- Where is the setter on the court? Look to see where the setter is coming from on the court, and serve to that area. This will make it more difficult for the setter to get out of the way of the serve. It will also make it more difficult for the passer to focus on the ball coming to her when the setter is running in front of her to get to the setting position near the net.

- Where is a weakness in a serve-reception pattern? Serve to the seams between players or to open areas to force passers to move to pass. This could also cause some confusion as the passers decide who should pass the ball.

- Do you want to put extra stress on one player? If so, make the same player pass every serve. By making her pass every serve, she will have less time to focus on preparing to hit. The level of concentration needed to pass every ball will wear her down.

- Where is the best place to serve to score a point? Serve to the opposing team's weakest receiver. Make that person pass the most serves, and put pressure on her to perform. Make the player move to pass the ball instead of serving directly at her.

- What will a receiving team player be thinking about after making a mistake? Serve to a player who just made a poor pass or got aced. She will most likely make another error and should be tested to see if she can handle the serve again.

- What can an opposing coach do to slow down a server? A coach will make a substitution for a variety of reasons, but one is to get the server to lose her concentration.

- Who should you serve to? Serve to a player who just substituted into the game.

- Is the libero their best passer? If a libero is on the court, serve to this player to test her passing ability.

- How can you get the passers to move on the court? Serve deep or short to the strongest hitter in the front row. Make the hitter move to pass the ball before she hits, possibly taking her out of a good hitting position, which means the setter will need to set another player.

- Can the middle hitter pass the serve? Serve it short to a middle hitter close to the net so she has to pass the ball before she can hit a set. This can take her out of the play offensively.

- Who should you serve to? Serve it to a player who just missed a serve. She will still be thinking about that error and may make a passing error.

- Where is the best area of the court to serve the ball? Serve it to zone 1 or deep near the end line (see figure 3.40 on page 64 for an example of the court zones). This will force players to back up to pass the ball.

- Is the ball going to be in or out? Serve it near the end line or sidelines to make the passer decide whether to play the ball or not.

Self-Knowledge

In addition to being aware of the opposing team's strengths and weaknesses, you and your players need to have knowledge about your own team's ability. In terms of serving, coaches and players should be aware of the following:

- Where will your strongest server start in the rotation order? Design the team rotation and serving order for maximum effect.

At a Glance

The following parts of the text offer additional information on serving:

Skill	Page
Underhand serve	25
Sidearm serve	29
Standing floater serve	34
Jump floater serve	39
Topspin serve	43
Roundhouse serve	46
Jump spin serve	50
Forearm pass	55
Overhead pass	59
Defending against the slide	168
Defending against a quick attack	183

(continued)

o How can players vary their serves? Players can use any of the area available behind the end line to serve. They will most likely want to serve from an area somewhere near their assigned defensive positions on the court. Players can vary not only where they serve along the end line but also their distance from the end line. These types of changes will help keep the opposing team's passers out of rhythm.

o Is every player on the bench mentally ready to come in and make a great serve? Every substitute must be mentally ready to come in and serve when called upon by the coach. The player should be aware of the serving strategy, weak passers, the opposing team's front-row players, and who passed the last serve and how she did.

o How can you dictate the opposing team's offense? An aggressive serve near a weak passer, in a seam between two players, or to a zone behind the setter will slow down a team's offense.

o What type of serve (or server) is needed in a particular situation? Certain situations in a game require a serve with a 100 percent success rate such as after a time-out or a substitution, after an opponent or a teammate misses a serve, or after the player has just come into the match.

Decision-Making Guidelines

When deciding the best way to gain an advantage when your team is serving, you and your players should be sure to consider the previous information. Also, consider the following guidelines:

o Change the serving pace and trajectory and where the serve comes from (along the end line and from varying depths behind the end line). Players should be able to serve a high short serve or a deep flat serve to keep the opponents guessing as to what type of serve will be coming at them.

o Servers must serve with the goal of scoring points. Servers want to be aggressive but not reckless. It is important that a player serve the ball as hard as she can control it.

o Ensure that players have a variety of serves in their repertoire to keep their opponents off balance when passing. Players should master at least two different types to use as needed.

o Serve a floater serve from as far back as possible, allowing the ball to move even more and making it difficult for the opponent to pass it accurately.

o Serve from directly behind the end line, reducing the amount of time the passer has to read and adjust to the serve.

o Serve down the line, near the end line, making it a difficult angle for the passer to get the ball back to the target (middle of the court).

o Serve near the sidelines or end line so the passer must make a decision whether the ball is going to land in or go out of bounds.

o Serve short to zone 3 (see figure 3.40 on page 64 for an example of the court zones) or to any of the middle hitters standing just back from the net. This may take them out of making a quick attack.

o Serve short to any of the front-row hitters, making the receiving player move forward to pass the ball and then back out to make her hitting approach.

o Serve deep to any of the front-row hitters, making the receiving player back up to pass the ball and then alter her spike approach.

o Serve deep to zone 1 or short to zone 2, making it more difficult for the setter to set the middle hitter because the ball is being passed from behind her.

o Serve to seams between zones or passers, making communication between the passers critical. It is more difficult for a player to move to pass a ball than to pass a ball aimed directly at her.

- Serve at a player who just made a passing error or was just substituted in. A player who has just made an error usually spends too much time focusing on the error instead of preparing to receive the next serve. A substitute should be tested immediately to see if she is mentally ready to pass a ball.

- Serve at the same player throughout the match to make her handle the constant pressure.

- Serve deep or short one time, and if the passers adjust their positions, serve even deeper or shorter for the next ball to keep them off balance.

- A good miss is better than a bad miss. A bad miss is into the net, where the opponent does not even have to think about whether to play the ball or not. A good miss is over the net but maybe long or to the side, requiring the opponent to decide whether to play the ball or not.

Being able to receive a serve accurately as a team lets you pass the ball to the target area, allowing your setter to make a variety of sets to the attackers. Passing to the target is known as being "in your offensive system." Making a poor pass where a player other than the setter has to set the ball is known as playing "out of system." Identifying your best passers and having them work together with their teammates is a key to a successful team. Working together means communicating whether the ball is in bounds or out of bounds and calling "Mine!" if they are going to pass the ball. Ultimately if there is a good pass, the setter can make a good set, trying to get an attacker isolated with one blocker so the attacker has a better opportunity to score.

 WATCH OUT!

The following circumstances may distract your athletes:

- Facing a jump server
- A loud crowd yelling at the team
- A previous serve-reception error
- Lack of communication among teammates when passing
- A low, aggressive serve

ACQUIRING THE APPROPRIATE KNOWLEDGE

When setting up your team serve reception, your athletes must understand the following:

Rules

You and your athletes need to know several main rules when setting up your team serve reception:

- Rules about overlapping
- Rules about time allowed for the server to contact the ball
- Rules about types of contacts allowed
- Rules about the ball hitting the net or going out of bounds during the serve
- Rules about substitution

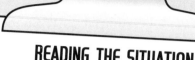

READING THE SITUATION

How do you and your players gain the best advantage when setting up your team serve reception? Teach your players to do the following:

- Know where they are on the court by looking around to see how close they are to the sidelines, end line, and teammates.
- Recognize the type of server and past serving tendencies.
- Know the seams of responsibility.
- Communicate immediately whether the ball is "in" or "out."

REMINDER!

You and your players must understand the team strategy and game plan and assess team serve reception based on those plans and the situation at hand. Make sure you and your players consider the questions on page 140.

Strengths and Weaknesses of Opponents

You and your players must account for the opposing team's strengths and weaknesses to know how to gain the best advantage when setting up your team serve reception. Teach your players to consider the following about your opponents:

- What types of servers does the opposing team have? Be ready to adjust the serve-reception pattern for a jump server by taking a step forward before the serve.

- What areas do the opponents serve from? Review the seam responsibilities for each server, and remind each other in between each serve what areas each specific player will need to cover.

- Where or who did the opponent serve to last time? Focus on what each server has done throughout the match, and be prepared for her to serve to the same zone or to the same person in that rotation again.

- What can you do to distract the server? If the server has scored 2 or 3 points, change the serve-reception pattern or move a passer who has been served to repeatedly out of the reception pattern. This could force the server to adjust her serve and may cause her to miss it.

Self-Knowledge

In addition to being aware of the opposing team's strengths and weaknesses, you and your players need to have knowledge about your own team's ability. In terms of team serve reception, coaches and players should be aware of the following:

- Which players work well together? When determining your lineup, strive to have passers who communicate and understand one another positioned next to each other.

At a Glance

The following parts of the text offer additional information on team serve reception:

Skill	Page
Underhand serve	25
Sidearm serve	29
Standing floater serve	34
Jump floater serve	39
Topspin serve	43
Roundhouse serve	46
Jump spin serve	50
Forearm pass	55
Overhead pass	59
Front-row attack	88
Quick attack	97
Slide	102

- Who are the best passers on the team? Some players receive serves better than others. Keep passing statistics in daily practice to make sure the best passers are in the team serve reception. Also, keep passing statistics for each player in various positions on the court. Some players may be better passers on the left side of the court than on the right side.

- What serve-reception pattern should be used? Depending on the number of good passers you have, you could pass with two, three, four, or even five passers in different patterns. Be ready to change patterns in each rotation order to distract the server. Note, however, that whatever the number of passers in the serve-receive formation, they should increase the rate of success in passing the ball to the setter.

- Can you get the best passer on the team to receive the most serves? Work on designing serve-reception patterns that have the best passer in the middle of the court and receiving the most serves as often as possible. Determine the best passer by keeping passing statistics in practice, and over time it will be obvious who the best passer on the team is. This will improve the team's offense if the ball is passed successfully to the setter so she can set the best hitter in the best situation.

- Who can change the serve-reception pattern? Either the coach from the bench, the setter, or the libero can instruct the team to change the pattern being used to receive the serve. Make sure this has been rehearsed in practice and that these players understand the reasons for making a change. In addition, all players must thoroughly understand each possible reception pattern for each rotation.

- What is the strategy for a player who is having trouble receiving a serve? Make sure the player focuses immediately on the next serve and what she needs to do to make a good pass. She should not be thinking about what just happened but what needs to happen next and the key technical points for passing.

(continued)

Decision-Making Guidelines

When deciding the best way to gain an advantage when your team is receiving the serve, you and your players should be sure to consider the previous information. Also, consider the following guidelines:

- Keep your serve-reception pattern simple. Fewer passers lead to fewer misunderstandings and fewer decisions, and even more important, those passers will get more practice passing serves.

- The passer closest to the server will be responsible for passing a ball in the short seam, and the player farther away will cover the deep seam. This needs to be discussed by all the players in the team serve reception before every serve, and time should be taken to practice passing in pairs or groups of three so players will be prepared to cover the seams in the serve-reception pattern.

- Players should take a look around before each serve to see how many steps they need to take to reach the sidelines or end line before a ball would land out of bounds.

- Use an overhead pass when the ball is high above the shoulders and is not traveling too fast. Players may have a starting position closer to the net so they can transition to hit faster or if they have trouble moving forward to pass a ball.

- The ball can hit the net legally on a serve and drop into your court. A front-row player needs to be assigned to be ready to react to this situation.

- Players must make a decision on whether the ball is out as quickly as possible and verbalize that to their teammates by calling "In" or "Out" so that teammates can make a decision to pass it or let it go out of bounds. Players who won't be passing the ball should strive to call it, as they will have a better view of the court and the trajectory of the ball.

- When receiving a serve, try to pass the ball to a target 5 feet (1.5 m) off the net and just to the right of the center of the court. This allows room for an error in passing without sending the ball over the net.

- Players should position themselves in the court so that if they are better at passing short serves, they can start deep and think *forward*. If they are better at passing deep serves, they should start up, or short, and think *back*.

- Passing a short serve can be challenging because the angle of the arms must be more horizontal since the ball will not travel forward as far as it does when passed from the back row. Be sure that players practice passing short serves from each zone across the front row and that they are able to make the pass and then become available as an attacker.

- Players not passing the ball should be involved by communicating whether the ball is in or out and should be ready to back up a passer in front of them.

successful attacker can hit a set ball from and to different areas of the court. She can hit the ball using different velocities, such as hard hits, off-speed hits, roll shots, or tips, as needed in a specific situation. She can also impart different trajectories on the ball and hit with range, meaning she can hit the ball in different directions such as down the line, through the seam of a block, or crosscourt.

⚠ WATCH OUT!

The following circumstances may distract your athletes:

o Passing the ball to the setter before beginning their attack approach

o A tall blocker in front of them

o A poor set from the setter

o Being blocked earlier in the match

o The ball being set from the back row

ACQUIRING THE APPROPRIATE KNOWLEDGE

When varying your attacks, your athletes must understand the following:

Rules

You and your athletes need to know several main rules when varying your attack:

o Rules about illegal hits

o Rules about the ball touching a blocker

o Rules about contacting the net

o Rules about contacting the center line

o Rules about the attack line if hitting from the back row

o Rules about the libero player delivering a hand set to an attacker in the front row

Strengths and Weaknesses of Opponents

You and your players must account for the opposing team's strengths and weaknesses to know how to gain the best advantage when varying your attacks. Teach your players to consider the following about your opponents:

o What type of blocking system are the opponents using? If the blockers are bunched inside, the set needs to go outside by the antenna. If the blockers are spread out, the set may need to go inside.

o What team defensive system are the opponents using? Knowing this can help the attacker determine where open spots on the court will be and where to hit.

o Can the back-row defenders move quickly enough to pick up a tip or off-speed shot to the middle of the court? If the back-row defenders are playing deep and don't read or move well, drop a tip over the block or an off-speed shot to the open court.

READING THE SITUATION

How do you and your players gain the best advantage when varying your attack? Teach your players to do the following:

• Know the blockers' starting positions and if they will be moving.

• Recognize where the blockers' hands are in the air.

• Look for a seam in the block.

• Be aware of defensive positioning of the opponents.

• Listen for teammates' verbal calls about the block or defensive formation.

REMINDER!

You and your players must understand the team strategy and game plan and vary your attacks based on those plans and the situation at hand. Make sure you and your players consider the questions on page 140.

(continued)

o Does the middle blocker get her inside hand over the net, or is the sharp angle open? If the middle blocker does not penetrate the net with her hand, look to hit a sharp crosscourt shot inside her hand.

o Do the opponents block the line or crosscourt in their defensive system? The player coming up behind the hitter to cover should call out whether the line or crosscourt is open.

At a Glance

The following parts of the text offer additional information on varying your attacks:

Skill	Page
Front-row attack	88
Back-row attack	93
Quick attack	97
Slide	102
Block	108
Dig	114
Run-through	118
Barrel roll (log roll)	129
Collapse dig (sprawl)	133
Pancake	136

Self-Knowledge

In addition to being aware of the opposing team's strengths and weaknesses, you and your players need to have knowledge about your own team's ability. In terms of varying your attacks, coaches and players should be aware of the following:

o What shots are your players capable of making? Use training time to work on various arm-swing speeds and hitting at different target areas on the court. Always have the hitter training against a block and a set coming from a passed ball so she will experience all the live situations, such as a bad pass, a tight set, a set outside the antenna, and so on. Some players may not be able to hit accurately down the line or to the deep corner.

o Does your team communicate well? Teammates need to talk during play to call out open shots for the attacker. In addition, the players covering the hitter should let them know any weaknesses they see in the blockers or back-row defenders.

o Is your hitter able to score against one blocker? The setter should work hard to make sure the hitter is hitting against one blocker. Then it is up to the attacker to put the ball away and score a point.

o Is the hitter able to focus on the next play after making a hitting error? The player must have enough confidence to want to hit the next ball after getting blocked or hitting the ball out of bounds.

Decision-Making Guidelines

When deciding the best way to gain an advantage when your team is varying their attacks, you and your players should be sure to consider the previous information. Also, consider the following guidelines:

o Use a variety of shots on good sets. A player does not have to spike hard. A well-directed tip over the block to a nondefended area is also effective, especially on a good set, which the opponents are expecting an attacker to hit hard.

o Set up the defensive team for an off-speed shot by scoring on a hard hit. Defensive players are usually ready to dig a hard-hit ball, and an off-speed shot catches them off guard. After a player hits a few hard hits, she needs to keep the defensive players guessing by changing her shots periodically.

o If the opposing team brings a second blocker into the middle to block a middle attack, the middle hitter can tip to where the blocker moved from. Many times when the outside blocker moves inside to block, the defender behind her forgets to move up to cover that open area of the court, so it is usually open for a tip.

o An attacker must be able to score on a hard hit before she will be effective using an off-speed hit or tip. The more gamelike the training in practices, the more the players will be able to vary their attack when necessary in the match.

o Just because there are two blockers in front of a hitter does not mean they will necessarily block the ball. Test the block by hitting into them to see if you can hit it through or off the blockers' hands.

ATTACKING VARIATIONS

A hitter needs to be able to make a consistent approach to the ball to get it in the same place relative to her body on every attack. Once she can do this and she can hit the ball hard, she needs to learn to vary the direction, speed, and trajectory. This will increase her ability to score points for her team.

Down-the-Line Shot

If the opponents are blocking crosscourt, the attacker wants to hit the ball down the sideline. She may also want to hit down the line if the blocker in front of her is not as strong as the middle blocker. To hit a ball down the line, the player contacts the top of the ball with the thumb facing up or toward her body.

Crosscourt or Sharp-Angled Shot

If the opponents are blocking down the line, the attacker wants to hit the ball crosscourt or at a sharp angle along the net toward the opposite front-row hitter. She may also want to hit the ball in this direction if the middle blocker is weak or doesn't get her hand over the net to cut the shot off. To hit a ball crosscourt or at a sharp angle, the player contacts the top of the ball with the thumb facing down toward the middle of the court or away from her body.

In-the-Seam Shot

If there is a hole in between the two blockers in front of the attacker, she should hit the ball through that seam. There may be a hole if the outside blocker is blocking down the line and the middle blocker has trouble getting far enough outside to close, or seal, the block. To hit a ball in the seam, the attacker should read the blockers to see the hole in their block and swing in that direction, with the thumb up as for the down-the-line shot.

Deep Corner Shot

Many teams do not do a good job of defending the deep corner of the court. Most players keep moving up in the court on defense and leave the court behind them open. Players need to learn to hit this area of the court, especially since it is a longer distance to that area (42 feet, or 12.8 m) than down the line (30 feet, or 9 meters). To hit a ball to the deep corner, the attacker must work on hitting a higher and flatter ball with not quite as much topspin so the ball travels deeper into the court.

Off-Speed Shot

Many defenders get into a defensive stance waiting for the attacker to hit the ball hard. Once an attacker has hit several hard spikes, she should change it up and hit an off-speed shot to catch the defense off balance. To hit an off-speed shot, the attacker takes a normal approach to the net just as she would when hitting the ball hard. The arm swing slows down slightly as she gets ready to make contact, and contact is a little more on the back of the ball, with topspin. The arm swing stops after contact is made, with no real follow-through.

Tip

If there is a solid two-person block in front of the hitter, she needs to be able to attack the ball over the top of the blockers' hands. Also, if your players have hit several hard hits, they should be ready to change it up just as in the off-speed hit. To tip the ball, the attacker takes a normal approach to the net just as she would when hitting the ball hard. The arm swing slows down slightly as she gets ready to make contact, and contact is made with an open hand using the inside pads of the fingers. The hand and wrist should be stiff in directing the ball over or around the block. Note that changing the direction of the ball may result in an illegal hit. Players are not allowed to catch, throw, or hold the ball when tipping it. The arm swing stops after contact is made, with no real follow-through.

Hitting Off the Block

hen an attacker is making an approach to hit the ball and a solid block is formed in front of her, taking away most areas of the court, a valuable tactical skill to have is a wipe-off shot, or what is called "tooling the block." This means the attacker hits the ball off the blocker's hand and out of bounds intentionally. Learn to hit off the block by aiming for the outside blocker's hand. The ball will deflect off of her hand and land outside the court on the hitter's side of the net or the opposing team's side of the court outside the sideline. The attacker can also aim for high off the blocker's hand so the ball will travel deep off the court, and the defenders have to chase it to play it up. It can prove to be very frustrating to the defensive team and a great option for the attacking team when the ball is set tight or close to the net and the hitter is trapped. There is really nothing the blockers can do to stop the attack except pull down their hands at the last second and let the attacker hit the ball out of bounds.

⚠ WATCH OUT!

The following circumstances may distract your athletes:

- A ball set tight to the net
- Being too afraid to hit hard into the block because the ball might be blocked back into the attacker's face
- Starting too far off the net to get in to make this play safely

> **REMINDER!**
>
> You and your players must understand the team strategy and game plan and assess hitting off the block based on those plans and the situation at hand. Make sure you and your players consider the questions on page 140.

> **READING THE SITUATION**
>
> How do you and your players gain the best advantage when hitting off the block?
>
> Teach your players to do the following:
>
> - Know the best situations to hit off the block.
> - See the blockers' hands while they are in the air hitting.
> - Recognize how close the ball is to the net, the sideline, and the outside blocker's hand.
> - Practice this particular shot against a wall to learn the angles.

ACQUIRING THE APPROPRIATE KNOWLEDGE

When hitting off the block, your athletes must understand the following:

Rules

You and your athletes need to know several main rules when hitting off the block:

- Rules about touching the net
- Rules about the ball hitting the antenna
- Rules about the ball touching the blocker's hands
- Rules about touching the center line
- Rules about the ball on top of the net
- Rules about line-judging responsibilities

Strengths and Weaknesses of Opponents

You and your players must account for the opposing team's strengths and weaknesses to know how to gain the best advantage when hitting off the block. Teach your players to consider the following about your opponents:

- Do the blockers' hands penetrate the net? If the blockers' hands are across the net, the attacker should contact the ball slightly off center, aiming just down the line or slightly outside of it, with the ball just touching the outside blocker's hand.

- What is the hand position of the blocker nearest the sideline? If the blocker nearest the sideline has her outside hand facing straight ahead instead of back into the attacking team's court, the outside of this hand should be the target for the attacker to hit the ball off of. The ball will deflect off the blocker's hand and go out of bounds because that is the direction the hitter is swinging when she hits the ball.

- Where is the back-row defense? If the defenders are playing shallow in the court, use the top of the blocker's hand to hit the ball high off the hand and deep out of bounds so the defense has to chase it. This is referred to as "high hands." Even if the back-row defenders are deep in the court, they will most likely have to run off the court to chase the ball to play it up. The attacker will swing up on the ball to hit it in that direction. If she misses the blocker's hand, the ball will fly deep out of bounds.

At a Glance

The following parts of the text offer additional information on hitting off the block:

Skill	Page
Front set	63
Back set	68
Front-row attack	88
Slide	102
Block	108
Covering the hitter	121

Self-Knowledge

In addition to being aware of the opposing team's strengths and weaknesses, you and your players need to have knowledge about your own team's ability. In terms of hitting off the block, coaches and players should be aware of the following:

- Where is the ball set? The ball needs to be set close enough to the net and the blockers' hands so the hitter can aim for the outside blocker's outside hand or hit high off either blocker's hands deep off the court. Players can't force a tool shot when the set is too deep. The ball needs to be set near the sideline for the attacker to use the wipe-off shot to deflect the ball outside the sideline.

- Can the hitter see the blockers' hands? During a training session, have the blockers wear brightly colored gloves so the attacker can learn to see their hands as she approaches the net to hit the ball. Have the blockers do different things with their hands such as leaving a hole, leaving the line open, and moving their hands to make the hitters try to hit the ball off of them. Another way to train hitters to see the block is to have other players stand on the floor on the other side of the net and hold up two to four foam "pool noodles" to simulate the blocker's or blockers' arms and hands. The attackers will learn to see these "blockers" out of their peripheral vision and learn to hit the ball through the seam, off the "blockers," or around them and down into the court.

Decision-Making Guidelines

When deciding the best way to gain an advantage when your team is hitting off the block, you and your players should be sure to consider the previous information. Also, consider the following guidelines:

- The attacker should first look to make a hard hit into the court, but if those shots are all covered, she can then use a blocker's hand.

- When hitting off the block, the attacker's arm must have the correct follow-through. The hand and wrist turn toward the outside of the court, or sideline, after contact.

(continued)

○ The players covering the hitter must be aware of where they are positioned according to the sideline. If the attacker hits off the blocker's hand and the ball comes back, the covering players need to determine if it will land out of bounds and let it hit the floor. If the ball comes back into the court, one of the players covering the hitter should dig the ball up and into the middle of the court near the attack line.

○ The players covering the hitter should surround her, with three players up close and the other two players deep in the court, making sure they have the court balanced. This will give the hitter confidence knowing that if she gets blocked, her teammates are ready to dig the ball up.

○ The player who was blocked will need to be ready to transition off the net, and get ready to hit the next ball, or cover the next hitter who is set the ball.

Setting a Quick Set

Your team's ability to receive serves and make accurate passes to the target area near the middle of the court will increase the setter's opportunity to set an in-system first-tempo set, or a quick set. Since most quick sets are set to hitters near the net, passing accuracy is very important. As discussed earlier, *in system* means the pass was good enough that the setter, rather than another player, could set the ball. Sets can vary in height depending on the attacker and jumping ability, but a first-tempo set is set only as high as the attacker can jump and reach.

WATCH OUT!

The following circumstances may distract your athletes:

- A tall middle blocker
- Poor serve reception
- Being blocked previously in the match
- An inexperienced setter
- Passing the ball at an inconsistent height

ACQUIRING THE APPROPRIATE KNOWLEDGE

When setting a quick set, your athletes must understand the following:

Rules

You and your athletes need to know several main rules when setting a quick set:

- Rules about contacting the net
- Rules about contacting the center line
- Rules about illegal hits
- Rules about overlapping
- Rules about back-row setters jump-setting a ball in the plane of the net

Strengths and Weaknesses of Opponents

You and your players must account for the opposing team's strengths and weaknesses to know how to gain the best advantage when setting a quick set. Teach your players to consider the following about your opponents:

- Where are the opposing team's blockers located? If the blockers are bunched inside and are starting near the middle of the court, the setter may not want to use a quick set in the middle of the court since the hitter has a better chance of being blocked. The setter should try to set a hitter who has only one blocker in front of her. If the blockers are spread out, the setter should look to set a quick set in the middle of the court to set up the hitter against one blocker ideally. Hitters should be able to score around one blocker since one blocker takes up less of the court.

READING THE SITUATION

How do you and your players gain the best advantage when setting a quick set? Teach your players to do the following:

- Know the range of the setter and the type of pass needed to be able to set a quick set to the middle hitter.

- Pay attention to the blockers' positions on the other side of the net.

- Know that the more often a quick set out of the middle is attacked, the more distracted the opposing middle blocker will be, and the team's outside hitters will be more open to hit the ball successfully. This is called isolating the hitter, or creating a one-on-one situation.

REMINDER!

You and your players must understand the team strategy and game plan and assess setting a quick set based on those plans and the situation at hand. Make sure you and your players consider the questions on page 140.

(continued)

At a Glance

The following parts of the text offer additional information on setting a quick set:

○ How well do all the blockers read the situation? If the middle blocker does a good job of paying attention to the setter and can detect a difference in the setter's position, the setter will need more training on looking the same for each type of set when she gets ready to set the middle. If the setter looks different when she is getting ready to set the quick hitter in the middle, there is a good chance the middle blocker will block that hitter.

○ What are the base positions for the left- and right-back defenders? Study your opponents to determine their back-row base positions and whether the attacker will be hitting against one, two, or three blockers. The hitter needs to be able to hit or tip around these blockers to an open spot on the court.

○ Does the middle blocker commit-block, or jump, with the middle hitter? If the middle hitter can follow the pass in toward the setter and be up in the air when the setter gets the ball, she will be more likely to hit the ball before the middle blocker jumps. This takes good timing between the setter and hitter but can be very successful.

Self-Knowledge

In addition to being aware of the opposing team's strengths and weaknesses, you and your players need to have knowledge about your own team's ability. In terms of setting a quick set, coaches and players should be aware of the following:

○ How well does your team receive serves? Evaluate your players' passes on a 3-point scale where the closer the number is to 3, the better the setter is able to set a quick set (strive for a team average of 2.4 or higher). A perfect pass with all setting options available is counted as 3 points; a pass that allows the setter to set only the other two hitters (not a quick set to the middle hitter) gets 2 points; if another player has to step in to set a ball that is passed, this gets only 1 point; and if the team gets aced, this is 0 points. The total number of points divided by the total number of attempts will give an average between 0 and 3.

○ Does the middle hitter always make herself available to hit the quick set? It is important that the middle hitter make an aggressive approach and jump with her arm and hand extended high in the air to give the setter confidence in setting the quick hit on every play. She will know the quick hitter is ready to hit the ball and is more likely to set her. If the middle hitter is coming in too late, the setter will not be able to set her accurately and will have to guess how high to set the ball. The middle hitter must also have a high hand and a quick forearm and wrist snap to quickly hit the ball down into the court.

○ Is the setter capable of setting a jump set accurately? If the setter can jump-set a quick set, this will speed up the offense even more and give the blockers less time to react and jump to get their hands over the net before the ball is hit.

○ Can the setter quick-set the ball to either the right or left shoulder of the attacker? If so, this will allow the attacker to hit around the middle blocker. If the attacker is right-handed and is trying to hit to the right (aiming for left back), the setter should set the ball in front of the hitter's right shoulder. If the attacker wants to hit a cut-back shot, which is away from her normal swing, she will hit to her left (aiming for right back), and the setter should set the ball in front of the hitter's left shoulder. The middle can signal the setter before the play which way she would like to set the ball, and the setter will set the ball to that shoulder so the hitter has a better chance of hitting by the blocker.

- Is the setter agile enough and quick enough to set quick sets in transition? The setter must be able to play her position in the back row on defense if the team is running a multiple offense (setters come in from the back row) and then get up near the net to set a dug ball. She may also need to block in the front row and then turn around and get in the correct position to set a ball that is dug up on defense.

- Does the setter understand the flow of the game? The setter needs to know which hitter to set in various situations, to set the ball away from a congested area of the court, to keep the offensive sets spread out along the net, and to set a quick hitter in the middle when it is the best time to do so.

- Has your setter convinced the opposing team that she can set the middle early in the match? It is important to establish a strong middle-hitter attack early in the match so the opposing middle blocker will have to pay attention to the middle hitter and cannot leave early to help block the outside hitters.

Decision-Making Guidelines

When deciding the best way to gain an advantage when your team is setting a quick set, you and your players should be sure to consider the previous information. Also, consider the following guidelines:

- If your team cannot receive serves accurately or has an inexperienced setter, then the quick set should not be attempted. The team does not want to lose points trying something the players can't do effectively. Remember, you should only attempt to do tactically what you can do technically.

- The middle attacker needs to stay farther off the net than her setter to not crowd the setter, ball, or net and to be able to keep the blocker in view. This is referred to as keeping the hitter–setter–ball triangle (see figure 5.1).

- Set the middle attacker if there is only one blocker up with her. A good middle should be able to score around one blocker.

- Any player can hit a quick set. The right-side player can come around the setter to the middle of the court and hit a quick set. The middle can approach to hit a variety of other higher sets. The left-side attacker can come inside the court to hit a low quick set.

- Keep the middle attacker jumping in the front row, ready to hit a quick set, even though she may just be a decoy to keep the middle blocker's attention so she cannot move outside to help block another hitter.

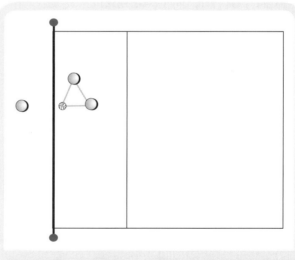

Figure 5.1 Hitter–setter–ball triangle.

Attacking or Dumping the Second Ball

Every pass or dig should be played up toward the middle right side of the court inside the attack line so the setter can set the ball to an attacker. If the setter is a front-row player, she can also become a surprise weapon for your team by hitting the ball over on the second contact (especially if left-handed) or dumping the ball at the last second after first looking as if she is getting ready to set the ball.

 WATCH OUT!

The following circumstances may distract your athletes:

- A tall middle or left-side blocker
- An illegal contact call by the referee
- An inaccurate jump set by the setter
- A pass that is too far off the net or too far away from the setter to attempt putting the ball over on the second contact
- The opposing setter dumping the ball

ACQUIRING THE APPROPRIATE KNOWLEDGE

When attacking or dumping the second ball, your athletes must understand the following:

Rules

You and your athletes need to know several main rules when attacking or dumping the second ball:

- Rules about contacting the net
- Rules about contacting the center line
- Rules about what constitutes an illegal hit
- Rules about overlapping and about the setter's needing to be a front-row player to jump up and attack the second ball
- Rules about a back-row attack violation when the ball is on top of the net
- Rules about the ball touching the blocker

READING THE SITUATION

How do you and your players gain the best advantage when the setter attacks or dumps the second ball? Teach your players to do the following:

- Recognize if the opposing team's left and middle blockers are not paying attention to the setter when they jump-set.
- Recognize if the opponents do not realize your setter is a front-row player.
- Know that a left-handed setter has a tremendous advantage in hitting the second ball aggressively.
- Observe the right- and left-back players to see if they are anticipating the ball coming over on the second hit.
- Be aware of the rhythm of the game and when it is appropriate to dump the ball.

REMINDER!

You and your players must understand the team strategy and game plan and assess attacking or dumping the ball based on those plans and the situation at hand. Make sure you and your players consider the questions on page 140.

Strengths and Weaknesses of Opponents

You and your players must account for the opposing team's strengths and weaknesses to know how to gain the best advantage when attacking or dumping the second ball. Teach your players to consider the following about your opponents:

- What are the opposing team's blocking strategies? If the blockers bunch into the middle of the court (in front of the setter's line of sight), a dump should go behind the setter over the net to the opposing team's left-front corner of the court near the net (zone 4). If the left-side blocker is behind the setter, then the dump should be aimed in the middle of the court (zone 3). See figure 3.40 on page 64 for an example of the court zones.

- What is the blockers' skill level? If the blockers have an advanced ability level, they may be able to get their hands over the net quickly for a possible middle attack and then again over quickly for the setter's dump. If they are not as advanced, they are likely to just stay on the ground with their hands high, ready to jump when the ball is hit over, either by the setter or a hitter.

- What are the opposing team's player responsibilities? Many teams will have their blockers focus on stopping the quick attacker in the middle or the slide hitter going to the right side and make their back-row players responsible for digging up the setter's dump or hit over on the second contact.

Self-Knowledge

In addition to being aware of the opposing team's strengths and weaknesses, you and your players need to have knowledge about your own team's ability. In terms of dumping or attacking the second ball, coaches and players should be aware of the following:

- How well does the setter disguise her intentions? If the setter can convince the defense that she will be setting the ball and at the last second attack or dump the ball down into the opposing team's court, she should do so every time the defense gives her this option. As you scout your opponents and your own team, you may notice a setter who tends to dump only in certain situations or too often to fool the defense. Also, look for a setter who tends to try to end a long rally each time by taking control and dumping or attacking the second contact. Some setters give away their intentions early by jumping with only one hand up to the ball.

- What is the setter's skill level? The setter must be tall enough and able to jump high enough to get her hand on top of the ball and dump it down into the court, not just over the net. If the setter can jump high or is tall enough, she should always be aggressive with the dump by contacting the top of the ball with the open hand and pads of the fingers, quickly pushing it down toward the floor. She should be careful not to break her wrist or change the direction of the ball. If she changes the ball's direction, she could be called for an illegal hit or thrown ball.

- What is the setter's ability level to dump the ball to different areas of the court? The setter should be able to dump the ball to different areas of the court. The areas where the setter is most likely to attack the ball are near the net in zone 3 or 4 based on the position of the blocker in front of her. She should also learn to dump the ball to the deep left-back corner (zone 5) which is left open when the defenders charge forward, expecting the dump to go down in front of them. See figure 3.40 on page 64 for an example of the court zones.

- Is your setter left-handed? A left-handed setter is a tremendous offensive weapon because she can set the ball or swing using her on-hand side approach, as discussed earlier, keeping the ball in front of her left shoulder. She has a great view of the defense and the blockers as well as what areas are open.

At a Glance

The following parts of the text offer additional information on attacking or dumping the second ball:

Skill	Page
Front set	63
Back set	68
Lateral set	72
Jump set	76
One-hand set	80
Slide	102
Block	108
Dig	114
Hitting off the block	152
Reading the attacker	165
Defending against the slide	168
Defending against a quick attack	183

(continued)

○ Can the setter jump-set accurately? If the setter is accurate with her jump sets, she should jump-set as often as possible. This speeds up the offense since the ball is in the air less time, meaning the blockers and the rest of the defenders have less time to react, and it gives the setter an advantage in dumping the ball because she is already in the air.

Decision-Making Guidelines

When deciding the best way to gain an advantage when attacking or dumping the second ball, you and your players should be sure to consider the previous information. Also, consider the following guidelines:

○ Players should dump the ball only when they believe they can score instead of just playing the ball over. The dump needs to be used as an offensive weapon to score points.

○ Back-row players who can see the opposing court clearly should communicate with the setter, letting her know what areas are open and where the blockers are.

○ Setters should attack or dump to the sidelines when the defense is moved inside and should attack or dump behind them, with the right hand closest to the net.

○ The dump needs to be one of the offensive options when the setter is in the front row. If the setter never dumps the ball, the three blockers will key on the other two attackers.

○ Tell your setter not to dump the ball right after the opposing setter has dumped the ball. Many times setters will do this as if they were just reminded of using the skill themselves.

○ If the left-side player in front of the setter does not pay attention to her or is a weak blocker, the setter should try to take advantage of this player by dumping it off the blocker's hand out of bounds near the sideline.

chapter 6

Defensive Tactical Skills

This chapter covers the defensive tactical skills players must know to be successful. In this chapter, you will find the following skills:

Positioning Defensively as a Team

When on defense, having all your players in the correct position on the court no matter what defensive system the team is playing allows a team to be successful. If the players are in the correct position it means the court is balanced, which increases their opportunity for touching a ball. Players who know where to be on the court, and why, in each situation that arises will pay off for your team because they will be in a good position to block balls back into the opposing team's court or dig them up to transition quickly to offense.

 WATCH OUT!

The following circumstances may distract your athletes:

- Playing in a certain place on the court out of habit
- Not understanding the team defensive concepts
- Being intimidated by a strong hitter or team
- Overplaying their position and trying to take balls away from teammates
- Being afraid to go to the floor after playing a ball up
- Not going for a ball because they might collide with a teammate

READING THE SITUATION

How do you and your players gain the best advantage when positioning defensively as a team? Teach your players to do the following:

- Be in a base position in order to move and get to any ball hit in their particular zone in three steps.
- Put the best defensive player on the court where the most hits go.
- Move in the same plane (keeping the head level) when adjusting to play the ball. This will save time and keep the vision accurate.
- Make sure they can see their teammates in their peripheral vision while moving into their defensive positions so they know where they are on the court in relation to their teammates.

REMINDER!

You and your players must understand the team strategy and game plan and assess positioning defensively as a team based on those plans and the situation at hand. Make sure you and your players consider the questions on page 140.

ACQUIRING THE APPROPRIATE KNOWLEDGE

When positioning defensively as a team, your athletes must understand the following:

Rules

You and your athletes need to know several main rules when positioning defensively as a team:

- Rules about the first contact
- Rules about overlapping
- Rules about screening the server
- Rules about illegal hits
- Rules about the ball hitting the line
- Rules about simultaneous contact
- Rules about the libero setting an attacker
- Rules about touching the net

- Rules about the center line
- Rules about the net antennas
- Rules about the back-row attacker

Strengths and Weaknesses of Opponents

You and your players must account for the opposing team's strengths and weaknesses to know how to gain the best advantage when positioning defensively as a team. Teach your players to consider the following about your opponents:

- Does the attacker give away her intentions? If the attacker tends to look in the direction she is going to hit the ball, your players can read this and determine the direction of the hit. Then they move into that area and are ready to block or dig the ball.

- To what area of the court does the attacker typically hit the ball? Most attackers feel comfortable hitting the ball to a certain area of the court. At most levels of play, attackers typically hit most balls crosscourt, so you should play the percentages unless attackers have shown they are capable of attacking line shots with consistency. Keep track of where the attacker typically hits the ball, and work to block those shots or put a defensive player in the area to dig it up.

- Does the attacker hit only one type of set or hit from one area of the net? Maybe the outside hitter can hit only high sets or the middle attacker hits only quick sets in front of the setter and never goes behind the hitter to hit a slide.

- What attacker does the setter set to most often? Most setters have a favorite hitter they like to set in each rotation no matter what the situation is. The closer the score, the more likely they will set the hitter they feel comfortable with and have the most confidence in.

Self-Knowledge

In addition to being aware of the opposing team's strengths and weaknesses, you and your players need to have knowledge about your own team's ability. In terms of positioning defensively as a team, coaches and players should be aware of the following:

- How well do your players "read" the situation? Have them train in gamelike situations as much as possible so they will learn to block and dig against live hitters. Help them learn what to look at and how they can then anticipate where to correctly position themselves on the court to successfully play the ball coming over the net.

- How well do your players move on defense? Spend some time training players to get in a ready position, read the hitter, move quickly to where they anticipate the ball is going to be hit, and get stopped and ready to play the ball hit at them. The players should lean into the ball and step forward toward the target area at the net after they dig the ball up. A player should always keep her head in front of her feet when playing defense, and she should rarely step back after making a defensive play. Rather, as mentioned, she should be moving forward to cover her hitter.

- Do all the players know their angle of pursuit from each position? Your players must be expected to move in any direction within a 120-degree range to dig a ball (see figure 6.1). Players cannot be expected to cover 180 degrees effectively and be equally ready to move to the left or to the right. The player closest to the ball goes in front to attempt to play the ball, and the player farthest

(continued)

from where the ball is coming goes behind. This is a great method for covering the area in the seams between two defensive players. Place the players in their positions on the court for each possible attack, and have them identify their range of coverage with their teammates.

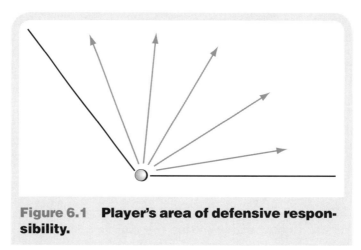

Figure 6.1 **Player's area of defensive responsibility.**

o How well can your players see their teammates? Players should be able to see their teammates when in their defensive positions or at least be aware of where they are. If they can't see other players or don't know where their teammates are on the court, they will not be able to correctly play up a ball hit into the seams.

Decision-Making Guidelines

When deciding the best way to gain an advantage when positioning defensively as a team, you and your players should be sure to consider the previous information. Also, consider the following guidelines:

o It is 42 feet (12.8 m) from one corner of the court diagonally to the other corner. Players need to be balanced around the court, with the deep crosscourt player making sure the deep corner is covered. This player should also have the rest of her teammates in view and would be the last possible person to play the ball before it lands in the corner because it will have gone past all the other players. Many attackers will aim to hit the ball into the deep corner when they are in trouble.

o It can be beneficial for your team if you study your opponents, specifically the attackers, on video or during the warm-up to determine where they are most likely to hit the ball. You can even keep an attack chart during the match to see where each hitter hits in each rotation and plan your defensive strategy around this.

o Players need to be aware of their positions on the court in relation to the sidelines and end line. This will help them let a ball go that is going to land out of bounds and know not to play it up. Players should position themselves just inside the court lines so that any ball coming toward them over their waist is out unless it was touched on the block by a teammate.

o Players need to start in a base defensive position on the court. The blockers in the front row should be somewhere in front of the attacker they expect to hit in their area or zone of the net. The back-row players should have the court balanced, with the middle back in the deep back middle of the court (or up on the attack line); the left- and right-back players should be 15 feet (4.6 m) back from the net and 7 feet (2.1 m) inside the sidelines facing the middle of the court. If the middle back is up at the attack line, 9 feet, 10 inches (3 m), the right and left-back players should be back about 20 feet (6.1 m) from the net.

Reading the Attacker

The key to being a successful defensive player, particularly a strong blocker, is possessing the ability to read the attacker's intentions by anticipating where the ball will go and how it will get there. This allows a defensive player to make the impressive digs that are so exciting in long rallies. It is the work done before the play that increases the opportunity to be successful. The more experienced the players and the more gamelike opportunities they get in practice, the more likely they are to anticipate what the attacker will do with the ball.

 WATCH OUT!

The following circumstances may distract your athletes:

- Being intimidated by a powerful hitter
- Watching the ball in the air instead of the setter and then the attacker
- A setter who can disguise which direction she is setting the ball
- A deceptive attacker who is capable of hitting a variety of shots in a variety of directions
- A setter who jump sets
- A left-handed setter
- A team that accurately passes a served ball to their setter

ACQUIRING THE APPROPRIATE KNOWLEDGE

When reading the attacker, your athletes must understand the following:

Rules

You and your athletes need to know several main rules when reading the attacker:

- Rules about overlapping
- Rules about net violations
- Rules about center-line violations
- Rules about illegal hits
- Rules about the ball contacting the antenna or going outside the antenna
- Rules about the back-row attack

READING THE SITUATION

How do you and your players gain the best advantage when reading the attacker?

Teach your players to do the following:

- Know which players are in the front row.
- Watch the ball briefly after the set to see where it is going and to determine how close it is to the net.
- Know that the attacker will typically hit in the direction of her attack approach.
- Look at the attacker's body orientation, shoulders, arm swing, and direction she is looking for keys to the direction and speed of the attack.

REMINDER!

You and your players must understand the team strategy and game plan and assess reading the attacker based on those plans and the situation at hand. Make sure you and your players consider the questions on page 140.

(continued)

Strengths and Weaknesses of Opponents

You and your players must account for the opposing team's strengths and weaknesses to know how to gain the best advantage when reading the attacker. Teach your players to consider the following about your opponents:

o   What does the attacker's arm swing look like? If the attacker's arm swing is slowing down or the elbow is dropping, then the hit will most likely be off-speed and land somewhere off the net in the middle of the court or near a sideline or the end line. If the arm swing is fast and the elbow is high, the blocker will need to jump and get her hands over the net quicker.

o   How can you tell if the hitter is going to tip the ball? If an attacker has been blocked several times or doesn't take a full-speed approach to attack, that is usually a sign that she may be going to tip the ball. Your players should stay in position and be ready to pursue a tipped ball, digging it up to the target area.

o   What is the attacker's hand position at contact? If the attacker's hitting hand is open and facing up, this may mean the attacker is going to tip the ball over or around the block, so blockers must communicate this as soon as they see an open hand. The back-row defense must pay attention and be ready to move forward to play the ball up because a deep tip is possible, and a back-row player may need to be ready to play the ball up with an overhead dig or overhead set to the target.

o   Where is the ball coming down in relation to the attacker's hitting-arm shoulder? If the ball is falling in front of the attacker's shoulder, she is likely to hit the ball straight ahead. If the ball is dropping inside or she is late on her approach, she may hit sharp crosscourt or tip the ball back toward the outside line.

o   Where is the ball set? The farther the ball is set off the net, the less likely the attacker will be swinging hard to hit the ball down into the court. Look for an off-speed hit or tip or possibly even a free ball. The farther the ball is set outside the antenna, the less area of the court is available for the attacker to hit the ball into since the ball must travel across the net inside the antenna. The blockers and back-row defense should shift inside to make sure they are in the playable area and can see the ball inside the antenna.

Self-Knowledge

In addition to being aware of the opposing team's strengths and weaknesses, you and your players need to have knowledge about your own team's ability. In terms of reading the attacker, coaches and players should be aware of the following:

o   Are your players in position to dig or block the ball? When on defense and reading the attacker, your players should start in the proper base position where they can get to the correct place to play the ball in their zone in three steps or less.

o   What area of the court do the blockers intend to take away? There needs to be good coordination between the front-row blockers and back-row players. Depending on the team defense being played, the diggers will move to be ready to dig a ball hit in the area the blockers are not taking away.

o   What if there is a hole, or seam, in the block? The back-row defense will need to be aware of this and fill in a hole if it is too big. They will also need to know how far off the net the ball has been set to decide if they need to take a step up in the court to be able to dig a ball that is set tight to the net.

o   Is the hitter off balance or not in a strong position to hit the ball down? There are times hitters do not make a good approach to the ball. It may be due to a poor set, poor timing by the attacker, or miscommunication between players about who should be hitting the ball. The defense should observe this and be ready to move deeper into the court. If the hitter is off balance, she will not be able to hit the ball down hard into the court.

Decision-Making Guidelines

When deciding the best way to gain an advantage when your team is reading the attacker, you and your players should be sure to consider the previous information. Also, consider the following guidelines:

- Know if the hitter is right- or left-handed. It will make a difference for the blocker to know which shoulder to be in front of when jumping to block the hitter.

- Know the hitter's tendencies. Hitters have favorite shots, and the defensive players should look for slight differences each hitter displays when getting ready to hit a certain shot such as a tip, a hit down the line, or a hit to the deep corner crosscourt.

- Make sure the blockers and back-row players communicate what they see as early as possible. Players should remind each other which hitters are in the front row, if the setter is in the front row, if they think they know if the setter is going to set the ball in front or behind her, where the hitter hit the ball last time, and any other information to help teammates be in the best position to play the ball.

- Have the players pay attention to the opposing team's warm-up to look for signs of what they might do when attacking. Study the setter as well as the hitters.

- Understand the angles in volleyball. For example, if the ball is set outside the antenna, the hitter will have to attempt to hit the ball crosscourt between the antennae, giving the defensive team an advantage by taking away part of the court they will have to cover.

At a Glance

The following parts of the text offer additional information on reading the attacker:

Defending Against the Slide

The slide is a fantastic offensive weapon because it is so difficult to stop defensively. For the slide, the attacker moves toward and then behind the setter and parallel to the net in the direction of the set. She decides when she wants to hit since the ball is not dropping down to a particular attack point. The ball is moving more horizontally and can be hit at any point along that path when the attacker decides to jump off one foot and swing at the ball. Add to the fact that the slide hitter can choose to rotate only slightly to hit down the line or delay and rotate at the last second to hit the ball crosscourt and back inside the blocker and it becomes even more difficult for the defense to read. Some advanced teams may have their outside attacker hit a front slide coming in toward the setter in the middle of the court. She must be careful not to land too close to the setter.

WATCH OUT!

The following circumstances may distract your athletes:

- The middle attacker successfully hitting quick sets from the middle of the court to start the match so the blockers become drawn in to that point and forget about watching for the middle attacker or slide hitter to come around behind the setter; an offensive team will try to establish the middle attack first and then begin sending the middle hitter back to hit the slide

- The middle attacker disguising her approach and coming from anywhere on the court

- The defensive left-side and middle blockers becoming confused when the opposing team's right-side and middle hitters cross paths, letting the hitter get by them, and they reach to the outside to block the ball

- The defensive outside blocker jumping laterally, drifting out with the attacker, and then the slide hitter hits back crosscourt

READING THE SITUATION

How do you and your players gain the best advantage when defending against the slide? Teach your players to do the following:

- Be able to serve short.

- Know the slide hitter's tendencies or strengths, and make her hit her weakest shot.

- The middle is the player who usually hits the slide, so the left-side blocker needs to see when she begins to come behind the setter and leave the setter to block her. The middle blocker will then be responsible for blocking the setter if she attacks or dumps the ball.

- Once the attacker runs past the ball, the only place she can hit it is crosscourt. The blockers can forget about blocking the line and can stay more inside the court.

REMINDER!

You and your players must understand the team strategy and game plan and assess defending against the slide based on those plans and the situation at hand. Make sure you and your players consider the questions on page 140.

ACQUIRING THE APPROPRIATE KNOWLEDGE

When defending against the slide, your athletes must understand the following:

Rules

You and your athletes need to know several main rules when defending against the slide:

- Rules about overlapping
- Rules about screening the server
- Rules about reaching over the net
- Rules about blocking the setter
- Rules about back-row setters
- Rules about the antenna
- Rules about touching the net
- Rules about touching the center line

Strengths and Weaknesses of Opponents

You and your players must account for the opposing team's strengths and weaknesses to know how to gain the best advantage when defending against the slide. Teach your players to consider the following about your opponents:

- Which of the opposing team's players are capable of hitting a slide? Pay attention to the hits they make during the warm-up to see which players can hit a slide effectively and where they tend to hit them. Watch to see who is hitting off one foot.

- How well does the setter disguise her sets? Watch the setter's hands and hips for clues to where she will set. Sometimes when a player is getting ready to back-set, she will lean backward just before setting the ball. The blockers who notice this can move in that direction to get ready to block the hitter.

- How well does the hitter disguise where she will hit the ball? Watch the hitter's face when hitting because she will usually look in the direction she intends to hit. If the blockers see the hitter's face looking toward the line, she will probably hit down the line. The blockers need to get their hands over the net in that area.

- Where does the slide hitter tend to hit the ball? If the slide hitter overruns the set, this allows only a crosscourt attack. If the slide hitter tends to let the ball stay well out in front of her, this may lead to more down-the-line attacks. If the ball is directly in line with her hitting shoulder, she can hit off the block, down the line, or back crosscourt.

- Be ready to back off the net instead of blocking if the set is several feet off the net. The slide hitter will probably not be able to hit the ball down, so the blocker can just drop off the net and be ready to play defense.

Self-Knowledge

In addition to being aware of the opposing team's strengths and weaknesses, you and your players need to have knowledge about your own team's ability. In terms of defending against the slide, coaches and players should be aware of the following:

- How well does your left-side blocker watch the court and her teammates? The left-side blocker has to watch the middle attacker since the left- and right-back diggers are primarily responsible for the setter dumping the ball over on the second contact. It is important the left-side blocker know she is primarily responsible for blocking the slide hitter and not the setter. Train blockers to move quickly along the net with hands high and to get hands over as soon as possible so they can block the ball being hit by the slide hitter. If your blockers tend to watch the ball too much

At a Glance

The following parts of the text offer additional information on defending against the slide:

Skill	Page
Hitting off the block	152
Setting a quick set	155
Reading the attacker	165
Determining blocking strategies	171
Defending against the back-row attack	174
Receiving a free ball	177
Using a libero	180
Defending against a quick attack	183
Chasing down a ball	187
Defending against a setter's dump or attack	190

(continued)

instead of the opponents, have them wear a baseball hat in practice to make them focus on the hitter and to keep them from looking up at the volleyball too long.

○ How well do your players communicate about the pass? All players need to recognize the pass or dig immediately and say "On," "Off," or "Over" to let all the players know whether the ball is on top of the net, off the net, or coming over. Each of those situations requires a different action.

○ Do your blockers coordinate well with the back-row defense? Your blockers must coordinate their block with the back-row players in order to fill in the holes and know seam responsibilities. If they intend to block the inside crosscourt shot hit by the slide hitter, the person playing defense behind them must know this to balance the court and stay deep down the line to dig the ball if hit in that direction.

○ Do you want your players to jump up to block if the slide hitter gets past them too quickly? Make sure your players know if you want them to go ahead and block where they are so they can take away an area of the court or if you want them to drop off the net and play defense.

Decision-Making Guidelines

When deciding the best way to gain an advantage when your team is defending against the slide, you and your players should be sure to consider the previous information. Also, consider the following guidelines:

○ The closer the opponent's pass is to the net, the more ready your blockers should be for quick hits and slides behind the setter since the setter is more likely to set them on a good pass that is not too far off the net. So, the tighter the pass, the higher the blockers should have their hands, which allows them to get their hands over the net quickly.

○ The defensive player should pay attention to the setter's range and how far off the net she can make a set for a slide hitter. If the setter is too far off the net, the slide hitter will not come around the setter to hit a slide but will most likely stay in front of the setter to hit a quick set instead.

○ Blockers should use a wide block with their hands and arms wide apart if they are unsure of the direction the ball will be hit. This allows them to take away more area of the court, and they may have the opportunity to touch or slow down the ball being hit.

○ The left-side blocker needs to get at least one hand up and over the net to take away some area of the court. The middle blocker may be able to reach over with her left hand to take away an area of the court. Using one hand to block the slide is OK since the hitter is approaching along the net, and the blockers cannot always get directly in front of the hitter as with other higher sets that drop straight down. This is a last resort but is better than leaving an open court for the slide hitter to hit into.

○ Instead of the blockers trying to move with the slide hitter, make a decision to commit-block an area and let the back-row defense position around it to dig the ball up.

○ Serve the ball to zone 2, or the right-front side of the court (see figure 3.40 on page 64 for an example of the court zones). This will overload that zone of the court and make it tougher for the setter, with the pass coming from that area and the slide hitter running into that area. It will congest that zone and hopefully force the setter to set away from that area to her outside hitter on the left side of the court.

○ Serve to the player who hits the slide, and force her to pass the ball up to the setter. This will make the slide hitter concentrate on passing the ball first before beginning her approach to hit the ball. This is a good way to take the slide hitter out of the play as a hitter.

Determining Blocking Strategies

There are several blocking strategies that teams may choose to use defensively. They may have a player commit-block, or jump, when the attacker jumps, whether or not the ball is set to them. They can read-block, meaning they read the pass, the setter, and the hitter to determine when and where they will block. They can also start bunched inside the court, closing up the middle of the court to stop quick hitters, or they can start with the blockers spread out along the net in an effort to stop the high outside set.

 WATCH OUT!

The following circumstances may distract your athletes:

- Attackers who hit the ball hard with a fast arm swing
- Attackers who start their approach in one zone of the net and hit from another
- A setter who can see the opposing blocker's position along the net
- An opposing team who seems to always pass the ball well, allowing the players to be in system

ACQUIRING THE APPROPRIATE KNOWLEDGE

When determining blocking strategies, your athletes must understand the following:

Rules

You and your athletes need to know several main rules when determining blocking strategies:

- Rules about overlapping
- Rules about consecutive contacts
- Rules about screening the server
- Rules about reaching over the net
- Rules about blocking the setter
- Rules about touching the net
- Rules about contacting the center line
- Rules about simultaneous contact

Strengths and Weaknesses of Opponents

You and your players must account for the opposing team's strengths and weaknesses to know how to gain the best advantage when determining blocking strategies. Teach your players to consider the following about your opponents:

- What did the opponents do with the ball during their last attempt in a specific position or rotation? Your team needs to know which attacker the setter gave the ball to, what type of set it was, and where the attacker hit the ball. If necessary, have someone on the bench keep track of this

READING THE SITUATION

How do you and your players gain the best advantage when determining blocking strategies? Teach your players to do the following:

- Scout the opponents so you become familiar with their hitting tendencies.
- Watch the entire play develop, from the quality of the pass to the set direction and location.
- Read the attacker by watching her approach to the ball and the way her head is facing.
- See if the opposing team has a strong middle hitter who likes to hit quick sets and shoot sets from the middle of the court.

REMINDER!

You and your players must understand the team strategy and game plan and determine your blocking strategies based on those plans and the situation at hand. Make sure you and your players consider the questions on page 140.

(continued)

and call out reminders so the blockers can be ready to take that shot away from the hitter. Many teams will set the same players in each rotation, so it is good to give your blockers the advantage of being ready to block down the line if that is what the hitter did last time she hit in this rotation.

○ Serve to the strongest hitter in the front row so she has to think about passing the ball before she can move to hit the ball.

○ Serve the front-row players deep to back them up or short in front of them to make them work hard to make a good pass to the setter before beginning an approach to hit the ball.

○ Make your defensive blocking strategy influence the opposing team's offense. Put your best blocker in front of their best hitter or the one most likely to get set the ball. You can even overload this player by putting two blockers in front of her early and make the setter set the ball to a weaker hitter.

Self-Knowledge

In addition to being aware of the opposing team's strengths and weaknesses, you and your players need to have knowledge about your own team's ability. In terms of determining blocking strategies, coaches and players should be aware of the following:

○ How strong is your blockers' technical ability? Your blockers should be ready to jump up, from their ready position, and block the ball, timing their jumps to get their hands over the net right before the hitter contacts the ball (the farther from the net the set, the later the blocker should jump; and the faster the hitter's arm swing, the sooner the blocker needs to jump).

○ How well do your players understand the game and the attack options available on each play? It is important to test your players' understanding of the game and the opposing team's offense. If the opposing team uses a variety of sets in different areas along the net, make sure your blockers know which one of them is responsible for each area of the net and whether you want a single, double, or triple block against a hitter.

○ Do your players move well laterally along the net? If they can read the setter and anticipate where the set is going to go, they need to use quick movements to get in the best area to block the ball with their hands over the net at the right time.

Decision-Making Guidelines

When deciding the best way to gain an advantage when determining blocking strategies, you and your players should be sure to consider the previous information. Also, consider the following guidelines:

○ If the opponent's set is tight to the net, your blockers need to make sure they have the line covered by blocking down the line or straight in front of the ball. This will protect the court directly behind them if they are playing a defense that leaves the line open and covers it with a defensive player. Although most attackers will try to hit the ball straight ahead, some highly skilled players may try to hit the ball off a blocker's hand on a tight set, so your blockers must make sure their outside hands (nearest the sideline) are turned in facing the opposing team's court to prevent the ball from being hit off a hand and out of bounds.

○ If the ball is set near the antenna, the blockers should have their outside hands turned in so the attacker cannot hit off their hands, or tool them. Tooling a block is another way to describe intentionally hitting the ball off the blocker's hand and out of bounds. This requires that a strategic decision be made because a great deal of the court will be cut off if the blockers have their hands up and over the net next to the antenna. The rest of the defensive players will have to move to position themselves around the blockers.

- If the ball is on top of the net, this will require jousting between two opposing players at the net. Usually the player who touches the ball second and is in the lowest position wins this battle. Short front-row setters can often win the battle against tall blockers. Have your players try to push second to gain an advantage.

- The blockers must communicate what they see their original hitter (whoever was in front of them at the beginning of the play) doing as they prepare to approach. As the hitter moves to a different area or zone, she needs to tell the other blocker to switch, and they change their focus to the hitter now in their zone. This can also be described as zone blocking.

- When a blocker is up against an attacker one on one, she must study the attacker's approach and get in front of her hitting shoulder (where the ball will cross the net) and the path of the approach.

- When blocking a back-row attack, blockers should jump and reach straight up for the ball. Reaching out causes the ball to hit the hands and land deep out of bounds or will misdirect a ball the defender was lined up to dig.

At a Glance

The following parts of the text offer additional information on determining blocking strategies:

Defending Against the Back-Row Attack

Since good teams always have at least one back-row attacker available in their offensive options, teams must now devise and use specific tactics to defend against this. The back-row attacker can score a lot of points if the defensive team is not prepared to handle it.

WATCH OUT!

The following circumstances may distract your athletes:

- The back-row attacker jumping high and hitting hard
- Backing off the net as soon as the ball is set to the back row
- A setter who disguises a set to a back-row attacker

ACQUIRING THE APPROPRIATE KNOWLEDGE

When defending against a back-row attack, your athletes must understand the following:

Rules

You and your athletes need to know several main rules when defending against a back-row attack:

- Rules about the attack line
- Rules about a libero hand-setting an attacker when in front of the attack line
- Rules about overlapping
- Rules about illegal contacts on a set ball
- Rules about net fouls
- Rules about center-line violations

READING THE SITUATION

How do you and your players gain the best advantage when defending against a back-row attack? Teach your players to do the following:

- Watch the play develop, and see what setting options will be available.
- Keep track of where the strong, or go-to, hitters are positioned in the back row (middle back or right back).
- Be aware of the back-row attacker coming in behind a quick hitter.
- Watch for the back-row attacker to tip the ball.

REMINDER!

You and your players must understand the team strategy and game plan and assess defending against a back-row attack based on those plans and the situation at hand. Make sure you and your players consider the questions on page 140.

Strengths and Weaknesses of Opponents

You and your players must account for the opposing team's strengths and weaknesses to know how to gain the best advantage when defending against a back-row attack. Teach your players to consider the following about your opponents:

- When do the opponents use a back-row attacker? They may have only one player who hits from the back row, or they may set the back row only when they make a bad pass or dig and are playing out of system.
- Are the opponents more likely to set a back-row attacker when their setter is in the front row? Many teams use a back-row attacker when their setter is in the front row because they have only two front-row attackers, so they add the back-row hitter as another option.

How well does the attacker jump? If the attacker has a good approach and strong broad jump, contacting the ball near the net, then your players may want to just play their regular defense, with at least two blockers in front of the attacker and the other players playing their normal defensive assignments based on the team defense they are playing.

How high is the ball set to the back-row attacker? If the ball is set very high, the blockers and back-row defense will have enough time to adjust their positions to block the ball. If it is set low, such as antenna height, the defense will have less time to react and move into the proper position to block or dig the ball.

Is the ball set out in front of the back-row attacker so she can make a powerful approach? If the ball is set so it would land just inside the attack line, the back-row hitter can hit the ball with more power, and the blockers and back-row defense must respond more quickly to play the ball. If the ball is set behind the attack line or directly to the back-row attacker, she will have a less powerful approach to hit the ball, and the defense should have more time to dig the ball up.

Self-Knowledge

In addition to being aware of the opposing team's strengths and weaknesses, you and your players need to have knowledge about your own team's ability. In terms of defending against a back-row attack, coaches and players should be aware of the following:

How well does your team understand the opposing team's offensive system and attack options available? Have the team study video and watch high-level teams play to see how the back-row attack can be effective. Players will see which areas of the court back-row attackers like to hit the ball and be ready to defend those with either blockers or back-row defenders.

Does your team understand their blocking and defensive responsibilities? When the opposing team uses a back-row attack, typically the middle blocker will stay up to block, with the rest of the players playing defense, filling in behind their block. The middle blocker must not reach outside her body to block the ball and possibly misdirect it to an area with no defender or deep out of bounds on the sideline or end line.

How well do your blockers time their jumps? If your blockers are skilled and have good timing and technique, they may choose to put up a double block against the back-row attacker. It is always better to block the ball first than to try to dig it. If they are likely to touch the net when attempting to block, they should back off the net.

How strong is your server? The tougher your team serves, the more likely your opponents will be caught out of system with a poor pass and be forced to set a back-row attack. Most teams would prefer to play defense against a back-row attacker than a strong attacker in the front row.

At a Glance

The following parts of the text offer additional information on defending against the back-row attack:

(continued)

Decision-Making Guidelines

When deciding the best way to gain an advantage when your team is defending against a back-row attack, you and your players should be sure to consider the previous information. Also, consider the following guidelines:

- When the opponents set the back row, the middle blocker can stay up to block and move along the net to get in front of the back-row attacker so that at least some portion of the court is taken away from the hitter by the blocker. The other five players on defense can fill in around that blocker to cover the court. Use this option if the attacker is not a strong threat to hit the ball down into the court but is just hitting the ball over the net.

- The middle blocker can sometimes try to block the back-row attacker and have the ball deflect off her hands out of bounds. If that happens frequently enough, then have your front-row players drop off the net and play the same defense as for a down ball, with the middle blocker backing up just inside the attack line and the outside blockers a little deeper. The back-row players will back up deep, with the middle back being the deepest along the end line, and the right and left backs being a step or two in front of the end line. This allows the players to easily go for balls hit into the seams, with the person closest to the ball going in front, and the one farthest from the ball going deep in the seam.

- Many teams prefer to block a back-row attack instead of dig it. If your team has strong blockers who can control their bodies along the net and not commit net fouls, use the block as the first line of defense.

- Make sure the blocker or blockers understand not to reach outside their bodies for a ball passing by them. If a blocker reaches laterally to try to block the ball, she will most likely just deflect it away from the back-row defense. The defenders position themselves in the back row around the blocker's hands, and when her hands move, the back-row players can be out of a good position to dig up the ball.

- Opponents may have more than one attack option (front and back row) within a blocker's zone—this is called overloading a blocker. Blockers must decide which hitter will be set the ball and not commit-block to the quick attacker in the front row and then be unable to recover and jump to block again when the back-row attacker is set the ball instead.

Receiving a Free Ball

A defensive team is set up to defend against the opposing team's attackers. However, there are times when there is a bad pass or bad dig, and the offensive team sends over a free ball—a ball that is sent over the net without being attacked by the opponents. It should be an opportunity for the defensive team to make a perfect pass to their setter and run any type of offensive set they want to. It is critical for the defensive team to immediately recognize this situation and get in the correct position to receive a free ball.

 WATCH OUT!

The following circumstances may distract your athletes:

o Not paying attention to a hitter who may be sending over a free ball instead of jumping to attack the ball

o Not concentrating on making a perfect pass off a free ball

ACQUIRING THE APPROPRIATE KNOWLEDGE

When receiving a free ball, your athletes must understand the following:

Rules

You and your athletes need to know several main rules when receiving a free ball:

o Rules about the three contacts a team is allowed

o Rules about the first contact on a side

o Rules about net fouls

o Rules about center-line violations

Strengths and Weaknesses of Opponents

You and your players must account for the opposing team's strengths and weaknesses to know how to gain the best advantage when receiving a free ball. Teach your players to consider the following about your opponents:

o How strong is the opposing team's blocker? Set the ball away from the strongest blocker. Once your team has received the free ball and passed it to the setter, being able to set your attacker in front of a weak blocker will give your team an advantage. You can also set to the quick hitter to try to beat the opponent getting into position on defense.

o Where are the opponents likely to play a ball if they can't attack it? Sending the free ball into the setter's defensive area of the court is an excellent strategy. If a team is sending over a free ball, the player should always try to send it deep to zone 1, or the right-back area of the court (see figure 3.40 on page 64 for an example of the court zones). Make sure your team has that area covered defensively. If your setter is in the back row and coming out of that area to move to the front row to set the ball, make sure your middle-back player shifts over to cover that corner of the court.

READING THE SITUATION

How do you and your players gain the best advantage when receiving a free ball? Teach your players to do the following:

- Receive the free ball overhead with their hands. This should be their most accurate skill and will speed up the play.

- Let the back-row players take most of the free balls so the front-row players who were blockers can transition off the net and get ready to hit.

- Watch the opponents' first two contacts to determine whether the ball can be set accurately to a hitter either in the front row or back row. Learn to recognize when the ball will not be sent over aggressively. The more experienced the team, the faster they will recognize this situation and back off the net to prepare to receive the free ball.

REMINDER!

You and your players must understand the team strategy and game plan and assess receiving a free ball based on those plans and the situation at hand. Make sure you and your players consider the questions on page 140.

(continued)

○ How high should your team pass a free ball? A free ball is usually sent over the net high enough that players can use their hands to set it. Ideally, the ball should be passed antenna height to the setter near the net so your team can hit the ball more quickly on offense. This will give the opposing team less time to set up their defense.

○ Which opposing players are most likely to send the ball over as a free ball if they get a poor set? Some players will not try to attack a poor set off the net. They want to just play a free ball over the net with a forearm pass or set the ball over the net instead of making a hitting error.

Self-Knowledge

In addition to being aware of the opposing team's strengths and weaknesses, you and your players need to have knowledge about your own team's ability. In terms of receiving a free ball, coaches and players should be aware of the following:

○ How well does your team communicate? As a free ball comes over the net, your middle attacker could audibly call the set. The middle attacker should have plenty of time to analyze the defense, call out the attack she wants, and approach and hit the ball to score. The middle attacker should try to attack the defense at a seam between the blockers or somewhere the defense looks vulnerable. The right-side hitter can also call out what set she wants to hit as well if the team has enough ball control and talent to do so. Teams may also use established free-ball plays instead of each hitter calling out their specific set. The setter can remind the team of the free-ball play she will use when the situation arises.

○ How does the setter know where she needs to set the ball based on the defensive blockers? Train the setter to be aware of the opposing middle blocker's body position to make the best decision on setting the attacker most open. If the blocker is leaning or beginning to move in one direction, the setter should set in the opposite direction to force the middle blocker to change her movement. This should make the middle blocker late to block the outside hitter.

At a Glance

The following parts of the text offer additional information on receiving a free ball:

Skill	Page
Forearm pass	55
Overhead pass	59
Block	108
Dig	114
Positioning defensively as a team	162
Reading the attacker	165
Determining blocking strategies	171
Using a libero	180

Decision-Making Guidelines

When deciding the best way to gain an advantage when your team is receiving a free ball, you and your players should be sure to consider the previous information. Also, consider the following guidelines:

○ When receiving a free ball, your team should strive to pass the ball at antenna height and about 2 to 3 feet (.6 to .91 m) off the net, just to the right of center. This will allow the setter to set the middle attacker for a quick hit or any other offensive options.

○ Your team can have several preset plays for your free-ball offense depending on the number of attackers in the front row and whether the setter is in the front row. Remember what plays have been successful in the past against the team you are playing. Plays that are predetermined will designate what type of set each of the hitters can expect. One play may have the middle hitter hitting a slide behind the setter, the right-side player coming into the middle of the court to hit a ball set about antenna height, and the left-side hitter hitting a high ball set outside. Another play may have the left-side hitter hitting a lower-set ball (antenna height) to the outside, the middle player hitting a shoot set, and the right-side player hitting a high set to the right side of the court. These plays should incorporate sets the players can execute successfully.

- If a free ball is directed to your setter in the right-back position, the setter should avoid taking the ball since she should already be transitioning up to the net. The middle-back player should shift over to the right to cover the back half of the court on the right side. However, if the setter does take the first ball, she should pass it up to the target area and the right-front player will set it to another attacker.

- There is no need for your blockers to risk committing a net foul or center-line violation when the ball is going to come over the net at a slow pace and high trajectory. This allows the blockers to back away or transition off the net and get ready to be hitters.

The libero is a specialized defensive player with an unlimited number of back-row substitutions, but she cannot attempt any type of offensive skills in front of the attack line such as attacking, blocking, or setting the ball to an attacker using her hands overhead. The libero often is a key position for a team's success, so this player should be your best at receiving serves and digging.

 ## WATCH OUT!

The following circumstances may distract your athletes:

- Players not wanting to be a libero since they cannot attack the ball or play in the front row
- Being limited in what they can do on the court
- Being under a lot of pressure to be good at serve reception
- Having to wear a different color uniform than their teammates

ACQUIRING THE APPROPRIATE KNOWLEDGE

When using a libero, your athletes must understand the following:

Rules

You and your athletes need to know several main rules when using a libero:

- Rules on libero restrictions
- Rules on tracking a libero in the game
- Rules on overlapping
- Rules on the libero uniform
- Rules on replacing the libero
- Rules on the libero serving

Strengths and Weaknesses of Opponents

You and your players must account for the opposing team's strengths and weaknesses to know how to gain the best advantage when playing against a libero. Teach your players to consider the following about your opponents:

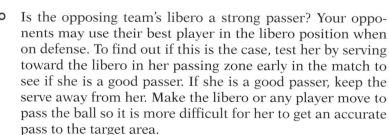

READING THE SITUATION

How do you and your players gain the best advantage when using a libero? Teach your players to do the following:

- Let the libero pass most serves.
- Train your libero to step into a secondary setter role if the primary setter takes a first ball over the net.
- Place your libero in the middle of the serve-reception pattern to receive the most serves.
- The libero should be the defensive leader on the court.
- Place your libero in a position in the back row where they will get the most digs.

REMINDER!

You and your players must understand the team strategy and game plan and assess using a libero based on those plans and the situation at hand. Make sure you and your players consider the questions on page 140.

- Is the opposing team's libero a strong passer? Your opponents may use their best player in the libero position when on defense. To find out if this is the case, test her by serving toward the libero in her passing zone early in the match to see if she is a good passer. If she is a good passer, keep the serve away from her. Make the libero or any player move to pass the ball so it is more difficult for her to get an accurate pass to the target area.

- Where on the court does the libero play? Your opponents will place the libero in a position on the court where they think she will receive the most attacks and be able to dig the most balls. If the libero is one of the opposing team's strongest players on defense, she might switch back and forth between the middle-back and left-back position depending on the team's rotation and your team's specific attackers. Know where the libero is on the court, and hit away from that position.

- How accurately can the libero set the ball? Can the libero set the ball accurately using a forearm set? If the libero is not very accurate in setting the ball to an attacker, your team may want to direct balls to another player in the right-back or right-front defensive position to make the set. Also note that the libero can use an overhand pass to set a front-row attacker as long as she is not inside the attacking area or past the attack line near the net.

- What type of serve does the libero use, and from where does she serve? Observe the libero during the match warm-up to see what type of serve the libero uses, and be ready to pass that type of serve and from that area along the end line.

Self-Knowledge

In addition to being aware of the opposing team's strengths and weaknesses, you and your players need to have knowledge about your own team's ability. In terms of using a libero, coaches and players should be aware of the following:

- Do your players have confidence in the libero? Since the libero is a player who will be on the court most of the time during a match, it is important the libero be respected by the team and can demonstrate good leadership skills on the court.

- How well does your libero pass the ball? Keep passing statistics during practice to see how well the person playing the libero position passes in all areas of the court. It is important to have a good serve-reception strategy to be successful, and having a libero who is an excellent passer is a key.

- How well does your libero play when on defense? If your libero is the best defensive player on the team, then put her in a position to receive the most digs in each rotation. However, if your team uses a back-row attacker, you will need to put the libero in a position on the court that the back-row attacker would not be hitting out of, which is usually left back. If you have a back-row player that attacks from the middle back position, the libero would not play there.

- How well does your libero serve? The libero will be one of the servers during the match, so it is important that she have a strong and accurate serve. The libero should be able to serve to all zones and to the serving target as designated by the coach or scouting report.

At a Glance

The following parts of the text offer additional information on using a libero:

Skill	Page
Forearm pass	55
Overhead pass	59
Dig	114
Run-through	118
Covering the hitter	121
Dig out of the net	123
Overhead dig	126
Barrel roll (log roll)	129
Collapse dig (sprawl)	133
Pancake	136
Reading the attacker	165
Defending against the back-row attack	174
Receiving a free ball	177
Defending against a quick attack	183
Chasing down a ball	187
Defending against the setter's dump or attack	190

(continued)

○ Can the libero hit a down ball overhead accurately? The libero is not allowed to jump up and attack a ball that is above the height of the net, but she should be able to stand on the ground and accurately drive or spike-roll the ball on the third contact over the net to an open area in the opposing team's court. She should train for this during practice by tossing the ball up and hitting it over to start some of the drills instead of a coach doing this.

Decision-Making Guidelines

When deciding the best way to gain an advantage when your team is using a libero, you and your players should be sure to consider the previous information. Also, consider the following guidelines:

○ Use the libero in every serving and passing drill in practice since she is on the court most of the time. Also, instead of having a coach start a drill, allow the libero to start drills with a serve or down ball, or put the libero in a position to receive a majority of serves. This will give her more opportunities to touch the ball and most likely improve her accuracy.

○ Use the libero in attacking drills to set hitters with a forearm set when she is in front of the attack line and an overhead pass when she is behind the attack line. The libero will need to do this in a game situation, so she should practice setting the ball, and the attackers need to hit those balls coming from the libero.

○ Train the libero to stand and drive a standing spike over the net on the third contact. Since it is against the rules for her to jump up and hit the ball, she needs to learn to play it over the net aggressively while standing on the floor. She should aim to place it deep in zone 1 of the opponent's court (see figure 3.40 on page 64 for an example of the court zones).

○ A libero does not have to be a short player. Do not make a player a libero just because she is not tall. Make sure she can pass serves and dig balls accurately.

○ Work with the libero to help her understand the defensive concepts you want your team to use. She can be the defensive leader on the team, just as the setter is the offensive leader on the floor.

Defending Against a Quick Attack

A quick attack is a short set, usually in the middle of the court, set to the middle hitter. The hitter makes her approach early and is in the air when the setter sets the ball to her. This set is popular because it gives the defense much less time to react to block or dig the ball. Defending it properly requires aggressive serving; a smart middle blocker who sees the play developing; and back-row players in the proper position on the court, ready to dig the ball.

WATCH OUT!

The following circumstances may distract your athletes:

- An intimidating quick hitter
- The middle attacker being a shorter player or one who doesn't jump very high, so the defense tends to think she can't hit the ball down
- More than one attacker approaching into the same zone of the net
- The opposing hitters running a crossing pattern, so the blockers lose sight of their hitters and are not ready to block a quick hitter coming into their zone at the net
- A setter in the front row that can dump the ball effectively
- A left-handed setter in the front row that can swing and hit the second ball instead of setting it

ACQUIRING THE APPROPRIATE KNOWLEDGE

When defending against a quick attack, your athletes must understand the following:

Rules

You and your athletes need to know several main rules when defending against a quick attack:

- Rules about overlapping
- Rules about let serves
- Rules about a ball on top of the net
- Rules about net violations
- Rules about center-line violations
- Rules about screening the server
- Rules about blocking the setter

READING THE SITUATION

How do you and your players gain the best advantage when defending against a quick attack? Teach your players to do the following:

- Serve short to the quick hitter in the front row, and force her to pass the ball before she approaches to hit.
- Serve to zones 1 or 2.
- Learn that the more accurate the opponent's pass, the higher the middle blocker's hands should be so she can get over the net quickly.
- Position the left-and right-back players about 15 feet (4.6 m) back from the net and about 7 feet (2.1 m) inside their respective sidelines. They must anticipate the middle hitter receiving a quick set and be in a low position, ready to react.

REMINDER!

You and your players must understand the team strategy and game plan and assess defending against a quick attack based on those plans and the situation at hand. Make sure you and your players consider the questions on page 140.

(continued)

Strengths and Weaknesses of Opponents

You and your players must account for the opposing team's strengths and weaknesses to know how to gain the best advantage when defending against a quick attack. Teach your players to consider the following about your opponents:

○ Where does the quick hitter start in the front row? The blockers must know which players are in the front row and which one is most likely to hit a quick set. Blockers need to physically point out the front-row hitters and verbally identify them to their teammates by calling out their uniform numbers. The middle hitter is most likely to hit the quick attack and will probably not be in the serve-receive formation, but more up near the net.

○ Where on the court is the quick hitter most likely to attack a quick set? This is typically based on the location of the passed ball and the skill of the setter. The higher the skill of the setter and hitter, the bigger range she will have from which to attack a quick set. A quick set may be a shoot set, which is in the seam between the middle- and right-front blockers. Another popular set is directly in front of the setter and is set as high as the quick hitter can reach.

○ Can the quick hitter attack behind the setter? Certainly an attacker can approach behind the setter and get up in the air, waiting for the setter to deliver a ball to her hitting hand. If she attacks close behind the setter and off of one foot, this is known as a tight slide. This set is used to confuse or surprise the blockers. Once they have scored on quick hits on the middle or maybe even blocked in the middle, they may try to hit from a different area.

○ Does the setter look different when she is getting ready to set a quick hitter? The more talented and experienced the setter, the more she will look exactly the same before contacting each set. Many times the setter will bend the knees to get a little lower when contacting the ball to set a quick hitter or will put the hands up higher to speed up the quick set. The setter may jump-set only when intending to set a quick hitter. Observing setters on video and in warm-ups may shed some light on what tendencies each has.

○ Does the setter use a jump set? If the setter is talented enough to jump-set, she may use this when she is getting ready to set a quick attack. She jumps up to set the ball, making the quick attack even faster since the ball is now in the air even less time before the quick hitter swings to hit it.

○ How good does the pass need to be for the setter to be able to get to the ball and set it to the quick hitter? A ball passed to the setter or target area can vary in height, speed, and position on the court. Most teams try to pass the ball at antenna height to give their quick hitter enough time to follow the ball to the setter and jump in the air to receive the set. If the pass is off or away from the net, the attacker will move away from the setter to open up the hitting shoulder to let the ball come inside the shoulder to hit it. Teams should be able to tell early in the match how good the setter is and if the quick hitter will jump every time to be an available option for the setter—and a threat to your blockers.

Self-Knowledge

In addition to being aware of the opposing team's strengths and weaknesses, you and your players need to have knowledge about your own team's ability. In terms of defending against a quick attack, coaches and players should be aware of the following:

○ How aggressively does your team serve the ball? The best way to stop an opponent's quick attack is to serve aggressively to keep the pass off the net and force the setter to move off the net to set the ball. If a team wants to see how well the opponents can hit a quick attack, then serve them an easy ball.

○ How many blockers should your team have up against a quick hitter? Have at least one blocker get her hands up and over the net in front of the quick hitter's shoulder to take away part of the court. If possible, the left-side blocker should help out and become part of the two-person block. This will depend on whether the setter is in the front row and has the potential to attack the second ball with a swing or dump the second ball over to score. If the setter is a threat, the left-side blocker may have to stay with the setter to defend the court. Also, if the quick hitter continues to score by hitting to left back, the left-side blocker will need to step in and get up to block, with the left-back player rotating to the outside of the court to be ready to pick up a tip to the left front (zone 4; see figure 3.40 on page 64 for an example of the court zones) by the quick hitter or a dump behind the head by the setter.

o Does the blocker responsible for blocking the quick hitter keep her hands high and knees bent, ready to get the hands across the net quickly? Most middle blockers start with their knees bent and hands high but then drop down to get ready to jump when the quick hitter goes up in the air, minimizing the effect of having the hands high to begin with. Blockers need to know that the better the pass, the higher their hands need to be to get them over the net quickly.

o What kind of defense should be played against a quick hitter? The team will always start in their base positions, so there is really not much change to defend the quick hitter. The left- and right-back players should be in a position about two steps in from their respective sidelines and about 15 feet (4.6 m) back from the net. This is an area most quick attackers aim for with their natural swings. If a quick hitter jumps and does not get set, the defense proceeds to read the set and move to their next defensive position.

Decision-Making Guidelines

When deciding the best way to gain an advantage when your team is defending against a quick attack, you and your players should be sure to consider the previous information. Also, consider the following guidelines:

o The key to blocking a quick set is to get the hands over the net low and tight to the top of the net, so blockers don't need to jump high to block a quick set. Most attackers try to hit the ball down in the court, so the hands being low will stop most of the balls. Keeping the forearms close to the top of the net will keep the ball from coming down inside the blockers' arms on their side of the net.

o Watch the angle of the hitter's approach and the direction of her face and head to determine the direction of the attack. Most hitters will hit in the direction they are facing. If right-handed, the attacker will most likely hit to the left-back area of the court. The setter can change the direction the attacker chooses to hit by setting the ball in front of the hitter's right shoulder (hit to left back) or to her left shoulder so she can hit a cut-back shot to the right-back area of the court.

o Be aware of who the quick hitters are. The front-row blockers need to pay attention to their attack approaches and know if they are going to hit a quick set or another type of set.

o Study the setter to see how skilled she is at setting quick sets. Many setters struggle with setting the quick set to their middle hitters. For this hit to be successful, it takes a great pass, good timing for the quick hitter, and a setter who can set the ball accurately to the quick hitter.

At a Glance

The following parts of the text offer additional information on defending against a quick attack:

(continued)

○ Use a smart serving strategy to make it tougher to set a quick attacker. Remember, you can serve short to the front-row attacker and maybe take her out of the play because she is too busy passing the ball to be able to make the approach and be in the air when the setter has the ball.

○ Most quick hitters like to hit the ball in the same direction every time they are set. Blockers need to remember this and take an attacker's favorite hit away by getting their hands over the net in that area when she is getting ready to hit the ball.

Chasing Down a Ball

There are times when a ball is hit down into the court and is deflected off a blocker's hands or when a back-row defender makes a poor dig and the ball goes off the court after the first contact. Your team needs to have a strategy for chasing down the ball and playing it back over the net. Once the ball has been deflected off the court on the first contact by your team, every player needs to run after the ball. The first person to get to it should attempt to pass it straight up in the air, and the next player there will stop underneath the ball, get her shoulders and back square to the net, and pass the ball backward over the net into the opposing team's court. The players then move back into their proper defensive positions on the court.

 WATCH OUT!

The following circumstances may distract your athletes:

○ Thinking the ball is unplayable so deciding not to go after it

○ Thinking another teammate will get the ball

○ Thinking they can't get to the ball to make a play

○ Being too tired or lacking the effort to sprint off the court

○ Not seeing or hearing a teammate say they touched the ball

ACQUIRING THE APPROPRIATE KNOWLEDGE

When chasing down a ball, your athletes must understand the following:

Rules

You and your athletes need to know several main rules when chasing down a ball:

○ Rules about the number of contacts allowed by a team

○ Rules about an unplayable ball

○ Rules about simultaneous contacts by teammates

○ Rules about a ball touching the blockers

○ Rules about the ball crossing the net in between the antennae

○ Rules about maintaining contact with the floor when playing a ball in the bleachers

Strengths and Weaknesses of Opponents

You and your players must account for the opposing team's strengths and weaknesses to know how to gain the best advantage when chasing down a ball. Teach your players to consider the following about your opponents:

○ How strong are the attackers at hitting? The attacker may be experienced at seeing the blockers' hands in front of her and be able to hit the ball high off the blockers' hands, deflecting the ball back off the court out of bounds and out of the reach of the back-row defenders.

READING THE SITUATION

How do you and your players gain the best advantage when chasing down a ball?

Teach your players to do the following:

• Follow the pursuit rule, which is explained later in this skill.

• Know where the sidelines and end line are and how much room is available around the court to retrieve a ball.

• Listen for their teammates to yell "Touch!" meaning the ball is in play and someone else on the team needs to contact it so it can be kept in play.

• Be aware of your teammates.

REMINDER!

You and your players must understand the team strategy and game plan and assess chasing down a ball based on those plans and the situation at hand. Make sure you and your players consider the questions on page 140.

(continued)

○ What is the attacker's arm swing? Attackers may attempt to tool the block (intentionally hit off a blocker's hand) toward the sideline by swinging the arm toward the sideline or deep off the court by swinging at a high seam in the block. Make sure your left-back and right-back players watch the hitter's arm swing, and if they notice the attacker swinging toward the sideline or high and deep, they need to be ready to pursue the ball as quickly as possible.

○ Does the attacker have a slow arm swing? This may cause the blockers to mistime their jumps, and the ball may be deflected off a hand and need to be chased down by the players on the team.

Self-Knowledge

In addition to being aware of the opposing team's strengths and weaknesses, you and your players need to have knowledge about your own team's ability. In terms of chasing down a ball, coaches and players should be aware of the following:

○ How well do your blockers time their jumps? If your blockers jump too late, the ball will hit off the top of the blockers' hands on their way up. Instead, blockers need to get their hands low and tight across the net as the attacker is contacting the ball. Blockers need to know how long it takes them to go from their ready position at the net to jumping and getting their hands over the net. They need to work on speeding up this movement by starting lower with their knees bent and only extending up instead of dropping down first, which takes away precious time.

○ Why is it important for everyone on the team to pursue the ball off the court? All players need to demonstrate to each other they are ready to pursue any ball to keep it off the floor. The more players who participate in this effort, the more likely they are to be successful.

○ Why does the first player who gets to the ball hit it straight up instead of back into the court? If the first player tries to dig the ball back into the court, there will be confusion about where it will go and who should play it over the net. It is simpler to hit it straight up, giving the next player, or the one making the third contact, enough time to get there and get her body set before sending it a long way back over the net.

○ Why is it important to practice this tactic? When teams hustle to chase a ball off the court and successfully get it back across the net, it can change the momentum of the match. It is such an exciting play the team will have more confidence every time they do it, while the offensive team will become frustrated and more likely to make hitting errors.

Decision-Making Guidelines

When deciding the best way to gain an advantage when your team is chasing down a ball, you and your players should be sure to consider the previous information. Also, consider the following guidelines:

○ The first person to arrive at the ball coming down off the court should attempt to play the ball with her forearms straight up and high enough for the next teammate to get there. This is the second of three contacts the team is allowed, unless the first contact was off the blocker. The ball touching a blocker's hands does not count as a contact unless it is not contacted again.

○ If there is to be a third contact, the player needs to get under where the ball is falling and get stopped with her back square to the net so she can direct the ball backward and over the net in between the antennae into the opponents' court. This ball should be sent deep enough into the opponents' court so they can't immediately attack it. This will give your players enough time to get back onto the court and set up their defense.

○ The player running to get to the ball will have more control if she plays it straight up. Running for a ball and trying to hit it back over her head while moving is not a recipe for success.

- Players must follow the pursuit rule when chasing down a ball. This means they will continue to attempt to play the ball unless they are in danger of hitting something (e.g., chair, wall), the ball contacts something (e.g., floor, ceiling) out of play, a teammate calls them off, or the referee stops play by blowing the whistle. This is called relentless pursuit.

- If the ball rebounds off a defender, that player doesn't go after it because she can't play the ball on the second contact. She should still pursue the ball with the rest of the team because she is allowed to make the third contact to send the ball back over the net.

- Players need to stay on their feet until they contact the ball. Players running after the ball may think they need to go to the floor to contact the ball. They should always attempt to play the ball first and then let the momentum of their movement take them to the floor to recover if necessary.

- Teammates should communicate as they are running toward the ball, letting each other know if they are in danger of contacting something such as the bleachers or a wall, reminding each other to play the ball straight up on the second contact, and letting each other know a teammate is right there with them to play the third ball over.

At a Glance

The following parts of the text offer additional information on chasing down a ball:

Skill	Page
Dig	114
Run-through	118
Dig out of the net	123
Overhead dig	126
Barrel (log roll)	129
Hitting off the block	152
Positioning defensively as a team	162
Defending against the slide	168
Defending against the back-row attack	174
Using a libero	180
Defending against a quick attack	183
Defending against the setter's dump or attack	190

The setter usually is the player who sets the pass to an attacker for her to hit over the net. If the setter is in the front row, she may attack the ball on the second contact instead of setting it. The defensive team must be ready to play this surprise attack, usually called a dump. The purpose of it is to catch the defense off guard. It is important for the defensive players to know if the setter is in the front row since she can't jump up and attack the ball over if she is in the back row. Blockers must be aware of the setter's movements and be ready to jump to block her, especially if she jumps up in the air to play the ball and has shown that she can effectively dump or attack the ball over the net. Although the blockers are considered the first line of defense, the left-side blocker may have another player to worry about blocking, such as the right-side hitter or the middle hitter approaching behind the setter to hit a slide. Therefore, the left- and right-back players must be ready to dig up the ball dumped or attacked over by the setter.

 WATCH OUT!

The following circumstances may distract your athletes:

- A tall setter
- A setter who jump-sets every ball, whether the setter is in the front or the back row
- A left-handed setter
- A team that passes well with a tall, left-handed jump setter
- An athletic setter that jumps well

READING THE SITUATION

How do you and your players gain the best advantage when defending against the setter's dump or attack? Teach your players to do the following:

- Study the setter on video or during the warm-up to determine what type of ball the setter likes to dump or attack on the second contact.
- Serve aggressively.
- Make sure the back-row players know the blocking strategy against the front-row setter.
- Make sure everyone knows when the setter is in the front row.
- Be aware of a left-handed setter since they are a real threat to swing and attack the second ball instead of setting it.

REMINDER!

You and your players must understand the team strategy and game plan and assess defending against the setter's dump or attack based on those plans and the situation at hand. Make sure you and your players consider the questions on page 140.

ACQUIRING THE APPROPRIATE KNOWLEDGE

When defending against the setter's dump or attack, your athletes must understand the following:

Rules

You and your athletes need to know several main rules when defending against the setter's dump or attack:

- Rules about a ball on top of the net
- Rules about a back-row attacker as the setter
- Rules about overlapping
- Rules about net violations
- Rules about center-line violations

- Rules about illegal hits
- Rules about blocking the setter
- Rules about the ball touching a blocker

Strengths and Weaknesses of Opponents

You and your players must account for the opposing team's strengths and weaknesses to know how to gain the best advantage when defending against the setter's dump or attack. Teach your players to consider the following about your opponents:

- What is the setter's body position? The setter must be in a good body position to jump up and play the ball over, either attacking it with a swing or dumping it down into the court. If your players recognize that the setter looks ready to make a play on the ball, your blocker directly in front of the setter should jump up and block, with her hands over the net taking away an area of the court. The back-row defense should fill in around her.

- Is the ball passed close enough to the net for the setter to attack it or dump it over the net? A tight pass will have the setter attempting to either set it to an attacker with one hand or to a quick hitter or to make a lateral set. The setter may also put both hands up as if to set the ball and then push the ball down into the court with the left or right hand.

- Does the setter jump-set? If the setter is highly skilled, she may jump-set the ball quite a few times during the match to set all of her hitters. She may also jump-set only when she intends to dump the ball over. Players need to pay attention and remember to watch her tendencies during the warm-up and throughout the match.

- What area of the court does the setter like to dump the ball to? If she is an advanced setter, she will observe where her opposing left-side blocker is and dump it around her. If the blocker is in front of her, she will dump the ball back toward the sideline, and if the left-side blocker is behind her, she may dump it in front of her in the seam between the left-side and middle blockers. The back-row players must see where their left-side blocker is playing and be ready to cover the area that is open for the dump, as explained previously. The left-side blocker should be in position to take away the setter's strongest shot and make sure the defenders fill in behind her. Some setters can dump the ball deep to the left-back corner over the left-back defender's reach.

- Is the setter left-handed? A left-handed setter can be very effective at dumping the second ball or taking a full swing at it as an attacker. The defensive team must know if the setter is talented enough to swing hard at the ball and be ready to block her accordingly, taking away her favorite shot or angle she likes to hit. A left-handed setter also is stronger with her left hand and is better at directing a dumped ball to different areas of the court, such as the deep left-back corner or straight down over the net.

- Does the setter (front or back row) like to set the ball over the net on the second contact? They will stay on the ground and set the ball laterally over the net with two hands instead of setting the ball to a hitter on their team. The back-row players must be ready to play this ball up.

Self-Knowledge

In addition to being aware of the opposing team's strengths and weaknesses, you and your players need to have knowledge about your own team's ability. In terms of the setter's dump or attack, coaches and players should be aware of the following:

- Do your left- and right-back players know their responsibilities? These two players should have the first responsibility of picking up the dump by the opposing setter. They do not have any blocking responsibilities, and therefore they can totally focus on the setter.

(continued)

They should be in a good base position on the court and be able to get their arms under any ball the setter puts over the net. They should be able to play the ball up when it is low to the ground using a variety of techniques.

o   What is the middle blocker's responsibility? The middle blocker is responsible for stopping the setter if the opposing middle attacker has gone behind the setter, and the setter is now the attacker in the middle of the court. The middle blocker should try to get at least one hand over the net in front of her when she sees the setter attempt to dump or swing at the ball. The left-side blocker and middle blocker need to communicate quickly as the hitter goes behind the setter to attack the ball.

o   What is the left-side blocker's responsibility? The left-side blocker keeps the setter from hitting the ball straight down in an area of the court behind her. She must decide on an angle to take away and make sure the setter has to go over her hands or around her, giving the back-row defenders more time to respond to play the ball up.

o   What is the right-side blocker's responsibility? This player needs to be ready to pull off the net and help play up any ball that comes into her area of the court near the net or help out on playing a ball deflected off one of the blockers. She may also need to be ready to set a dug ball if the ball is hit toward the right-back defensive player, who may be the setter.

Decision-Making Guidelines

When deciding the best way to gain an advantage when your team is defending against the setter's dump or attack, you and your players should be sure to consider the previous information. Also, consider the following guidelines:

o   When playing against a team that has a left-handed setter (or a talented right-handed attacking setter) who plays in the front row, the defensive team must know how they want to keep that person from scoring a point on the second contact or at least slow her down a little bit. This will require a decision whether the left-side blocker is going to commit-block (jump in the air) if the setter jump-sets, where the left-side blocker will position himself in relation to the opposing setter, taking away her favorite shot. The back-row players must know the strategy that is going to be used so they can fill in the holes on defense.

o   Another common situation is for the setter to try to end a long rally by taking charge and dumping it herself. Sometimes she thinks she will catch the defensive team by surprise, and many times she does. The teams are in such a habit of watching the setter make a set to a hitter they forget about the setter as an attacker option.

o   If the left-side blocker is in front of the setter, this will encourage the setter to dump the ball behind her to zone 4 along the net (see figure 3.40 on page 64 for an example of the court zones), so the left-back player should shift to that area. If the left-side blocker is even with the setter and can take away the dump to zone 4, then the left-back defender should shift toward the middle of the court and be ready for the setter to dump the ball in that direction. In other words, the digger goes in the opposite direction of the blocker, or the position the blocker is taking away.

o   If the opposing team has a middle hitter who can attack behind the setter, it is difficult to ask the left-side blocker to be responsible for blocking both the setter and the middle hitter who comes into her zone. The left-side blocker and middle blocker will need to communicate quickly as the hitter comes around.

o   If your setter dumps the ball during a rally, be ready for the opposing setter to dump the ball immediately. This is an odd phenomenon in volleyball that seems to occur frequently. The defensive team should prepare for it to happen by anticipating a dump once their setter has dumped the ball over.

- Use serving tactics to limit the setter's ability to dump. Serve to a zone behind the setter, or serve aggressively to hopefully keep the pass off the net and reduce the chance of the setter's dumping or attacking since she is away from the net.
- Right back has to be ready to dig a ball the setter hits since she will most likely hit crosscourt. If this happens and the defensive setter is playing right back, be prepared for another player, usually right front, to set the second ball to an attacker.

At a Glance

The following parts of the text offer additional information on defending against the setter's dump or attack:

Skill	Page
Slide	102
Block	108
Dig	114
Barrel roll (log roll)	129
Pancake	136
Attacking or dumping the second ball	158
Positioning defensively as a team	162
Reading the attacker	165
Defending against the slide	168
Determining blocking strategies	171
Defending against a quick attack	183
Chasing down a ball	187

Planning for Teaching

Part IV helps you apply what you learned in the previous chapters to developing a plan for the upcoming season. By having a season plan that outlines your practices for the year and then creating specific practice plans that make up your season plan, you will be ready to coach and get the most out of your season.

Chapter 7 explains how to create your season plan, which is a framework for the practices that make up your season. Besides teaching you about the six essential steps to developing the season plan, this chapter provides a sample season plan using the games approach. After you have created your season plan, you must create what is called a practice plan, which outlines how you will approach each practice. Chapter 8 helps you do this by explaining the components of a good practice plan and then providing samples of the first eight practices of your season based on the season plan using the games approach.

chapter 7

Season Plans

John Wooden, the legendary UCLA basketball coach, followed a simple coaching philosophy that emphasized execution over winning. He believed that if his Bruins concentrated on executing the basics, winning would follow. In that regard, his well-planned practice sessions created a foundation for 10 national titles in a 12-year span in the 1960s and 1970s. As Wooden said, "Failure to prepare is preparing to fail." Before the first practice of the season, you should review your coaching philosophy and reflect on the upcoming year. By doing so, you can avoid the pitfalls of previous years and set goals for the one to come. No matter what sport, a good coach always takes the time to make plans.

Developing a Coaching Philosophy

Successful planning begins with developing a good coaching philosophy. Do you like to run a fast offense or a more conservative one? Do you want to have a quick hitter available on every pass or dig, or do you like to set the ball high outside? No matter what your coaching philosophy is, you must develop guiding principles for your team and only attempt to do tactically what your team can do technically.

So how exactly do you form a coaching philosophy? First, you should determine your beliefs and values. You shouldn't try to adapt or use a philosophy that goes against your personal beliefs. You will have difficulty getting the players to buy into a system and coaching philosophy that isn't really yours. That being said, you shouldn't be afraid to borrow parts of a philosophy from successful coaches you have played for or studied closely. Pay close attention to the programs and teams that win often. What makes those teams successful? Don't be afraid to ask other coaches how they prepare for a season, run their practices, or discipline their players. Good coaches will be flattered and be more than willing to share their knowledge with you. Attend the USA Volleyball Coaching Accreditation Program

(CAP) certification courses, and join the American Volleyball Coaches Association (AVCA) to stay educated on the latest information and advancements in volleyball.

But as you know, gathering information from other coaches or from books provides only the basic material for a coach. The next step is to process this information and organize it into a useful plan. Successful coaches are good teachers. Just as a teacher wouldn't walk into a classroom without a well-thought-out lesson plan, a volleyball coach shouldn't begin a season without a plan. You need to organize information into an annual training plan by carefully analyzing, observing, and prioritizing what you need to cover.

Six Steps to Instructional Planning*

Chapter 1 of Rainer Martens' *Successful Coaching, Third Edition*, provides a framework for creating and implementing coaching values. You may want to read that chapter and refine your coaching philosophy.

After you have your coaching philosophy down on paper, you can begin planning for the upcoming season by following a simple six-step approach called Six Steps to Instructional Planning, as shown here:

Step 1: Identify the skills your athletes need.

Step 2: Know your athletes.

Step 3: Analyze your situation.

Step 4: Establish priorities.

Step 5: Select methods for teaching.

Step 6: Plan practices.

Step 1: Identify the Skills Your Athletes Need

To help athletes become excellent volleyball players, you need to know what skills players need to play volleyball. Not all the skills will be within the reach of most high school players, so you must filter this all-encompassing list. First, you need to isolate the skills the team needs to be successful, as shown in column one of figure 7.1.

Figure 7.1 provides an overview of the basic to intermediate skills needed in volleyball, based on the skills described in chapters 3 through 6, along with additional basic skills that aren't covered in a book of this level, since we are assuming the coaches and players have a basic knowledge and aptitude of volleyball. It also includes communication and physical, mental, and character skills from Rainer Martens' *Successful Coaching, Third Edition*. At this stage, you should examine the list of skills and modify as desired based on what skills are applicable to your team's skill level (step 4 of the planning process further explains how you can put this list to work).

Step 2: Know Your Athletes

Before going into a season, you should be familiar with your athletes. If you trained the team the year before, review the list of returning players and evaluate them—their strengths, their weaknesses, how much they still have to learn, and so on. If you are a new coach with no knowledge of the skill level of a team, the process is more difficult. Review the guidelines for evaluation discussed in

---

*Reprinted, by permission, from R. Martens, 2004, *Successful coaching*, 3rd ed. (Champaign, IL: Human Kinetics), 237.

Figure 7.1 Identifying and Evaluating Skills

STEP 1	STEP 4							
	Teaching priorities			Readiness to learn		Priority rating		
Skills identified	Must	Should	Could	Yes	No	A	B	C
OFFENSIVE TECHNICAL SKILLS								
Underhand serve	M	S	C	Yes	No	A	B	C
Sidearm serve	M	S	C	Yes	No	A	B	C
Standing floater serve	M	S	C	Yes	No	A	B	C
Jump floater serve	M	S	C	Yes	No	A	B	C
Topspin serve	M	S	C	Yes	No	A	B	C
Roundhouse serve	M	S	C	Yes	No	A	B	C
Jump spin serve	M	S	C	Yes	No	A	B	C
Serve receive (forearm pass)	M	S	C	Yes	No	A	B	C
Serve receive (overhead pass)	M	S	C	Yes	No	A	B	C
Free ball (forearm pass)	M	S	C	Yes	No	A	B	C
Free ball (overhead pass)	M	S	C	Yes	No	A	B	C
Setting (overhead pass)	M	S	C	Yes	No	A	B	C
Setting (front set)	M	S	C	Yes	No	A	B	C
Setting (back set)	M	S	C	Yes	No	A	B	C
Setting (jump set)	M	S	C	Yes	No	A	B	C
Setting (one-hand set)	M	S	C	Yes	No	A	B	C
Setting (lateral set)	M	S	C	Yes	No	A	B	C
Setting (dump)	M	S	C	Yes	No	A	B	C
Setting (forearm set)	M	S	C	Yes	No	A	B	C
Attacking (left side)	M	S	C	Yes	No	A	B	C
Attacking (middle)	M	S	C	Yes	No	A	B	C
Attacking (right side)	M	S	C	Yes	No	A	B	C
Attacking (back row)	M	S	C	Yes	No	A	B	C
Attacking (quick)	M	S	C	Yes	No	A	B	C
Attacking (slide)	M	S	C	Yes	No	A	B	C
Attacking (off-speed)	M	S	C	Yes	No	A	B	C
Attacking (tip)	M	S	C	Yes	No	A	B	C
Attacking (high set)	M	S	C	Yes	No	A	B	C
Attacking (off blocker)	M	S	C	Yes	No	A	B	C
Attacking (line)	M	S	C	Yes	No	A	B	C
Attacking (crosscourt)	M	S	C	Yes	No	A	B	C
Attacking (deep corner)	M	S	C	Yes	No	A	B	C
Attacking (sharp angle)	M	S	C	Yes	No	A	B	C
Attacking (seams)	M	S	C	Yes	No	A	B	C

(continued)

Figure 7.1 *(continued)*

STEP 1	STEP 4							
	Teaching priorities			Readiness to learn		Priority rating		
Skills identified	Must	Should	Could	Yes	No	A	B	C
DEFENSIVE TECHNICAL SKILLS								
Blocking	M	S	C	Yes	No	A	B	C
Digging (underhand)	M	S	C	Yes	No	A	B	C
Digging (overhead)	M	S	C	Yes	No	A	B	C
Run-through	M	S	C	Yes	No	A	B	C
Collapse dig (sprawl)	M	S	C	Yes	No	A	B	C
Pancake	M	S	C	Yes	No	A	B	C
OFFENSIVE TACTICAL SKILLS								
Serving zones	M	S	C	Yes	No	A	B	C
Serving situations	M	S	C	Yes	No	A	B	C
Setting (training)	M	S	C	Yes	No	A	B	C
Setting (variety of attack options)	M	S	C	Yes	No	A	B	C
Setting (signals and plays)	M	S	C	Yes	No	A	B	C
Attacking (from serve receive)	M	S	C	Yes	No	A	B	C
Attacking (from defense)	M	S	C	Yes	No	A	B	C
Attacking (from different positions)	M	S	C	Yes	No	A	B	C
Serve receive (floater serve)	M	S	C	Yes	No	A	B	C
Serve receive (jump floater serve)	M	S	C	Yes	No	A	B	C
Serve receive (jump spin serve)	M	S	C	Yes	No	A	B	C
Serve receive in various team formations	M	S	C	Yes	No	A	B	C
Specialize players by position	M	S	C	Yes	No	A	B	C
Serve-receive offense	M	S	C	Yes	No	A	B	C
Free-ball offense	M	S	C	Yes	No	A	B	C
Transition offense	M	S	C	Yes	No	A	B	C
Out-of-system offense	M	S	C	Yes	No	A	B	C
DEFENSIVE TACTICAL SKILLS								
Blocking (bunch)	M	S	C	Yes	No	A	B	C
Blocking (spread)	M	S	C	Yes	No	A	B	C
Blocking (read)	M	S	C	Yes	No	A	B	C
Blocking (commit)	M	S	C	Yes	No	A	B	C
Blocking (overload)	M	S	C	Yes	No	A	B	C
Blocking (swing)	M	S	C	Yes	No	A	B	C
Left-side blocking	M	S	C	Yes	No	A	B	C
Middle blocking	M	S	C	Yes	No	A	B	C
Right-side blocking	M	S	C	Yes	No	A	B	C
No block (free ball)	M	S	C	Yes	No	A	B	C
No block (down ball)	M	S	C	Yes	No	A	B	C
Defense (base position)	M	S	C	Yes	No	A	B	C
Defense (seams)	M	S	C	Yes	No	A	B	C
Ball in net retrieval	M	S	C	Yes	No	A	B	C
Saving a ball off court	M	S	C	Yes	No	A	B	C

STEP 1	STEP 4							
	Teaching priorities			Readiness to learn		Priority rating		
Skills identified	Must	Should	Could	Yes	No	A	B	C
PHYSICAL TRAINING SKILLS								
Strength	M	S	C	Yes	No	A	B	C
Speed	M	S	C	Yes	No	A	B	C
Power	M	S	C	Yes	No	A	B	C
Endurance	M	S	C	Yes	No	A	B	C
Flexibility	M	S	C	Yes	No	A	B	C
Quickness	M	S	C	Yes	No	A	B	C
Balance	M	S	C	Yes	No	A	B	C
Agility	M	S	C	Yes	No	A	B	C
Jumping	M	S	C	Yes	No	A	B	C
MENTAL SKILLS								
Emotional control: anxiety	M	S	C	Yes	No	A	B	C
Self-confidence	M	S	C	Yes	No	A	B	C
Motivation to achieve	M	S	C	Yes	No	A	B	C
Ability to concentrate	M	S	C	Yes	No	A	B	C
Other	M	S	C	Yes	No	A	B	C
COMMUNICATION SKILLS								
Sends positive messages	M	S	C	Yes	No	A	B	C
Sends accurate messages	M	S	C	Yes	No	A	B	C
Listens to messages	M	S	C	Yes	No	A	B	C
Understands messages	M	S	C	Yes	No	A	B	C
Receives constructive criticism	M	S	C	Yes	No	A	B	C
Receives praise and recognition	M	S	C	Yes	No	A	B	C
Credibility with teammates	M	S	C	Yes	No	A	B	C
Credibility with coaches	M	S	C	Yes	No	A	B	C
CHARACTER SKILLS								
Trustworthiness	M	S	C	Yes	No	A	B	C
Respect	M	S	C	Yes	No	A	B	C
Responsibility	M	S	C	Yes	No	A	B	C
Fairness	M	S	C	Yes	No	A	B	C
Caring	M	S	C	Yes	No	A	B	C
Citizenship	M	S	C	Yes	No	A	B	C

From American Sport Education Program, 2011, *Coaching volleyball technical and tactical skills* (Champaign, IL: Human Kinetics). Adapted, by permission, from R. Martens, 2004, *Successful coaching,* 3rd ed. (Champaign, IL: Human Kinetics), 250-251.

chapter 2 before attempting this process. You may want to conduct a tryout session on the first day of practice or before the season, if the rules allow. The tryout session could include the physical testing of the players as discussed in chapter 2 as well as some on-the-court skill evaluation such as serving, passing, setting, hitting, and defensive drills to assess their volleyball ability. Include some type of competition (3v3 or 6v6) to look at their ability to play the game where you can also assess teamwork, communication, and court awareness.

Step 3: Analyze Your Situation

As you prepare for the season, you must also weigh the external factors that will both guide and limit you. Budgetary issues and related fund-raising options will affect scheduling, training facilities, practice equipment, and court time.

Administrative and community support will influence goal setting and expectations. Teaching loads will set limits for both off-season and in-season programming. Clearly, then, many factors influence your planning, In analyzing these factors, you may find it helpful to spend some time working through the questions in figure 7.2.

Step 4: Establish Priorities

You must institute a set of priorities before a season. Given the limited practice time available to most high school teams, you cannot do everything possible within the sport of volleyball. You should also consider the abilities of the athletes before establishing priorities. Refer to figure 7.1, paying special attention to the columns under "Step 4." Here you examine the list of essential skills and evaluate them to establish practice priorities for the season. First, you must give each skill a priority according to its importance. Ask yourself, "Is this a skill I *must, should,* or *could* teach?" You should then ask, "Are my athletes ready to learn this skill?" And possibly even "Does the level of play of our opponents necessitate spending time developing this skill?" The results from step 2 may help you with this phase. Finally, on the basis of those two factors—the teaching priority and the athletes' readiness to learn—you can give each skill a priority rating in column 4. The A-rated skills are those you think are essential to teach, so you should teach them early and often. Likewise, you should teach as many B-rated skills as possible. Finally, depending on the ability and rate of progression of the players, you can teach C-rated skills.

Although you may believe that most of the skills are must-teach skills, circumstances may arise that make teaching some skills impractical at various times during the season. For example, you might think that teaching the middle hitters to hit a quick set is important, but the team might not be ready or able to learn this more difficult skill. Remember, you should only attempt to do tactically what your team can do technically.

Step 5: Select Methods for Teaching

Next you should choose the methods you want to use in daily practices to teach the skills you have decided are necessary. Take care in implementing this important step. The traditional approach to practice involves using daily drills to teach skills, interspersed with serving and passing practice. This approach emphasizes technical skill development, the thinking being that the more players repeat the skills in drills, the better they become at performing them in matches.

Although this traditional method might cover the techniques of volleyball adequately and even cover some of the tactical situations a team will face during matches, it does have serious shortcomings. First, a traditional session overemphasizes individual techniques at the expense of tactics. Second, too much direct instruction usually occurs. Typically, a coach would explain a skill, show how to

Figure 7.2 Evaluating Your Team Situation

How many practices will you have over the entire season, and how long can practices be?

How many contests will you have over the entire season?

What special events (team meetings, parent orientation sessions, banquets, tournaments) will you have and when?

How many athletes will you be coaching? How many assistants will you have? What is the ratio of athletes to coaches?

What equipment will be available for practice?

How many courts will you have available during practice?

How much money do you have for travel and other expenses?

What instructional resources (videos, DVDs, books, charts, CDs) will you need?

What other support personnel will be available?

What other factors may affect your instructional plan?

From American Sport Education Program, 2011, *Coaching volleyball technical and tactical skills* (Champaign, IL: Human Kinetics). Adapted, by permission, from R. Martens, 2004, *Successful coaching*, 3rd ed. (Champaign, IL: Human Kinetics), 247-248.

perform it, and then set up a situation in which players can learn the skill. Unfortunately, volleyball coaches like to be part of the drills, especially initiating the play, which is not recommended. The more the players are involved in running the drill, the better they will become at the game and the more time the coach will have to observe and give feedback rather than perform as a ball machine.

Recent education research has shown, however, that students who learn a skill in one setting, say the library, have trouble performing it in another setting, such as the classroom. Compare this finding to the common belief among coaches that young players today don't have volleyball sense, or the basic knowledge of the game that players used to have. For years, coaches have been complaining that today's players don't react as well to game situations, blaming everything from video games to the increasing popularity of other sports. But external forces are not entirely to blame for this decline. All coaches love drills and use as many as they can get their hands on to help teach the technical skills. Perhaps learning techniques and performing drill after drill just creates the ability to do drills rather than to develop expertise, and this does not transfer into the competitive game. Any team can be great at performing drills, but are they great at playing the game?

An alternative and better way to teach volleyball skills is the games approach. As outlined in chapter 1, the games approach allows players to take responsibility for learning skills. A good analogy is to compare the games approach in sport to the holistic methods of teaching writing. Traditional approaches to teaching students to write included doing sentence-writing exercises, identifying parts of speech, and working with different types of paragraphs. After drilling students in these techniques, teachers assigned topics to write about. Teachers used this method of teaching for years. When graduating students could not write a competent essay or work application, educators began questioning the method and began to use a new approach, the holistic method. In the holistic method of teaching writing, students write compositions without learning parts of speech or sentence types or even ways to organize paragraphs. Teachers look at the whole piece of writing and make suggestions for improvement from there, not worrying about spelling, grammar, or punctuation unless necessary. This method emphasizes seeing the forest instead of the trees.

This forest versus the trees approach is applicable to teaching volleyball skills as well. Instead of breaking down skills into their component parts and then having the athletes attempt to put the pieces back together, you can impart the whole skill and then let the athletes discover how the parts relate. This method resembles what actually occurs in a game, and learning will occur at game speed. These latter two concepts are crucial for understanding the games approach.

This method does not take you, the coach, out of the equation; in fact, you must take a more active and creative role. You must shape the play of the athletes to get the desired results, focus the athletes' attention on the important techniques, and enhance the skill involved by attaching various challenges to the games played.

You can use the games approach to teach almost any area of the game of volleyball. Instead of having players work on just serving and passing, you can create games around those skills to encourage competition among the players. You can work on serving and passing while involving the setters and middle hitters—which is more gamelike—by shaping, focusing, and enhancing. Using this type of drill makes the players serve aggressively to force a bad pass so the middle can't be set a quick set, the passer must concentrate on a perfect pass, and the setter and middle hitter get practice on live balls. This approach also gives players opportunities to practice decision making as well as the all-important, all-encompassing skills of reading, anticipation, judgment, and timing in a gamelike and competitive manner.

Step 6: Plan Practices

In Step 6, you sketch a brief overview of what you want to accomplish during each practice for the season. Using the information compiled in the previous five steps, you can sketch an outline for an entire season, both practices and matches, which can be called the season plan. Figure 7.3 shows a sample season plan for the games approach, using a 12-week season plan that includes a 2-week period for postseason play-offs.

This plan presumes that the first 3 weeks of the season will be devoted primarily to practice, with matches beginning in the 4th week. The early practices are more detailed and complete, but after playing a few matches, practice plans become more open-ended so you can focus on problems that may have occurred in past matches and can develop practices according to the game plan (see chapter 9).

Figure 7.3 shows a season plan for the games approach. Although this season plan was created in isolation, you can and should employ both traditional and games approaches when considering your season planning. For example, you may find that you are more comfortable teaching skills in a more traditional way through repetitive drilling early in the season and early in each practice, but then you move to more gamelike drilling as the season or practice progresses. Remember to work through the six steps yourself to create a season plan best suited for your team. And then be sure to extend your planning into a more detailed daily practice plan.

After completing the season plan, you can further refine step 6 of the process by adding specifics to your individual practices. The next chapter helps you in this procedure by showing the components of a good practice session and providing a sample of the games approach to practices.

Figure 7.3 Games Approach Season Plan

		Purpose	New skills to introduce
WEEK 1 – PRESEASON	**Practice 1**	Establish team and practice culture; introduce basic offensive skills	Serving, serve receive, setting, attacking
	Practice 2	Review offensive skills; introduce basic defensive skills	Blocking, digging
	Practice 3	Basic ball-control drills; introduce basic team offense	Team serve-receive patterns
	Practice 4	Basic ball-control drills; introduce basic team defense	Team defensive concepts
	Practice 5	Position training; offensive skills: serving, passing, hitting	Training by positions
	Practice 6	Position training; competition: 2v2, 3v3, 4v4	Training by positions (Keep track of individual player scores)
WEEK 2 – PRESEASON	**Practice 7**	Team serve receive with front-row attack options	Setter and hitter timing off serve receive; hitters learning shots; different types of serves
	Practice 8	Team serve receive with attack options v. blockers	Setters and hitters seeing blockers; blocking footwork
	Practice 9	Team defense against attack options	Blockers and diggers reading hitters; free-ball and down-ball reception
	Practice 10	Team defense and transition offense	Transition from blocking to hitting
	Practice 11	6v6 using one offensive system and one team defensive system	Team play concepts
	Practice 12	Scrimmage competition using various lineups (Keep player statistics)	Evaluate all players in game situations
WEEK 3 – PRESEASON	**Practice 13**	Video review of scrimmages; review basic skills	Serving, passing, setting, hitting, blocking, digging
	Practice 14	Position training; team serve receive adding back-row attack options	Back-row attackers
	Practice 15	Introduce emergency individual defensive skills; team defense v. attackers	Collapse and barrel roll
	Practice 16	Position training; team serve receive v. team defense	Focus on correcting unforced errors
	Practice 17	Introduce a second team defense	Review team defensive concepts
	Practice 18	Match warm-up, scrimmage competition using various lineups (Keep player statistics)	Match warm-up routine (Evaluate all players in game situations)
WEEK 4 – IN-SEASON	**Practice 19**	Full-team scrimmage using officials and regulation-match format	Keep player statistics
	Match 1		
	Practice 20	Video review of match; team serve-receive offense v. team defense	To be determined (TBD)
	Match 2		
	Practice 21	Video review of match; team defense v. serve-receive offense	TBD
	Matches 3, 4 & 5	Tournament	

		Purpose	New skills to introduce
WEEK 5 – IN-SEASON	**Practice 22**	Video review of matches; evaluation of unforced errors (serving, passing, hitting)	TBD (Focus on correcting unforced errors)
	Match 6		
	Practice 23	Video review of match; basic skills; position training; 6v6 drills	TBD
	Match 7		
	Practice 24	Video review of match; basic skills; position training; 6v6 drills	TBD
	Matches 8, 9 & 10	Tournament	
WEEK 6 – IN-SEASON	**Practice 25**	Video review of matches; basic skills; position training; 6v6 drills	TBD
	Match 11		
	Practice 26	Video review of match; basic skills; position training; 6v6 drills	TBD
	Match 12		
	Practice 27	Video review of match; basic skills; position training; 6v6 drills	TBD
	Practice 28	Basic skills; position training; team concepts; 6v6 drills	TBD
WEEK 7 – IN-SEASON	**Practice 29**	Basic skills; position training; team concepts; 6v6 drills	TBD
	Match 13		
	Practice 30	Video review of match; basic skills; position training; 6v6 drills	TBD
	Match 14		
	Practice 31	Video review of match; basic skills; position training; 6v6 drills	TBD
	Practice 32	Basic skills; position training; team concepts; 6v6 drills	TBD
WEEK 8 – IN-SEASON	**Match 15**		
	Practice 33	Video review of match; basic skills; position training; 6v6 drills	TBD
	Match 16		
	Practice 34	Video review of match; basic skills; position training; 6v6 drills	TBD
	Practice 35	Basic skills; position training; team concepts; 6v6 drills	TBD
	Match 17		

(continued)

Figure 7.3 *(continued)*

		Purpose	New skills to introduce
WEEK 9 – IN-SEASON	**Practice 36**	Video review of match; basic skills; position training; 6v6 drills	TBD
	Match 18		
	Practice 37	Video review of match; basic skills; position training; 6v6 drills	TBD
	Practice 38	Basic skills; position training; team concepts; 6v6 drills	TBD
	Match 19, 20 & 21		
	Practice 39	Video review of match; basic skills; position training; 6v6 drills	TBD
WEEK 10 – IN-SEASON	**Practice 40**	Basic skills; position training; team concepts; 6v6 drills	TBD
	Match 22		
	Practice 41	Video review of match; basic skills; position training; 6v6 drills	TBD
	Match 23		
	Practice 42	Video review of match; basic skills; position training; 6v6 drills	TBD
	Practice 43	Basic skills; position training; team concepts; 6v6 drills	TBD
WEEK 11 – PLAY-OFFS	**Practice 44**	Basic skills; position training; team concepts; 6v6 drills	TBD
	Match 24	District match	
	Practice 45	Video review of match; basic skills; position training; 6v6 drills	TBD
	Match 25	District match	
WEEK 12 – STATE PLAY-OFFS	**Practice 46**	Video review of match; basic skills; position training; 6v6 drills	TBD
	Practice 47	Scouting review of upcoming opponent, basic skills; position training; team concepts; 6v6 drills	TBD
	Practice 48	Basic skills; position training; team concepts; 6v6 drills	TBD
	Match 26	State championship match	

chapter **8**

Practice Plans

To get the most out of your practice sessions, you must plan every practice. Completing the season plan, as described in the last chapter, helps you do this. But you have to take that season plan a step further and specify in detail, and on paper, what you will be doing at every practice.

As described in *Successful Coaching, Third Edition*, every practice plan should include the following:

- Date, time of practice, and length of practice session
- Objective of the practice
- Equipment needed
- Warm-up
- Practice of previously taught skills
- Teaching and practicing new skills
- Cool-down
- Coaches' comments
- Evaluation of practice

Using those elements, we developed eight practice plans based on the games-approach season plan in chapter 7, beginning on page 197.

Some programs may have larger equipment such as a volleyball-tossing machine and hitting or blocking boxes or platforms that may be left on the court or stored in a storage area. The equipment listed in the practice plans does not include all this equipment but rather focuses on the equipment that needs to be brought to practice each day.

Note that these practice plans have been developed for a program of 10 to 15 players and approximately two coaches. If your program has a smaller or larger number of players or staff, you may need to tailor your practices to fit your situation better.

Please pay special attention to practice sessions that call out skills to be done by all players. In these instances, if you have players who will not do those skills in games, and you have enough coaches and court space, take those players aside and work on other more pertinent skills. For example, you will not need to have your setters working on receiving serves or your liberos working on attacking.

The following games-approach practice plans were developed based on the season plan from chapter 7. The early practices focus on volleyball as a whole, including the essential tactical skills. Then, because players need to refine technical skills, those skills are brought into the practices. When athletes play focused games early in the season, they quickly discover their weaknesses and become more motivated to improve their skills so they can perform better in game situations.

Note that research shows that prepractice sitting and static stretching do not prepare the body for the dynamic movements of volleyball. Rather, players should warm up to increase body and muscle temperature and then do five minutes maximum of individual active stretching as needed. Save the static stretching for the cool-down and flexibility training. Note that a player dealing with an injury may need to do more prepractice warming up, however.

Date

August 9

Practice Start Time

3:00 p.m.

Length of Practice

Two hours

Practice Objectives

- Team building
- Establishing practice culture by setting the tone of how you want your practices to run
- Introducing basic offensive technical skills (serving, passing, setting, hitting)
- Using the net in every drill
- Having fun

Equipment

Net standards, padding, net, antennae, volleyballs, ball cart, portable flip scoreboard

Time	Name of activity	Description	Key teaching points
3:00-3:10 p.m.	Announcements, practice partners, and team building	*Team juggle:* Players stand in a circle and toss a volleyball to another player across the circle until everyone has been involved, keeping the pattern going. Coach keeps introducing another ball to see how many they can keep going without dropping.	• Assigned practice partners ensures all have an opportunity to work with everyone else throughout the season. • Get acquainted. • Have fun. • Focus on the ball coming to you and on throwing to another player.
3:10-3:25 p.m.	Warm-up	*Short-court tipping game:* Players play 3v3 inside the attack line using only half the court and all nets; rotate groups around every 2 min.	• Warm up the body. • Make lots of contacts with the ball. • Improve ball control.
3:25-3:30 p.m.	Individual stretch	Players can use this time to stretch if needed, get a drink of water, and prepare for the next activity	• Prepare for next activity.
3:30-3:40 p.m.	Partner activity	Practice partners position at each attack line and throw and catch the ball over the net using a proper throwing motion, with elbow high, 10 times in a row without dropping the ball. Add another component after every 10 repetitions. Players call the ball by saying "Mine" before catching it; move to catch the ball in the middle of their bodies; and watch the ball all the way into their hands.	• Begin practice with concentration and focus. • Add components important for playing the game (communicating, watching the ball, moving, and so on).

(continued)

(continued)

Time	Name of activity	Description	Key teaching points
3:40-3:55 p.m.	Passing	*Butterfly passing:* Players are in groups of 3, and a player puts the ball into play using deep and short throws or serves. The 1st player throws the ball over the net, 2nd player passes it, and 3rd player sets it high outside to the target (middle of the court). Players must make 5 good passes before rotating.	• Review key points for passing skills beginning on page 55. • Work on movement up and back in the court, staying level.
3:55-4:00 p.m.	Core exercises and drink break	Practice partners do 20 slow, full sit-ups with 1 person counting and switch; 30 sec. drink break; practice partners do 20 slow push-ups with 1 person counting and switch.	• Develop core strength. • Drink break is length of time-out (30 sec.).
4:00-4:15 p.m.	Setting and attacking	*Pass, set, hit:* Player throws ball over the net to a hitter, who passes the ball to a setter. Setter sets the ball to the attack line (off the net), and the hitter attacks the ball. Hit 3 in the court and rotate so that everyone sets and hits.	• Review key points for setting skills beginning on page 63 and attacking skills beginning on page 87. • Use both sides of the net for this drill.
4:15-4:35 p.m.	Serving	*Triples:* Play 3v3 where a player on one team serves, and the 1st player on the opposing team passes the serve, 2nd person sets, and 3rd player hits the ball over. Winners stay on the court, and a new 3-player team rotates in to replace the losing team.	• Review key points for serving skills beginning on page 25. • Evaluate passing. • Work on moving on the court and problem solving. • Keep score, awarding a point for each player on the winners' side of the net.
4:35-4:40 p.m.	Core exercises and drink break	All players go to the end line and hold front bridge for 30 sec.; 2 min. drink break; all players go to the opposite end line and hold back bridge for 30 sec.	• Develop core strength. • Drink break is length of time between sets (2 min.).
4:40-4:55 p.m.	Scrimmage	Play a regulation 6v6 game with regular scoring; video scrimmage for coaches review.	• Evaluate skills. • Players need to play to improve.
4:55-5:00 p.m.	Cool-down and stretch	Players get in a circle, with 1 person leading a slow stretch.	• Cool down body temperature.
5:00 p.m.	Brief practice evaluation and announcements	Have players stand (or sit) so you can see all of them.	• Give praise for things they did well in practice. • Remind of next practice time or team activity. • Answer questions.

Date

August 10

Practice Start Time

3:00 p.m.

Length of Practice

Two hours

Practice Objectives

- Team building
- Reviewing basic offensive technical skills
- Introducing basic defensive technical skills
- Having fun

Equipment

Net standards, padding, net, antennae, volleyballs, ball cart, portable flip scoreboard

Time	Name of activity	Description	Key teaching points
3:00-3:10 p.m.	Announcements, practice partners, and team building	*Birthday lineup:* Players have 3 min. to line up along the end line according to their birthdays without talking. The players must figure out how to communicate with each other using hand signals.	• Develop nonverbal communication. • Learn more about their teammates.
3:10-3:25 p.m.	Warm-up	*Narrow-court tipping game:* Players play 3v3 using only half the court at full length and all nets; rotate groups around every 2 min.	• Warm up the body. • Make lots of contacts with the ball. • Improve ball control.
3:25-3:30 p.m.	Individual stretch	Players can use this time to stretch if needed, get a drink of water, and prepare for the next activity.	• Prepare for next activity.
3:30-3:40 p.m.	Partner activity	Practice partners position at each attack line and throw and catch the ball over the net using a proper throwing motion, with elbow high, 10 times in a row without dropping the ball. Add another component after every 10 repetitions. Players call the ball by saying "Mine" before catching it; move to catch the ball in the middle of their bodies; and watch the ball all the way into their hands.	• Begin practice with concentration and focus. • Add components important for playing the game (communicating, watching the ball, moving, and so on).

(continued)

(continued)

Time	Name of activity	Description	Key teaching points
3:40-3:55 p.m.	Defense v. live hitter	Players play 2v3. For team A, a digger positions down the line from the other team's attacker, and another player on team A sends the ball over the net, putting it in play. A passer on team B passes the ball to a setter, who sets the ball high to the left-front hitter. The hitter attacks the ball down the line toward the digger on team A. Rotate players in each of the positions after they have made 2 good contacts.	• Review key points for attacking beginning on page 88 and digging beginning on page 114. • Set ball 3 ft (.9 m) off the net so the hitter can swing without getting caught in the net. • Get feet to the ball so it is hit in front of hitting shoulder. • Hitter's arm follows through toward digger down the line. • Digger starts in a base position and moves into a defensive position, then digs the ball up to the middle of the court. • Diggers learn to read the hitters.
3:55-4:00 p.m.	Core exercises and drink break	All players go to the end line and hold left-side bridge for 30 sec.; 2-min. drink break; all players go to the opposite end line and hold right-side bridge for 30 sec.	• Develop core strength. • Drink break is length of time between sets (2 min.).
4:00-4:15 p.m.	Blocking	*Blocking circuit:* Players go through various blocking body positions while standing or sitting on the floor with practice partner; each position is held for 15 sec. for each player: 1. Player standing as partner checks for wide hands with fingers spread. Switch. 2. Player standing as partner checks for wide hands with fingers spread and wrists stiff. Switch. 3. Player standing as partner checks for wide hands with fingers spread and wrists stiff, with arms extended up overhead and strong shoulders. Switch. 4. Player lies on floor in sit-up position, and partner checks for wide hands with fingers spread and wrists stiff, with arms extended up overhead and strong shoulders. Switch. 5. Player lies on floor with legs extended and body in a pike position, and partner checks for wide hands with fingers spread and wrists stiff, with arms extended up overhead and strong shoulders. Switch. *Block jumps:* Have 3 lines of players on the court, with the first 3 at the net in ready-to-block position. Have them perform 3 block jumps with the correct technique just learned and go to the end of their line.	• Review key points for blocking beginning on page 108. • Watch technique.

Time	Name of activity	Description	Key teaching points
4:15-4:35 p.m.	1 blocker and 2 diggers v. a live hitter	Players play 3v3. For team A, a digger is positioned down the line, and one is crosscourt from the other team's attacker. A third player on team A acts as a blocker and must protect the middle of the court so the other team's attacker cannot hit the ball down in that area of the court. A player on team A sends the ball over the net, putting it in play. A passer on team B passes the ball to a setter, who sets the ball high to the left-front hitter. The hitter attacks the ball down the line or crosscourt toward one of the diggers on team A. Rotate players in each of the positions after they have made 2 good contacts. Use two courts to keep all players involved.	• Review key points for attacking beginning on page 88, blocking beginning on page 108, and digging beginning on page 114. • Set ball 3 ft. (.9 m) off the net so the hitter can swing without getting caught in the net. • Get feet to the ball so it is hit in front of hitting shoulder. • Hitter's arm follows through toward digger down the line or crosscourt. • Digger starts in a base position, moves to her defensive position in the court and then digs the ball up to the middle of the court. • Blocker focuses on getting hands over the net at the correct time. • Diggers position around the blocker so they can see the hitter and the ball. • Blocker and diggers call out where they think the ball is going to be hit based on reading the hitter.
4:35-4:40 p.m.	Core exercises and drink break	All players go to the end line and hold front bridge for 30 sec.; 2-min. drink break; all players go to the opposite end line and hold back bridge for 30 sec.	• Develop core strength. • Drink break is length of time between sets (2 min.).
4:40-4:55 p.m.	Scrimmage	Play a regulation 6v6 game with bonus points for a block or a dig to the target (middle of the court) during a rally.	• Review key points for serving, passing, and hitting. • Evaluate skills players need to play to work on more.
4:55-5:00 p.m.	Cool-down and stretch	Players get in a circle, with 1 person leading a slow stretch.	• Cool down body temperature.
5:00 p.m.	Brief practice evaluation and announcements	Have players stand (or sit) so you can see all of them.	• Give praise for things they did well in practice. • Remind of next practice time or team activity. • Answer questions.

PRACTICE PLAN 3

Date

August 11

Practice Start Time

3:00 p.m.

Length of Practice

Two hours

Practice Objectives

- Team building
- Reviewing basic defensive technical skills
- Introducing a basic team offense
- Overlapping on serve receive
- Serve-receive responsibilities
- Hitter coverage
- Having fun

Equipment

Net standards, padding, net, antennae, volleyballs, ball cart, portable flip scoreboard

Time	Name of activity	Description	Key teaching points
3:00-3:10 p.m.	Announcements, practice partners, and team building	*Back-to-back communication:* Players sit on the floor back-to-back with a partner so that one person is facing the coach and the other is facing away, holding a sheet of paper and a pencil or pen. The coach holds up a sheet of paper with different shapes drawn on it. One partner describes it to the other, who tries to draw it by listening to the partner's directions. Players have 2 min. and then switch roles using a different diagram.	• Learn to communicate clearly and specifically. • Learn to listen carefully. • Learn how to communicate better with teammates and coaches.
3:10-3:25 p.m.	Over-the-net, on-the-ground pepper	Players play 3v3, using only half the court at full length and all nets. The ball is tossed up and hit over the net, dug, set, and standing-hit over the net, continuing in this fashion for 2 min.	• Warm up the body. • Make lots of contacts with the ball. • Improve ball control. • Read the hit coming over the net. • Move to get into a good position to play the ball on each contact.
3:25-3:30 p.m.	Individual stretch	Players can use this time to stretch if needed, get a drink of water, and prepare for the next activity.	• Prepare for next activity.

216

Time	Name of activity	Description	Key teaching points
3:30-3:40 p.m.	6-person pepper	All the players are on the same side of the court, spread out in their normal positions, except the 2 outside players at the net face away from the net toward their back-row teammates. Those two players act as hitters, and one player in middle front sets the dug ball back to either hitter at the net. The rest of the players on the court read and dig the ball up to the setter. This can continue until they have dug up a certain number of balls. The team rotates so everyone gets to practice every position or plays for a set time (e.g., 1 min.) in each position.	• Players start in base defense positions on the court. • Defensive players need to read and call out where they think the ball is being hit. • Players receive lots of opportunities to learn to control their hitting, digging, and setting. • Ensures lots of reading and defensive movement on the court.
3:40-3:55 p.m.	15 perfect passes	Divide your team in half. Half the players are servers and the other half are passers. For the passing team, 3 players position on the court with a setter, and the rest of the players wait off the court along the sidelines. A player on the serving team serves a ball over the net, and one of the 3 passers must receive the ball and pass it to the setter. The passers get a point for each perfect pass to the setter, and a point is deducted for an ace or a ball that is passed back over the net. When the ball is passed to the setter, she sets a high ball to the right or left side of the court, and the players along the sidelines can gather the balls. The goal is to get to 15 perfect passes. Start with a lower number if needed.	• Review key points for serving skills beginning on page 25 and serve-receive skills beginning on page 55. • Make sure serves are aggressive, but watch for too many serving errors. • Use a portable scoreboard to keep track of points or perfect passes.
3:55-4:00 p.m.	Core exercises and drink break	All players go to the end line and do crunches for 30 sec.; 2-min. drink break; all players go to opposite end line and do full push-ups for 30 sec.	• Develop core strength. • Drink break is length of time between sets (2 min.).
4:00-4:30 p.m.	Offensive team concepts	Place a full team on the court based on the positions of the team offense that will be used (5-1, 6-2, and so on), and set up a team-serve reception pattern (3 or 4 passers). Have a player send an easy ball over the net so the setter can transition into the target position and set to one of the hitters. Rotate players around after 5 receptions until they are back to their starting positions.	• Discuss overlapping on serve reception. • Discuss seam responsibilities for serve reception. • Discuss hitter coverage responsibilities.

(continued)

(continued)

Time	Name of activity	Description	Key teaching points
4:30-4:35 p.m.	Core exercises and drink break	All players stand in a squat position at the end line and hold for 30 sec.; 2-min. drink break; all players go the opposite end line and do front lunge steps for 30 sec.	• Develop leg strength. • Drink break is length of time between sets (2 min.).
4:35-4:55 p.m.	Scrimmage	Play a regulation 6v6 game with regular scoring. Decide on a focus for this game, such as communicating what is open for the hitter, covering the hitter, etc.	• Evaluate skills. • Video record scrimmage and keep statistics (serving, passing, hitting, and so on). • Players need to play in a game situation to improve.
4:55-5:00 p.m.	Cool-down and stretch	Players get in a circle, with 1 person leading a slow stretch	• Cool down body temperature.
5:00 p.m.	Brief practice evaluation and announcements	Have players stand (or sit) so you can see all of them.	• Give praise for things they did well in practice. • Remind of next practice time or team activity. • Answer questions.

Date

August 12

Practice Start Time

3:00 p.m.

Length of Practice

Two hours

Practice Objectives

- Team building
- Reviewing basic team offense
- Basic ball-control drills
- Introducing basic team defense
- Having fun

Equipment

Net standards, padding, net, antennae, volleyballs, ball cart, portable flip scoreboard

Time	Name of activity	Description	Key teaching points
3:00-3:10 p.m.	Announcements, practice partners, and team building	Pass out a player questionnaire with a series of questions for each player to answer such as favorite food, favorite music, best vacation, favorite subject in school, and so on.	• Learn more about teammates.
3:10-3:25 p.m.	Warm-up	*Short-court tipping game*: Players play 3v3 inside the attack line using only half the court and all nets; rotate groups around every 2 min.	• Warm up the body. • Make lots of contacts with the ball. • Improve ball control.
3:25-3:30 p.m.	Individual stretch	Players can use this time to stretch if needed, get a drink of water, and prepare for the next activity.	• Prepare for next activity.
3:30-3:40 p.m.	3 deep with setter	Players are in groups of 4, with 3 players positioned in the back row (behind the attack line) and one player as a setter. An extra player serves the ball over the net, and one of the 3 deep players digs the ball to the setter, who can dump the ball back over the net or set to one of the 3 hitters in the back row, who will attack it over the net. If players miss a dig, set, or hit, the coach gives them another ball to play so they can have an opportunity to perform the skill better. Other players stand along the sidelines to gather balls and will enter the game on the coach's instruction.	• Players get an opportunity to experience success when the coach gives them another ball. • Review key points for serving, passing, setting, attacking, reading, and defensive skills from chapters 3 through 6. • Work on transition movement for all players.

(continued)

(continued)

Time	Name of activity	Description	Key teaching points
3:40-3:55 p.m.	Offensive team concepts review	Repeat drill from previous day reviewing all the concepts.	• Review team serve-receive passing responsibilities. • Review overlapping. • Review seam passing responsibilities. • Review hitter coverage.
3:55-4:00 p.m.	Core exercises and drink break	All players go to the end line and do lateral lunge steps for 30 sec.; 2-min. drink break; all players go to the opposite end line and do tuck jumps for 30 sec.	• Develop leg strength. • Drink break is length of time between sets (2 min.).
4:00-4:30 p.m.	Defensive team concepts	Place 6 players on the court and have them move as the concepts are discussed; switch front- and back-row players. Rotate players in from off the court each time, or have them shadow the movements outside the court. Have a player throw a ball over the net, and have them dig the ball up to the target (middle of the court). Have them continue and play the ball over the net if they are ready for the transition from defense to offense.	• Teach basic team defensive concepts (p. 162). • Discuss base positions. • Discuss positioning around the blockers. • Discuss seam responsibilities. • Discuss pursuit rule (going for every ball).
4:30-4:35 p.m.	Core exercises and drink break	All players go to the end line and hold front bridge for 30 sec; 2 min. drink break; all players go to the end line and hold back bridge for 30 sec.	• Develop core strength. • Drink break is length of time between sets (2 min.).
4:35-4:55 p.m.	6v6 wash drill	Play regulation 6v6 game. The team that wins the first rally has to win a free-ball rally in order to score a point and rotate. If they do not win the free-ball rally, it is called a "wash," and neither team rotates. The team that rotates the most times wins the game.	• Evaluate skills. • Players need to play the game to improve.
4:55-5:00 p.m.	Cool-down and stretch	Players get in a circle, with 1 person leading a slow stretch.	• Cool down body temperature.
5:00 p.m.	Brief practice evaluation and announcements	Have players stand (or sit) so you can see all of them.	• Give praise for things they did well in practice. • Remind of next practice time or team activity. • Answer questions.

Date

August 13

Practice Start Time

3:00 p.m.

Length of Practice

Two hours

Practice Objectives

- Team building
- Position training
- Reviewing offensive skills (serving, passing, and hitting)
- Reviewing basic team defense
- Having fun

Equipment

Net standards, padding, net, antennae, volleyballs, ball cart, portable flip scoreboard

Time	Name of activity	Description	Key teaching points
3:00-3:10 p.m.	Announcements, practice partners, and team building	*Human knot:* Players form a circle, standing shoulder to shoulder. Each player places a hand in the middle of the circle and grasps another player's hand. Players then put the other hand in the middle, grasping a different player's hand. Now they attempt to untangle themselves without letting go. If done correctly, when untangled they will be in a circle.	• Teach players how to work together. • Build group understanding of communication, leadership, problem solving, team work, trust and persistence.
3:10-3:25 p.m.	Free balls to target	Players get in three lines behind the end line and move into the court to pass a free ball coming over the net when the person in front of them completes a pass. The ball is sent over by a player across the net. After passing the ball, they must jog to the back wall and return to the end of another line before they enter the court to pass another free ball. The goal is to get 20 perfect passes to the target area as a team.	• Warm up the body. • Make lots of contacts with the ball. • Improve ball control.
3:25-3:30 p.m.	Individual stretch	Players can use this time to stretch if needed, get a drink of water, and prepare for the next activity.	• Prepare for next activity.

(continued)

(continued)

Time	Name of activity	Description	Key teaching points
3:30-3:40 p.m.	Over-the-net, *crosscourt*, on-the-ground pepper	Players play 3v3, using only half the full-length court and all nets. The ball is tossed up and hit *crosscourt* over the net, dug, set, and standing hit-crosscourt over the net, continuing in this fashion for 2 min.	• Warm up the body. • Make lots of contacts with the ball. • Improve ball control. • Work on reading the hit coming over the net. • Move to get into a good position to play the ball on each contact. • Improve hitting and digging crosscourt.
3:40-3:55 p.m.	Position training	• Middles, libero, and setters work on one court for timing of sets. The ball is sent over the net by a player to the libero, who passes to the setter. The middle player comes from a serve receive position near the net and transitions off the net to hit the ball around a blocker. Middle players rotate blocking and hitting and rotate after attempting 5 hits, 5 block attempts, and so on. • Outsides and defensive specialists are on another court, serving and passing in groups of 3.	• Setters focus on timing of sets to middle and outside hitters. • Outside hitters and defensive specialists work on their serving and serve reception. • There is one coach on each court to work with groups.
3:55-4:00 p.m.	Core exercises and drink break	All players go to the end line and hold a full push-up position for 30 sec.; 2-min. drink break; all players go to the opposite end line and hold a full push-up position in the down position for 30 sec.	• Develop upper body and core strength. • Drink break is length of time between sets (2 min.).

Time	Name of activity	Description	Key teaching points
4:00-4:30 p.m.	Team defense v. 4	Play 6v4, with 6 players playing defense for team A and 3 hitters and 1 setter playing offense for team B. Team A serves to team B, and one of the 3 players passes the ball to the setter, who dumps it over the net or sets it so that one of the hitters can attack it over the net. Team A attempts to block the ball or digs it to the target (middle of the court) for a point. Team B scores if they get a kill v. the defense. Rotate or switch out players after 5 points.	• Review team defense concepts. • Defensive team works on reading, moving, and blocking and digging the ball up. • They can play the ball out, but they get a point if they dig the ball up to the target area successfully.
4:30-4:35 p.m.	Core exercises and drink break	All players go to the end line and hold front bridge for 30 sec.; 2-min. drink break; all players go to the end line and hold back bridge for 30 sec.	• Develop core strength. • Drink break is length of time between sets (2 min.).
4:35-4:55 p.m.	Scrimmage	Regulation 6v6 game with regular scoring. Have a certain focus for the players either offensively or defensively.	• Video to evaluate skills. • Players need to play the game to improve.
4:55-5:00 p.m.	Cool-down and stretch	Players get in a circle, with 1 person leading a slow stretch.	• Cool down body temperature.
5:00 p.m.	Brief practice evaluation and announcements	Have players stand (or sit) so you can see all of them.	• Give praise for things they did well in practice. • Remind of next practice time or team activity. • Answer questions.

Date

August 14

Practice Start Time

3:00 p.m.

Length of Practice

Two hours

Practice Objectives

- Team building
- Position training
- Competition (2v2 and 4v4)
- Having fun

Equipment

Net standards, padding, net, antennae, volleyballs, ball cart, portable flip scoreboard, bingo cards, pencils

Time	Name of activity	Description	Key teaching points
3:00-3:10 p.m.	Announcements, practice partners, and team building	*People bingo:* One coach creates a 5 by 5 sheet of squares with 25 interesting traits that describe different aspects of the players and staff they shared with the coach but that others may not know (e.g., plays the bongos, once lived in Sweden, has a karate trophy, is a twin, won a science fair). Players have 5 min. to figure out which players have that particular characteristic and place the player's name in the corresponding box. The first player to fill five boxes across or down yells "Bingo!" and the game is over.	• Getting to know new things about their teammates and coaches.
3:10-3:25 p.m.	Run-throughs	One player is on the other side of the net with a basket of balls. The other players line up along one sideline. The player at the net stands and tips the ball over the net and the first player in line moves forward to receive a ball that is tipped. The player runs in and passes it to the target (middle of the court) and jogs off the court back to the end of the line. After 10 good passes up to the target area, switch the players to the other sideline and replace the player at the net.	• Warm up the body. • Make lots of contacts with the ball. • Improve ball control. • Stay on their feet to play the ball. • Learn the angle of the arms needed to pass the ball to the middle of the court.

Time	Name of activity	Description	Key teaching points
3:25-3:30 p.m.	Individual stretch	Players can use this time to stretch if needed, get a drink of water, and prepare for the next activity.	• Prepare for next activity.
3:30-3:50 p.m.	Position training	• Middles, libero, and setters work on one court for timing of sets. The ball is sent over the net by a player to the libero, who passes to the setter. The middle player comes from a serve receive position near the net and transitions off the net to hit the ball around a blocker. Middle players rotate blocking and hitting and rotate after 5 hits, 5 blocks, and so on. • Outsides and defensive specialists are on another court, serving and passing in groups of 3. • Middles and outsides switch after 10 min. so outsides can work with setters and middles can work on blocking footwork on the other court.	• Setters focus on timing of sets to middle and outside hitters. • Outside hitters and defensive specialists work on their serving and serve reception. • There is one coach on each court to work with groups.
3:50-3:55 p.m.	Core exercises and drink break	All players go to the end line and hold a left-side bridge for 30 sec.; 2-min. drink break; all players go to the opposite end line and hold a right-side bridge for 30 sec.	• Develop core strength. • Drink break is length of time between sets (2 min.).
3:55-4:20 p.m.	2v2 competition	Play 2v2 on all available courts, playing narrow-court doubles by placing an antenna in the middle of the net to create the narrow court and some floor tape to divide the court. Play a rally-scoring game to 7 points.	• Have a round-robin doubles competition. • Keep track of wins and losses for each team. • Players needing more individual work on ball control will become evident.
4:20-4:25 p.m.	Core exercises and drink break	All players go to the end line and do twisting sit-ups for 30 sec.; 2-min. drink break; all players go to the opposite end line and do stomach crunches for 30 sec.	• Develop core strength. • Drink break is length of time between sets (2 min.).
4:25-4:55 p.m.	4v4 competition	Create even groups of 4 players by combining 2 doubles teams based on wins from 2v2 competition. Play rally-scoring games to 10, and rotate teams on the court.	• Have a round-robin competition. • Keep track of wins and losses for each team.
4:55-5:00 p.m.	Cool-down and stretch	Players get in a circle, with 1 person leading a slow stretch.	• Cool down body temperature.
5:00 p.m.	Brief practice evaluation and announcements	Have players stand (or sit) so you can see all of them.	• Give praise for things they did well in practice. • Remind of next practice time or team activity. • Answer questions.

Date

August 15

Practice Start Time

3:00 p.m.

Length of Practice

Two hours

Practice Objectives

- Team building
- Ball control
- Small-group competition
- Team serve receive with front-row attack options
- Having fun

Equipment

Net standards, padding, net, antennae, volleyballs, ball cart, portable flip scoreboard

Time	Name of activity	Description	Key teaching points
3:00-3:10 p.m.	Announcements, practice partners, and team building	*Clusters or clumps:* Coach calls out a number between 2 and the total number of players on the team. Players must immediately get in groups of that number (e.g., 4 means that 4 players get in a group as quickly as they can); whoever is left out of the groups must do 5 sit-ups. Keep repeating using different numbers for a few minutes.	• Quickly respond to the number the coach yells out. • Follow directions quickly.
3:10-3:25 p.m.	Warm-up	*Short-court tipping game:* Players play 3v3 inside the attack line using only half the court and all nets; rotate groups around every 2 min.	• Warm up the body. • Make lots of contacts with the ball. • Improve ball control. • Learn to move around the net.
3:25-3:30 p.m.	Individual stretch	Players can use this time to stretch if needed, get a drink of water, and prepare for the next activity.	• Prepare for next activity.
3:30-3:40 p.m.	Warm-up hitting	3 players start at the attack line on one side of a court. They self-toss the ball up near the net, make an approach, and hit it, rotating out after 5 hits. Other players at the opposite end line pick up the balls and keep them from rolling under the net.	• Toss the ball up and toward the net with the hitting hand. • Make a full approach to hit the ball over the net. • Reach, hit, and snap the wrist over the ball to hit it down over the net.
3:40-3:55 p.m.	3v3 competition	Play 3v3 on all available courts. Play rally-scoring games to 10, and rotate teams on the court.	• Have a round-robin competition. • Keep track of wins and losses for each team. • Have players work on different types of serves.

Time	Name of activity	Description	Key teaching points
3:55-4:00 p.m.	Core exercises and drink break	All players go to the end line and do lateral lunges for 30 sec.; 2-min. drink break; all players go to the opposite end line and do forward lunges for 30 sec.	• Develop lower-body strength. • Drink break is length of time between sets (2 min.).
4:00-4:20 p.m.	1 min. passing	1 player is ready to serve outside each of the 4 corners of the court, with a supply of volleyballs, and 1 passer is positioned in each court to receive serves. 1 server starts play by serving the ball down the line to the passer on the other side of the net. The passer attempts to pass the ball and quickly shuffles in a low position toward the other sideline. This pattern continues, with servers serving the next ball as soon as the passer has passed the previous serve. Continue for 1 min. and rotate players. The drill continues until each player has been through as a passer 4 times.	• Review key points for serving and passing from chapter 3. • A coach or player watches the target area (middle of the court) on each side of the net to count the number of perfect passes each passer makes. • Keep statistics on passers. • Passers must concentrate on each ball served and stay low as they move across the court after each pass.
4:20-4:25 p.m.	Core exercises and drink break	All players go to the end line and hold front bridge for 30 sec.; 2-min. drink break; all players to to the end line and hold back bridge for 30 sec.	• Develop core strength. • Drink break is length of time between sets (2 min.).
4:25-4:55 p.m.	Team serve receive	Divide teams up evenly. Play a 6v6 game, with one team needing to score on 3 out of 5 serve receptions to rotate. The serving team or the receiving teams that loses that small game steps off the court and does 5 sit-ups, push-ups, or tuck jumps before stepping back out onto the court to try again. Work on each team getting through 2-3 rotations they need to work on the most.	• Evaluate skills. • Keep statistics on serving, passing, and hitting, and work to see what offensive options are working well. • Video scrimmage.
4:55-5:00 p.m.	Cool-down and stretch	Players get in a circle, with 1 person leading a slow stretch.	• Cool down body temperature.
5:00 p.m.	Brief practice evaluation and announcements	Have players stand (or sit) so you can see all of them.	• Give praise for things they did well in practice. • Remind of next practice time or team activity. • Answer questions.

PRACTICE PLAN 8

Date

August 16

Practice Start Time

3:00 p.m.

Length of Practice

Two hours

Practice Objectives

- Team building
- Ball control
- Team serve receive with attack options versus blockers and diggers
- Having fun

Equipment

Net standards, padding, net, antennae, volleyballs, ball cart, portable flip scoreboard

Time	Name of activity	Description	Key teaching points
3:00-3:10 p.m.	Announcements, practice partners, and team building	*Team mission:* Players take time to discuss their team mission for the season and make a list of 5 things they will each commit to doing to achieve that mission.	• Focus on season goals. • Identify what it will take to get there. • Remind players of their team mission in practice.
3:10-3:25 p.m.	Warm-up	*Short-court tipping game:* Players play 3v3 inside the attack line using only half the court and all nets; rotate groups around every 2 min.	• Warm up the body. • Make lots of contacts with the ball. • Improve ball control.
3:25-3:30 p.m.	Individual stretch	Players can use this time to stretch if needed, get a drink of water, and prepare for the next activity.	• Prepare for next activity.
3:30-3:55 p.m.	Ball-control tip scrimmage	Players on team A start in team defense and send the ball over the net to team B, who attempt to make a perfect pass to the setter. If the pass is good, the setter sets the ball to a hitter, who tips the ball over the net back to team A, who attempt to make a perfect pass to their setter and so on. The coach stops the drill if the pass is not made properly to the setter, and the drill starts over. After 3-5 passes for each team, switch front and back rows. You can also add proper coverage of the hitters for the drill to continue.	• Work on ball control for a slow-moving ball. • Work on good court movement while reading the hitter.

Time	Name of activity	Description	Key teaching points
3:55-4:00 p.m.	Core exercises and drink break	All players go to the end line and hold a right-side bridge for 30 sec.; 2-min. drink break; all players go to the opposite end line and hold a left-side bridge for 30 sec.	• Develop core strength. • Drink break is length of time between sets (2 min.).
4:00-4:30 p.m.	Attack options v. blockers	Divide players into 3 lines of hitters near the net who will transition off the net and attack the ball after it is sent over the net to a passer and set by a setter. The hitter must be ready to hit against blockers and diggers positioned on the other side of the net.	• Only attempt tactically what your team can do technically—this is the time to see what that might be. • Review placement of sets and timing of attacks.
4:30-4:35 p.m.	Core exercises and drink break	All players go to the end line and do full sit-ups for 30 sec.; 2-min. drink break; all players go to the opposite end line and do full push-ups for 30 sec.	• Develop core strength. • Drink break is length of time between sets (2 min.).
4:35-4:55 p.m.	3 before 5	Put a starting line up together and play 6v6, where the starting team must receive the serve and score 3 points before the serving team scores 5 points. When the receiving team scores 3 points, they rotate and continue the drill receiving serves and working on their offense. The losing team has a quick consequence, such as a sprint to the opposite wall or 10 tuck jumps or 10 lunges.	• Evaluate skills. • Keep statistics on certain skills (serving, passing, hitting, and so on).
4:55-5:00 p.m.	Cool-down and stretch	Players get in a circle, with 1 person leading a slow stretch.	• Cool down body temperature.
5:00 p.m.	Brief practice evaluation and announcements	Have players stand (or sit) so you can see all of them.	• Give praise for things they did well in practice. • Remind of next practice time or team activity. • Answer questions.

PART V

Coaching Matches

You can plan and have your players practice all day long, but if they do not perform to the best of their abilities during matches, what has all that planning done for you? Part V helps you prepare players for match situations.

Chapter 9 teaches you how to prepare long before the first match, addressing concepts such as communication, scouting opponents, and creating a game plan. Chapter 10 teaches you how to prepare your players for situations before, during, and after the match such as a prematch warm-up routine, substitution protocol, and tactical changes you may make as a coach.

After all the preparation you have done, match day is when it really becomes exciting, especially if you and your players are ready for the challenge.

Preparing for Matches

The performance of a volleyball team on game day reflects its preparation during practices. A well-prepared team will be fundamentally sound, organized, and efficient, opening the game with a strong offensive attack and handling critical situations effectively because the players have rehearsed those skills and situations. If practices in preparation for the match have been effective, the coach will be able to sit back and watch the team perform while offering some timely advice and feedback. Following are the areas you should consider when preparing yourself and your team for a game.

Communication

As a coach, you must communicate well at many levels—with players and team captains, parents, your coaching staff, game officials, school and community officials, and the media. You must be aware of your nonverbal communication, which can be just as loud as what you say with your voice. Make an effort to keep your communication positive and encouraging to your players. They will work hard for you as a coach if you help them gain more confidence in themselves.

Players

When you communicate well, you engage your players in the learning process. When players become partners and have a stake in their own development, you become a facilitator, not merely a trainer. The players' participation in the learning process is the key to the games approach and what makes it such a valuable approach to coaching. Although shaping, focusing, and enhancing play is difficult, and it may take a bit more time and patience for the players' internalized learning process to occur, this is ultimately more rewarding because it allows players to take ownership of their development. It is important that you begin to ask the players more questions and stop giving them the answers for how to do things without making them think. You will actually be coaching smarter, and your teams will respond by playing smarter.

As part of the communication process, you may want to assemble a team handbook that covers your coaching philosophy, the season match schedule, the season practice schedule, basic skill techniques, offensive and defensive systems, the season training plan, volleyball terminology, and various tactics. Distribute this resource to players several weeks before the first day of practice. The manual should not be too long because the longer it is, the less likely the athletes are to read it. Meet with players often, possibly individually, by position and as a team, and encourage them to study the manual thoroughly. Use a three-ring binder so they can continue to add material throughout the season.

Before the beginning of a season, you should prepare a list of expectations that outlines the policies you expect players to follow. The term *expectations* is preferable to the term *rules*, which conveys a sense of rigidity. The term *expectations* also communicates to players that they are responsible for living up to them. The coaching staff must reinforce expectations daily so they become second nature to the team. Any breaches of discipline that arise should be handled immediately and evenhandedly. You must treat all players alike, starters no differently from subs. It is highly encouraged that the team members be involved in determining the expectations and team rules. Players are more likely to follow rules they helped develop and believe in.

In addition, the selection of the right captain or captains is critical for a team's success. It is important the team understands the roles and responsibilities of the captains. Players should be asked to write down whom they feel they would like as their team captain and why they selected those people. Those players must have "personal power" with the team if you expect the team to follow them. If they have personal power, they can then assist you in communicating with the team. However, just because an athlete is a great player, or one who is well liked by teammates, does not mean she is automatically a good leader or captain. You need to devote time to developing and training captains and leadership skills. Take time to look for younger players who may become captains as they get older to make sure you are laying the groundwork for them. Emphasize to captains that their main role is to help make their teammates better players. Show captains the many ways to accomplish that—by encouraging teammates, helping them work on their skills, supporting them, and modeling good practice habits.

Parents

Before the season begins, you should schedule a preseason meeting with the parents of all volleyball players, separate from the meeting that most schools already sponsor during each sport season. A few weeks before the season begins, mail a letter to the homes of players, with an RSVP attached. This personal touch will pique the interest of parents and make them feel valuable to the program. A special invitation letter should go to the superintendent, the principal, and the athletic director, who should be present to explain school policies, athletic codes, and general school issues.

Prepare an agenda for this meeting, and follow it to keep the meeting on track and to convey to parents a sense of your organizational ability. Besides setting an agenda, you should prepare and distribute material outlining the roles of parents, players, and coaches. Parents want to be involved in their child's progress, so stating the method of communication between parent and coach is important. Having a good orientation session will contribute to a successful relationship with the parents. The communication between coaches and all parents should continue throughout the season on a regular basis.

Coaching Staff

Coaches need to constantly communicate with their assistants. Each season, you should hold a formal preseason meeting with your coaching staff to outline expectations and responsibilities as well as program goals for the season. Discuss your coaching philosophy, staff expectations, and specific techniques you will emphasize, especially if changes have occurred from the previous year or if new members have joined the staff. You should write out the roles of assistants or volunteer coaches, including how to deal with parents, who should be referred to you. Assistants should be firm and fast in noting breaches of discipline and bringing them to your attention. Assistant coaches need to keep the head coach informed, with no surprises. Loyalty to the head coach is key to having a good staff. Although you can disagree in private, it is imperative to show a united staff to the team and parents. Consider using players who may not make the team as your managers. They can serve a useful role in a variety of ways and enjoy their experience with the team even though they may not be on the court.

Game Officials

Coaches must also communicate well with officials. You should treat officials as the professionals they are, even when they have made a mistake. When questioning a ruling, approach the official slowly and respectfully. If the rules do not allow you to speak with the official directly, make sure your captain is respectful. Players, parents, and even fans will model your behavior with officials. Because most states and leagues provide outlets for evaluation of officials, you can address shortcomings and commendations of officials through that process.

Community and Media

Involvement with the community and the media demands that you be a good communicator. You speak each day the way you behave. If you become rattled or easily frustrated, players will assume that demeanor. If you are coolheaded, the players will be calm too. By maintaining composure, you convey an attitude of control under pressure even in intense, challenging situations.

You should be accommodating to the press and instruct players in how to talk with the media. Players need to understand that the role of the media may come in conflict with the goals and expectations of the team. Players should respectfully answer questions that deal with matches but defer questions about philosophy or game management to the coaching staff. Your athletes must be careful not to say anything disrespectful about an opponent that might find its way onto an opposing team's locker room bulletin board.

Scouting an Opponent

Another essential step in preparing for matches is scouting. Scouting helps eliminate the element of surprise from the game equation. Most of the scouting for volleyball teams today is done using video analysis. By reviewing match footage, you can develop more accurate scouting reports than you can by watching matches in person, allowing you to better prepare your team for competition.

The most important element of scouting is the breakdown, or evaluation, of the video. The final scouting report may come in different forms, from fancy computer spreadsheets to handwritten notes, but it will be only as accurate and meaningful as the information recorded on the original breakdown. Allowing the team to watch the video and develop their own scouting report gives the players ownership of the game plan. The players are able to focus on their own position and what they need to do to be successful in the match. A combination scouting report with input from the coaches and the players is the best way to prepare for an opponent.

The coaching staff must first decide what elements they are going to chart as they break down the video. Most breakdowns include the following about the opponents:

- Who are their players (setter, middles, outsides, right side [opposite], and libero or defensive specialist)?
- What do their serve-receive formations look like?
- Who are their best and worst passers?
- What are their plays from serve reception by each rotation?
- Who are their favorite hitters, and what do they hit in each rotation?
- Who do they set as their back-row attackers?
- What are their free-ball plays?
- What do they do on a down ball?
- What blocking systems do they use?
- What team defense or defenses do they play? Does it vary based on hitters?
- What are the strengths and weaknesses of blockers by rotation?
- Where are the open areas of the court on defense?
- What are the matchups favored by rotation?

The scouting report must also include an evaluation of the opponent's serving game because many games are won or lost on receiving serves. This should include different types of servers (jump, floater, topspin, and so on) and where they serve from. Any other serving tendencies should be noted.

Finally, no scouting report is complete until you have completed a self-scout of your team's tendencies, which your opponent will be evaluating. Although the self-scout doesn't have to be as elaborate or detailed as the scouting report on the opponent, you should prepare it carefully, consider it in the game plan, and make an effort to break the tendencies your team has established in previous games. Think like your opponent will, and ask yourself, *How would I beat this defense?* Otherwise, the opponent will have the advantage on game day of knowing what you are going to do before you do it.

Developing the Game Plan

After completing and analyzing the scouting report, the coaching staff begins the process of developing a game plan for the opponent. You formulate the game plan by carefully considering the scouting report, your overall strategy, and your team's offensive and defensive capabilities. The game plan, simply put, is the particular concepts you have chosen to give your team the best chance for success against the systems the opponent uses. Remember, only attempt to do tactically what your team can do technically. Keeping the game plan simple and reducing unforced errors on your side of the net gives your team a better chance of being successful. The game plan should include a serving strategy, an offensive strategy, a defensive or blocking strategy, and a reminder of the key things the team must do to be successful during the match.

Controlling Your Team's Performance

By establishing a consistent routine on match day, you help your athletes prepare themselves physically, mentally, and emotionally for their best possible performance. You have great flexibility in designing your pregame ritual. Whatever schedule you choose, staying with that schedule for the entire season is more important than its actual elements. When the team is on the road, your routine should remain as similar as possible to the one used at home. This regularity produces consistency in performance that might not exist if the timetable were erratic. See "Sample Prematch Routine" for a routine you may want to use with your team.

SAMPLE PREMATCH ROUTINE

Routine should become part of the events leading up to the match itself to provide a comfortable atmosphere and help players feel relaxed and ready to give their best. Following is a suggested routine for the hours leading up to a match.

Three to Four Hours Before the Match

Players should eat a meal that provides them with the proper diet and nutrition for a strong performance in volleyball. This meal should include food that is comfortable for each player. If players get in the habit of eating the same meal at the same time before every game, they will learn exactly how much to eat and what choices to make so they feel their best throughout the contest. This may be something you need to discuss with the parents. For more information on your athletes' diet, refer to chapter 16, "Fueling Your Athletes," beginning on page 357 of Rainer Martens' *Successful Coaching, Third Edition* (Champaign, IL: Human Kinetics, 2004).

One Hour Before the Match

After meeting in the locker room or quiet area to quickly review the game plan, players should take to the court to warm up an hour before the match. The warm-up should get the players used to the court surroundings, serving and passing, setting various attacks, and playing defense. The warm-up should end in time for the team to return to the sideline bench for final details and instructions. Having the team leaders help design the prematch warm-up will make sure the players are involved in activities that get them mentally and physically prepared for the match.

During a match is not the time to offer criticism. You may desire outstanding performance during the game, but if you berate players' mistakes during a match, their performance will likely diminish rather than improve for the rest of that day. Instead, allow time during practice the day after the match to critique the players, point out errors, and provide suggestions for improvement and elimination of mistakes. A good rule to use is "praise in front of the team, and criticize in private." Take a player aside if you need to be critical of his play and you think it will help him improve.

Team Building and Motivation

All the best game planning and physical training will not produce successful performance on match day unless the athletes work together and are inspired to play hard. We talked earlier in this chapter about preparing players for their responsibilities in the game plan, but you need to extend your planning for the match into the mental area as well. Although a motivating talk right before the match might produce an early burst of energized play, the physical demands of the match require a more substantial basis for the players to keep playing hard. Work to give a consistent pregame talk, reviewing key points necessary for players to be successful during the match. These points should also be the topics discussed during time-outs. By always referring to the game plan, you can keep the team focused on the right concepts.

As players work during the week to prepare for certain opponents, they have to know why it is important to grasp the concepts and learn how to execute the plays. They must make the connection between preparation and performance and realize they can reach their goals only if they practice diligently and deliberately. Then, when match time comes, they are confident in their abilities, committed to the goal, and ready to play the match.

Despite your best efforts to plan and prepare your team, one factor trumps everything else in the sport of volleyball. One of the main reasons young people play volleyball is that they enjoy the friendship, camaraderie, competition, and life lessons they share with their teammates. Because they go through tough and exciting experiences together, both positive and negative, they develop deep and committed bonds of friendship. The commitment of team members to each other is the most powerful form of motivation in sport. You must strive to find ways to encourage and enhance opportunities for players to spend time together, work to break down barriers between isolated groups on the team, and help players develop the kind of friendships that will last a lifetime.

chapter 10

Before, During, and After the Match

The three-step tactical triangle approach to analyzing a game situation detailed earlier in this book (in chapter 1 on page 6) creates a blueprint for you and your players to follow in making important decisions on match day. As the triangle shows, inevitably, you will need to accurately read the cues presented, apply technical and tactical knowledge on the spot, and adjust your game plan accordingly by making immediate decisions. The logical format of the triangle helps you slow the speed of the game and apply organized, logical thinking to several key situations that commonly occur before, during, and after your matches.

Before the Match

For a team to be prepared physically and mentally, there are several areas a coach needs to plan for such as a good game warm-up and a starting lineup to begin the match.

Warm-Up

Pay attention as the opponents warm up to see if you can pick up anything you may not have noted in the scouting report. This is a final opportunity to see if you need to be prepared to make any tactical changes as the match progresses. The opponents may have learned some new skills, or there may be other players getting ready to start because of injuries. During a drink break off the court, plan to have your athletes watch the opposing team's warm-up to see if they can read the players and to think about how they will respond to situations they see during the match. This is also the time to make sure your team is warming up properly. You can tell if the players are focused and ready to begin strongly.

Starting Lineup

The starting lineup will have players in a certain rotational order on the court based on their positions and the offense your team is playing. The starting rotation is a decision you need to make based on a variety of things such as starting with your strongest server serving first or in the rotation that you usually score the most points in, or the order may be based on matching players up with their opponents to take advantage of your strengths and delay your weakest rotations. This rotational order may change from one set to the next based on winning, losing, or how well the team is matched up with the opponent.

During the Match

As the match progresses, be aware of patterns you see and actions you can take as a coach to help your team be successful. This may include making substitutions, serving toward different players who may be struggling receiving serves, or blocking a hitter down the line instead of blocking crosscourt.

Tactical Adjustments

During the match is not the time for you to focus feedback on technical skill performance. Rather, it is the time to give feedback on the tactics and strategies of the game, as coaches must make numerous tactical decisions in a match. For example, suppose the opponents have been setting the left side to hit over the setter the entire match because they believe she is a weak blocker. The match has reached the fifth and deciding game, or set, of the match. You decide whether to make a substitution to take your setter out of the game when your team is serving and put in a stronger blocker to stop their left-side attacker. The ability to adjust and read the match as it develops is a critical application of the tactical triangle. The rest of this section shows how to apply the tactical triangle to match management in key situations that commonly occur.

Time-Outs

Develop a plan for how you will run time-outs. Time-outs are very short, and this time needs to be used efficiently. Share your philosophy with the team on why you might call time-outs in certain situations. Where do you want the players in the match to sit, who hands them their water bottles (player name or number marked on them) and individual towels (player name or number marked on them), who speaks to the team, where do the substitutes stand, and what information will you be sharing with them? These are all details to be worked out so that time-outs run smoothly. Take time to practice your time-out routine.

Substitutions

Substitutions will be made for a variety of reasons. A player may need to come out of the match to get a mental break for a few minutes, or you may make a substitution to slow down the tempo of the match or for a tactical reason. Players need to be ready to go back into the match immediately and should cheer for the player who took their place on the court.

Make sure you have reviewed the proper format for substituting during the match with your players. Rehearse the format during a practice scrimmage with a referee present to make sure substitutions are made properly and in a timely manner. Share your philosophy with the team on when and why you might be substituting in certain situations so players are prepared for when they might enter the game.

Bench Behavior

The bench area during a match should be set up so coaches and players know where everything is located. Decide if you want the players not currently in the match to stand or be seated on the bench, depending also on what the rules allow. Make sure you have gone over with all the players the behavior you expect from the bench, emphasizing that their focus and concentration on the match are critical for the team to be successful. They must also be mentally ready to go into the match immediately to replace a player for a variety of reasons. Share those concepts with the team ahead of time so they know those situations. To help eliminate problems, you should assign one coach or manager to keep an eye on the bench area. The bench should be organized, with players' bags, towels, water bottles, and other equipment lined up in an orderly fashion, either under the chairs or behind the bench.

Between-Set Adjustments

You have a lot to accomplish during the short two-minute break. The coaching staff should orchestrate that time carefully. In general, the teams will go to their respective end lines and run around the net to the opposite end line before being dismissed by the official. The coaches and staff will move to the other bench and meet briefly to discuss adaptations to the game plan while the players get water and sit on the bench. Substitutes may want to use volleyballs to warm up on their court briefly if this is allowed. The coach will then make brief comments referring to the game plan and any adjustments needed, giving the players the starting rotation before they head back out onto the court.

After the Match

Immediately following the match, coaches and players must be aware of several things. After shaking hands with the opposing team, gather up your items from the bench and then begin taking care of the other required activities.

Postmatch Meeting

When the match is over, the coaches and players should meet at the net and shake hands with the opponents and officials. After the handshakes, you must always meet with your team quickly on the court. Players' families and friends must understand that this postmatch meeting is important for you and your team and that their time with the players will follow. At this time, you must briefly address the team, regardless of the outcome.

Remember to take a deep breath, think before you speak, and be careful and understated, whatever your emotional condition may be. In defeat, console the team and praise their effort without indicating that you are not satisfied with the outcome. Find positives to build on, and move forward to the next opponent. In victory, let the team know you are happy, but follow up by pointing out any areas where they still need to improve. Refer to the game plan, and reinforce how a productive week of practice prepared them for their performance. Whether a win or loss, point out achievement of team goals during the match and indicate goals for the next match or next practice. Remind them of their next activity together, whether it is practice the next day or another match in a few hours.

Postmatch Interviews

When the brief meeting ends, players should be able to visit with family and friends, while you and certain players may have to meet with the media. Again, you must train the players before the season starts about how to handle interviews. They must be complimentary of their teammates and their opponents and avoid making excuses or commenting about the officials. They should be polite, brief, and positive about future matches but not overconfident. They should answer only the specific questions asked, and they should not provide extraneous information. Players should also decline to comment about injuries, coaching decisions, and playing time.

As the head coach, you should again take a deep breath and slow the racing tempo of your thoughts before beginning to answer questions. Many of the instructions for the players apply to you as well, but the media will ask you about your team. In victory, give your players the credit. Talk about how hard they practiced, how well they executed, how hard they competed, and so on. In defeat, deflect the blame from your players by talking about how well the opponent played and possibly referring to what the coaching staff might have done to change the outcome.

At all costs, avoid two common pitfalls of the postmatch interview—first, the comment that "our team didn't show up today" or "we didn't come to play," and second, the comment that "the players just didn't execute today." Both comments blame the players for the loss; either they lacked motivation or they played poorly. But it is your job to motivate the players and teach them the skills of the game. If the players aren't motivated, you have to do a better job of motivating; if the players aren't executing, you have to do a better job of teaching. Coaches can't separate themselves from their teams, even when you are tempted to do so after a heartbreaking loss. You and your players are in this game together, all the time, especially in the postgame crucible.

Be aware that leadership does not just happen; it is a gradual process of education and experience. You should describe to the team how you expect them to look on game day—how they should act on the sideline, how they should talk (or not talk) to the officials or the opponents, how they should react to adverse situations, and how they should respond to success. This must be done in the practice setting. Then you must subsequently follow up by insisting on those behaviors through reinforcement during and after the match. Everything your team does on game day is something you have taught or something you have allowed to happen in practice. Teach game day the right way, and your team will perform admirably.

index

NOTE: Page numbers followed by an italicized *f* or *t* indicate that there is a figure or table on that page, respectively.

about the authors

Cecile Reynaud ranked in the top nine in career victories (630 matches over 26 years, including 7 conference championships and 14 postseason appearances) among active Division I coaches when she retired from Florida State University in 2001. She received the prestigious George J. Fischer Volleyball Leader Award from USA Volleyball in 1996 in recognition of her contributions to the sport. Reynaud is a former president of the American Volleyball Coaches Association. Reynaud served 12 years on the USA Volleyball board of directors and 3 years on its executive committee. She is currently a faculty member in the sport management program at Florida State University.

The American Sport Education Program (ASEP), a division of Human Kinetics, is the leading provider of youth, high school, and elite-level sport education programs in the United States. Rooted in the philosophy of "Athletes first, winning second," ASEP has educated more than 1.5 million coaches, officials, sport administrators, parents, and athletes.